DATE DUE

European Community Decision Making

European Community Decision Making

Models, Applications, and Comparisons

Edited by

Bruce Bueno de Mesquita and

Frans N. Stokman

Yale University Press   New Haven and London

29357703
DLC

2-16-95

Set in Times Roman type by DEKR Corpora-
tion, Woburn, Massachusetts.
Printed in the United States of America by
BookCrafters, Inc., Chelsea, Michigan.

Library of Congress Cataloging-in-Publication Data
European community decision making : models,
   applications, and comparisons / edited by
   Bruce Bueno de Mesquita and Frans N.
   Stokman.
        p.   cm.
   Includes bibliographical references and
   index.
   ISBN 0-300-05759-8
   1. Policy sciences — European Economic
Community countries. I. Bueno de Mesquita,
Bruce, 1946–   . II. Stokman, Frans N.
H97.E86   1994
320'.6'094 — dc20   93-43875
                       CIP

A catalogue record for this book is available
from the British Library.

The paper in this book meets the guidelines for
permanence and durability of the Committee on
Production Guidelines for Book Longevity of the
Council on Library Resources.

10 9 8 7 6 5 4 3 2 1

To Samuel Eldersveld with our admiration and appreciation

Contents

Preface

This book is the final product of an integrated study in which two classes of models are systematically compared and applied to decision making in the European Community (EC). In political science, there is a longstanding discussion among two contending groups of scholars. The first group maintains that the nature of politics is primarily conflictual so that social outcomes are obtained primarily by competition among individuals and groups over the social use of material things or over values. The second group emphasizes the cooperative nature of many political processes and their similarity with exchange processes in economics, where social outcomes are determined by the cooperation of buyer and seller.

We find the same controversy among scholars of EC decision making. Some of them stress the importance of logrolling in EC decision making, whereas others dispute the significance of bargains across issues, emphasizing instead conflicts, threats, and compromises on one issue at a time. One reason for the persistence of this dispute is that results of noncooperative and cooperative models have been difficult to compare. The difficulty arises in part because incommensurable approaches have been used to think about the political process. A second difficulty has been the general reluctance of researchers to compare one approach directly to another, preferring instead to focus only on how well a given analytic scheme does in a specific context. It is altogether too rare, in our opinion, that alternative explanations are investigated simultaneously in the study of politics.

In this book two directly comparable models are presented: the noncooperative expected utility model of Bueno de Mesquita on the one hand, and the cooperative exchange model of voting positions of Stokman and Van Oosten on the other. These models are based on similar assumptions and on exactly the same three variables, namely, the capability or potential control of actors to determine the outcomes of decisions, the salience of the issues for the actors, and the actor's preferred outcomes (denoted as the policy positions of the actors). Despite the fact that they use the same variables, these alternative approaches model the underlying political process in fundamentally different ways.

Each model is investigated here in the context of sixteen past issues resolved by the European Community's Council of Ministers and an additional six banking issues that occupy the EC's membership at the time of this writing. Because the models have been applied to the same issues, their performance can be directly compared. And it is this comparison that motivates the writing of this book.

Two central objectives of this volume are to evaluate the predictive and explanatory value of the models we examine in the light of decision making within the European Community. Not only do the tools we discuss provide quite specific policy predictions, they also provide rich, detailed, extensive analyses of the underlying political bargaining, expectations, coaxing, and cajoling that, according to the logic of the models, produces the political outcomes that we observe. Although the empirical value of all of these simulated processes cannot be tested directly in this book, the rich implications of the models help us understand the processes that actually take place in collective decision making in general and within the EC in particular. And, in specific cases, despite the secrecy of EC decision making, we can detect anecdotal evidence regarding our evaluations of simulated underlying processes. With regard to predicted outcomes, we can and do go well beyond anecdotal evidence. Here we are able to provide rigorous, systematic evaluations of the possibility of making reliable predictions about EC policy through the use of these models.

This combination of features makes the book interesting for three audiences: researchers who are primarily interested in model development, researchers who are interested in collective decision-making processes, and researchers and politicians who are primarily interested in the European Community.

The initiative for the book followed from two conferences. The first conference was initiated by Samuel Eldersveld and was organized in April 1988 by the Department of Political Science and the Center for Political Studies at the University of Michigan. The second conference was initiated by Frans Stokman and organized in June 1990 at the University of Groningen by its Department of Sociology, the Interuniversity Center for Social Science Theory and Methodology (ICS), and the CARIAN Group.

The conferences had two objectives. First, they explicitly aimed to bring together the model-oriented and policy-oriented approaches in political science and international relations. Second, it was hoped that they would enhance discussions among American and European scholars. We noted at the time that such a double confrontation is very rare and might open new perspectives. In this respect we were not disappointed. The policy-oriented presentations gave concrete significance to a number of abstract aspects of the modeling approach, whereas the modeling approach gave a number of new perspectives to those who are policy oriented.

At first, we aimed to publish a selection of the papers of the two conferences, but gradually a much more coherent approach was chosen, resulting in this book. Despite our departure from our original intentions, the two conferences were vital for the success of this undertaking. Without the conferences it is unlikely that we would have made an attempt to bridge the two worlds of model development and close observation of policy processes. We hope that we will succeed in keeping the interest of both audiences and in providing each with some useful links to the other. If we do succeed in fostering some integration between these two normally separate enterprises, it is largely because of the help we have been given by the participants in the conferences. If we fail, it is surely due to our own inability to grasp the enormous difficulties of applied researchers to understand models like ours.

The conferences also served as the venue that brought the two editors together. Until then, we each were developing our models independently, each working in a different discipline (political science and sociology), and each ignorant about the work of the other. It was at these conferences that we discovered a common orientation in model development and testing. The result is the presentation of two classes of comparable models and their application in the context of the European Community.

We have accumulated many debts in developing this volume. The specification of the models in the context of the European Community requires a detailed understanding of the EC's decision-making process, as well as knowledge about important issues, which neither editor has. We are grateful particularly to Jan Van den Bos for bringing this knowledge to our undertaking and for his willingness to write two chapters.

We are also grateful to Samuel Eldersveld, A. F. K. Organski, and Roy Pierce for their critical evaluation of our efforts, for their insightful critiques during the two conferences, and for their contributions. We also wish to thank Jacek Kugler and John H. P. Williams, who helped broaden the scope of our undertaking by studying the evolution of banking policy within the European Community through the lenses of the models presented here.

The conferences and this book would never have occurred without the initiative of Samuel Eldersveld. As a token of our gratitude and esteem for Sam, and to demonstrate our admiration for his enormous contribution to the political science literature and to the advancement of the social sciences, we dedicate this book to him.

Roy Pierce

1 Introduction: Fresh Perspectives on a Developing Institution

This book, as its title indicates, lies at the intersection of three subjects that are of great importance to contemporary social scientists: modeling as an analytical method, decision making as a focus of investigation, and the European Community (EC) as a political institution. It is, in consequence, directed at three groups of readers. One group is the community of modelers in the social sciences, those scholars who, when confronted with some collective problem — whether it be an effort to predict next year's gross national product or an attempt to explain why almost all popular music evaporates while the classics endure (McPhee 1963, ch. 1) — instinctively turn to the technique of modeling in order to derive answers. Another group is students of decision making, those scholars who tend to believe that the inner dynamics of institutional arrangements can best be understood by examining how conflicting interests are transformed into common policy at points of ultimate decision. The third group consists of those people who have a special interest in the development and operation of the European Community.

Interest in the European Community has waxed and waned during the comparatively short period since the current institution originally took shape in the guise of the European Coal and Steel Community (ECSC), more or less according to the levels of interest displayed in the further development of the institution by the European nations involved. The second half of the 1980s, however, culminating with the signing of the treaty of Maastricht at the end of 1991, ushered in a period of renewed and heightened interest in the process of European integration as it is expressed in the European Community. This book is meant to be a contribution to the growing literature on the European Community that has been inspired by this dramatic and unprecedented impulse toward European integration.

The hope that this book will reach several audiences reflects the multiplicity of its objectives and its inspiration. These are, simply put: to persuade the specialized scholars of the European Community of the usefulness of modeling as an instrument for furthering their understanding of how the Community works; to encourage modelers to direct their attention more than they often do toward the institutions whose operations they are modeling; and to suggest that the focus on decision making is particularly well designed for analyzing several of the major issues that confront the EC and whose resolution will inevitably have great importance for its future structure and operation.

The first goal of the book — to try to win over students of the EC to the merits of political modeling — was inspired by the observation that students of the EC tend, more than most social scientists, to be unlikely to employ quantitative methods of analysis. From one point of view, this form of underrepresentation is perfectly understandable. The kinds of information available to students of the EC do not lend themselves very easily to quantification. The official documentation relating to the growth and development of the EC is enormous, but it is mainly legalistic in form. The "politics" of the EC is regularly expressed in the speeches of the European nations' political leaders, party programs, official communiques issued after the numerous high-level meetings associated with the EC, and occasional memoirs, but these are seldom amenable to systematic analysis. Indeed, we are indebted to the dedicated efforts of the community of EC watchers for their patient mining of these multifarious sources for those nuggets of information that give us some confidence in our ability to generalize about the workings of the EC.

Yet it is also true that the activities of the EC lend themselves particularly well, if not necessarily to all forms of modeling, at least to the kinds of models elaborated in this book. I will spell out shortly in more detail just why this is so. For the moment, it should be enough to point out that the main decision-making agency of the EC, the council (which will be more fully discussed in chapter 2), makes hundreds of decisions each year, almost every one of which must satisfy the interests in the relevant matter of each of the twelve member nations of the EC. We have here a dozen major actors, each of which can be regarded as expressing a single interest, operating in an arena that literally churns out hundreds of decisions each year. This very structure is not only uniquely appropriate for systematic analysis of the kind that modeling permits, but it virtually requires such analysis if the processes by which the decisions are made are to be properly understood.

At the same time that we hope this book will produce converts to the modeling approach among specialized students of the EC, we also hope it will help persuade the community of modelers to broaden their substantive horizons. Some of our best friends are modelers, so we know perhaps better than most people that it is all too easy for modelers to become so preoccupied with their models that they lose sight of the institutions or processes they are modeling.

Just as the disinclination of most EC specialists toward quantitative analysis is understandable in the light of their informational constraints, so the propensity of modelers to subordinate what they model to how they model it is understandable in the light of the constraints that operate on modelers. All modelers are naturally consumed by the question of whether their models "work," to the point that there is a risk that making the model work becomes the exclusive goal of the modeler. But most people are more interested in what is being modeled than in the model that is being applied. The challenge to modelers, therefore, is to exploit their models as fully as they can to illuminate the institutions or processes being modeled. A major goal of this book, therefore, is to focus on what models can tell us about the European Community, even as we will be concerned with the relative merits of the various models employed.

Finally, we approach EC activities at the point of decision making, not only because the EC regularly generates large numbers of decisions, but also because decision making more generally lies at the heart of some of the most critical issues the EC will eventually have to decide. The agenda of the EC contains several major items, each of which will have great importance for the way in which the EC will make its decisions. In that sense, decision making is itself an issue for the EC. At the same time, the kind of modeling approach that is employed in this book has great promise for estimating the outcomes of alternate ways in which the EC might resolve its future decision-making problems.

The Models

Models are simplified versions of reality. When one models a process, such as the decision-making process of the EC council, it is essential to reduce the process conceptually to the minimum number of elements that are logically necessary to account for what the modeler assumes is going on in the real world. Simplifying assumptions must be made about who the principal actors are, what their motivations are, what they know about themselves and the other actors, what each actor is likely to do in order to achieve its goals, and how other actors are likely to respond to another actor when it does thus or so to achieve its goals.

Models are usually expressed in mathematical form. Assigning numerical values to the elements of the model, as appropriate, ensures consistency of definition, permits mathematical manipulation (such as deducing relations between variables, drawing means, establishing rankings, and determining degrees of association), makes direct comparisons possible, and generally allows for precision in describing what is going on.

Models are normally evaluated on the basis of three criteria: their parsimony, their verisimilitude, and their predictiveness. Parsimony refers to how economical the model is with regard to its elements and its assumptions. The leaner and less cluttered the model, the more likely it is to be admired by modelers. Unfortunately, how parsimonious a model is may run counter to the extent to which the model displays verisimilitude with regard to the process being modeled. The real world is complex, and sometimes the kind of processes that we might want to model do not look simple at all to an outside observer. Instead of appearing clean, neat, and easy to follow, some processes take on the qualities of an onion, which exposes layer after layer of internal structure in response to persistent efforts to get at its core. This is all the more likely to happen when the observer is particularly knowledgeable about the broad context in which the process is embedded. Privileged observers of that sort are likely to be so aware of the history of the situation, the idiosyncracies of the participants, and the details of the institutional framework, that they are naturally skeptical about the possibility of understanding what is going on without considering all the conceivable factors that might have some relevance for the process under examination. In this sense, verisimilitude is always at war with parsimony.[1]

Even so, it should be clear that we are not dealing here with polar opposites, but rather that the trade-off between parsimony and verisimilitude is always a matter of degree. Every description of a process, every explanation of an outcome, is partial in the sense that it emphasizes some factors over others. By focusing on some elements of a situation, we naturally diminish or exclude others. Reality cannot be grasped in its totality; and even those sections of reality that we think we can circumscribe are linked with forces outside the circumference by ties that we can never completely identify and pursue to their points of anchorage. No description can ever be complete. The great French moralist, Albert Camus (1956, p. 270), pointed out in a different context that "to be really realistic a description would have to be endless. Where Stendhal describes in one phrase Lucien Leuwen's entrance into a room, the realistic artist ought, logically, to fill several volumes with descriptions of characters and settings, still without succeeding in exhausting every detail. Realism is indefinite enumeration." Just as an artist gives bold relief to a situation or a character through selection and exclusion, so the modeler tries to get to

1. Fiorina (1975, p. 153) puts it this way: "All modeling involves a trade-off between simplicity and realism."

the heart of the matter by concentrating on what seems essential and ignoring everything else.[2] The trick is to account for as much as possible with as little as possible, without stretching the credulity of experienced observers.

The third criterion on the basis of which models are customarily evaluated is their predictiveness. How well do they account for known outcomes? Do they retroactively predict what we know to have happened in the past? Even better, do they successfully predict what has not yet happened but what we will know to have happened in the not too distant future?

Indeed, there are some people who argue that predictiveness is the main criterion by which a model should be judged. In this view, properties such as parsimony or, especially, verisimilitude are clearly secondary in importance. They are incidental attributes that might make a model superficially attractive, but the real test of a model is its predictiveness. "Theoretical models should be tested primarily by the accuracy of their predictions rather than by the reality of their assumptions," writes Anthony Downs (1957, p. 21), echoing an earlier elaboration of that position by Milton Friedman (1953). That austere, confident proposition invariably induces antagonism, but there is much to recommend it.[3] Verisimilitude is useful for building confidence among people inclined toward skepticism, but who is to say what the properties of the real world are that any given model must reflect? The path of scientific development is strewn with discarded images of reality that once were received opinion. The symbol of willful obsolescence is membership in the flat earth society. Modelers might well argue that if their models predict accurately, their assumptions *must* express the real world, for there is no other way to determine what the real world is.

I have some sympathy for that view and would not want to reject it out of hand. But it is too narrow to be accepted without reservation. Predictive accuracy is essential for a successful model, but models can and should be employed not only for predictive purposes but also for increasing our understanding of the institutions or processes being modeled. It is in this connection that a fourth criterion for the evaluation of models is added: the extent to which they help us understand how the object of the modeling works. A good model should predict accurately. A model also should be parsimonious in its structure, not only for aesthetic reasons but also be-

2.   At least provisionally. There is no reason why simple models cannot be refined to bring additional elements into the equation by the process of decreasing abstraction (Lindenberg 1992).

3.   I do not think a single student of mine, on first being introduced to that proposition, has ever accepted it.

cause simplicity enhances clarity. The assumptions of the model should display verisimilitude with the process being modeled, if only to try to ensure that minimum degree of general acceptance among expert observers necessary for forestalling premature objections. Finally, a model ought to tell us things about the object of the model that we would not have known had we not applied the model in the first place.

The models deployed in this book are fully described in chapters 4 and 5, where — among other aspects of the models — their basic assumptions are set forth unambiguously. The models are applied to decision making in the European Community in chapters 6, 7, and 8. The predictiveness of the models, and their unique contribution to understanding how decisions are made within the EC, are analyzed in chapter 9. An overall assessment of the contribution of the earlier chapters both to modeling as a method of political analysis and to our understanding of the European Community as an institution appears in chapter 10.

The models themselves belong to the family of social science analysis that is generally referred to as rational-choice theory. This is an intellectual strand that is at the core of the liberal tradition, in both its economic and political expressions. Although, like all powerful ideas, its ancestry can be traced back to the remote past, its modern origins lie in the radical individualism of Thomas Hobbes and the utilitarians who built on the foundations that Hobbes had laid.

The most familiar and widespread applications of rational-choice theory are in the domain of classical economics, but it is increasingly employed in the analysis of political behavior as well. The central notion that underlies the theory is that people have ordered preferences, and that given the opportunity to do so, they will seek to satisfy their top preference. It is easy to understand why such a simple notion should have quickly found its main application in economics, where people are always exchanging things. Persons exchange things that they do not value particularly highly for things that they prefer. The circulation of money makes it easier than it otherwise would be to order one's preferences for purposes of exchange. One will pay the most for what one prefers the most, everything else being equal. When a buyer and a seller agree on a price for a given object, they have reached an equilibrium in that both actors are satisfied.

The concepts of exchange and equilibrium are not limited to the realm of economic behavior. The concept of exchange is broad enough to embrace the domain of bargaining more generally, and the notion of equilibrium can be applied to any kind of agreement that represents the agreed position of negotiating partners who are seeking to satisfy their preferences. And, of course, the bargaining agents do not have to be individuals; they can be any kind of actor who has ordered preferences and is in a position to seek to satisfy them, such as firms, political parties, or nation-states. Indeed, it can be argued that rational-choice theory is more appropriately applied to collectivities than it is to individuals. Classical economics has always been more readily accepted in its theoretical formulation than in its applied form because of doubts about the extent to which its assumptions are legitimate. Individuals do not always behave as though they had ordered preferences; there are large information gaps concerning alternate prices and sources of supply; there is tremendous variation in people's capacity for mobility; and so forth.[4]

There are fewer doubts about the behavior and resources of nation-states, which Charles de Gaulle once described as the most selfish of human enterprises. They shamelessly calculate what is to their advantage and then pursue it. Indeed, their leaders further their own personal interests by proclaiming that they are achieving some national interest. They expend vast resources gathering information about one another and maintaining large corps of professional bargainers. They are given to bullying and cajoling in ways that are foreign to ordinary citizens seeking some modest bargain in the marketplace. If rational-choice theory works anywhere, it should work with regard to international bargaining.

And if rational-choice theory is more unreservedly applicable to the analysis of international relations than to economic or political behavior at the individual level, it is particularly appropriate for the study of decision making within the European Community. For international bargaining in the general sense occurs intermittently, involves shifting groups of nations, and operates within a variety of institutional frameworks. While rational-choice models, including those employed in this book, may be applied to any form of international bargaining, lack of regularity in performance, inconsistency in the cast of characters, and the absence of institutional stability reduce the possibility of considering the decision-making process being analyzed as a system. The models may "work" in the sense that they predict outcomes, and in that sense they also tend to sustain the assumptions underlying the models. But in the absence of a structured system of decision making, there is no opportunity to derive implications from the models with regard to the operation of a system.

The European Community, however, provides an ordered framework for the investigation of international bargaining. It makes large numbers of decisions on a regular basis, the number and identity of the participating member states remain constant, and the decisions are taken according to a fixed set of rules. It is difficult to imagine an arena for international bargaining whose decision-making process can be more fruitfully analyzed by modeling than the European Community.

4. Of course, such confounding factors as information gaps, inadequate resources, and the like, alter the expected utility of alternative outcomes, even though the unconstrained preferences of the decision maker remain fixed.

The European Community

The European Community is the most original new constitutional system of any kind — national or international — to have been constructed since the Second World War. The institutional development of the EC has occurred at an uneven pace, and that irregularity, combined with inevitable tensions and setbacks, has both frustrated enthusiasts and encouraged cynics. The fact remains that in the postwar world, the EC is the most creative new work of political architecture, a field in which real innovation is rare and variety is limited.

The European Community engages in four main activities:

1. it is trying to establish, and police, a common market in goods, services, capital, and labor;
2. it adopts common policies in a limited but growing number of domains, including agriculture, regional development, and the environment;
3. it tries to create common foreign policies on an ad hoc basis, under the guise of political cooperation; and
4. it studies and plans its own constitutional development, including the admission of new members, on which it occasionally takes important new steps.

Decision making in the EC is complex, and it is conducted in secrecy — both factors that make it difficult to study on a systematic basis. The decisions on which the most light is thrown and, consequently, about which scholars know the most are those that fall within rubrics 3 and 4, relating to political cooperation and the constitutional development of the EC itself. This is because decisions in those areas require the participation of the top political leaders in all of the member states, often on a sustained basis, and because the issues themselves are normally the subject of highly charged political debate within each of the member states. Those conditions ensure publicity and permit the followers of EC affairs to reconstruct with tolerable accuracy how eventual decisions (or nondecisions) were arrived at.

The decisions in those two domains are always of major, and sometimes even of historic, importance, but they are also comparatively infrequent. The vast majority of EC decisions fall within categories 1 and 2, related to the common market and the areas of common policy. The EC regularly makes hundreds of decisions each year in those areas (see table 2.1 for an exact accounting), all of which are negotiated in secret and about which the public at large learns little or nothing.

This book will analyze one set of major decisions concerning the creation of a European central banking system (see chapter 8). In addition, sixteen separate decisions relating to three important areas of common policy-making will also be analyzed (in chapters 6 and 7). In that way, the analysis will be distributed across both what one may call the exceptional and the more routine aspects of EC decision making.[5]

When thinking about decision making within the EC, it is important to keep in mind that analogies with decision making in parliamentary systems of government are of strictly limited usefulness. All major decisions, and most routine decisions, must be unanimous. Even when unanimity is not required, a qualified majority is necessary to carry the day, the larger states entitled to more votes than the smaller ones. These rules are spelled out in chapter 2, and our inventory of routine decisions includes issues for which a qualified majority was adequate, as well as issues for which unanimity was required.

There are no a priori governing coalitions, majorities, or opposition. Each decision is situation-specific. Each actor is its own court of last resort (at least juridically). There are no reserves of shared loyalty on which beleaguered participants can draw. Such checks and balances as exist are very different from, say, those that operate in the United States political system. The European Community combines novelty, complexity, and secrecy. It is, therefore, both a challenge and a unique target of opportunity for the student of political decision making.

Application of the Models to the EC

In later chapters of this book, seven variants of two basic decision-making models are applied to sets of decisions made by the European Community in four issue domains. The importance and contemporary relevance of the issues can hardly be doubted.

One of the issues examined relates to the establishment of a central European banking system. The complexity and constitutional importance of this issue are such that it is accorded a single chapter (chapter 8) and treated in greater depth than the other issues. In particular, the analysis of this issue includes consideration of a series of decisions made at three different European summit meetings between 1989 and 1991. It also takes into account the positions on the issue of various groups and countries

5. Strictly speaking, the decisions relating to banking were not EC decisions, but rather decisions made by the heads of the member states at successive European summit meetings with the aim of negotiating a new treaty relating to the EC. Summit meetings became formalized in 1974 as the European Council, which was reaffirmed in 1985. The European Council, which must meet at least twice a year and includes the heads of state or government of the member states, their foreign ministers, and the president and one other member of the EC commission, is not itself an organ of the EC and is distinct from the EC Council of Ministers discussed in chapter 2. The banking decisions treated in this book were so directly and exclusively related to the EC that we feel no pangs of guilt at referring to them as EC decisions.

Table 1.1
Inventory of Issues Investigated

	Source of Initiative	Time under Consideration	Number of Decisions	Decision Rule	Date of Latest Decision
Banking	Commission	4 years	6	unanimity	December 1991
Nuclear energy	Commission	20 months	2	qualified majority	December 1987
Air pollution	Germany	4.5 years	9	unanimity	December 1987
Transport liberalization	Parliament	8 years	5	unanimity	December 1987

Note: All decisions are scored on continuous scales except for two dichotomous (yes/no) decisions (one relating to nuclear energy and the other to transport liberalization) and another, also relating to transport liberalization, for which the scores are discrete and range from 0 to 4.

that were not actually member states of the EC. These include East Germany, both before and after reunification with West Germany, as well as the German central bank; the internal opposition to British Prime Minister Margaret Thatcher; both West European and East European non-EC member states; and several international organizations, including EFTA (the European Free Trade Association), GATT (the General Agreement on Tariffs and Trade), and COMECON (the vanishing Soviet bloc's Council for Mutual Economic Assistance). The banking analysis also explicitly includes Jacques Delors, the president of the EC commission, as a separate actor. In that fashion, the broad perspective appropriate for European summit meetings is incorporated into the analytical models applied.

The other three sets of issues, which are analyzed in chapters 6 and 7, relate to problems that are at the center not only of European preoccupations but also of governments worldwide: nuclear contamination, air pollution, and economic liberalization — in this case, the liberalization of air transport. The latter is a particularly thorny issue because air transport has traditionally been under tight government control (and even ownership) in Western Europe, and consequently evokes nationalistic reflexes as well as considerations of comparative competitive advantage. Table 1.1 summarizes the issues considered and provides information illustrative of their diversity.

The two basic models, which are spelled out in detail in chapters 4 and 5, are an expected utility model and a logrolling model, respectively. Both basic models require the same information in order to be applied: the position on the issue of each member state, the degree of salience attached to the issue by each member state, and the potential power of each member state to affect the outcome. The expected utility model treats each vote on each issue as a separate and complete act, isolated from any others. The logrolling model, as the name connotes, considers the possibility that member states might trade their votes on one aspect of an issue in exchange for support on another aspect of the same issue. Variations of each model, usually produced by altering the definition of potential power, are explored. The two basic models are also combined in various ways, making it possible to test the hypothesis that the decision-making process occurs in two stages — first independently and then via logrolling.

These two models are not merely alternate ways of expressing a common political process. They relate to different basic conceptions of the political process itself. The expected utility model reflects an orientation toward the noncooperative side of politics, in which power relations are predominant. The logrolling model puts the emphasis on politics as exchange, in which cooperation is emphasized.

There is, therefore, more at stake than modelers' curiosity in any assessment of which model(s) predict best. What we hope to learn is just how the EC member states bargain in the effort to serve their subjective interests, or — in the language of rational choice theory — to maximize their utility. Do they operate in a manner that suggests that they perceive the EC as an arena of political competition? Or is there a discernible pattern of exchange that suggests that the institutionalization of decision making within the EC framework may have contributed toward habits of cooperation?

Chapter 9 summarizes the findings of the various models and both evaluates the models for their predictiveness and indicates the ways in which the models enlighten us about the operation of the European Community.

Implications

This book is illustrative of a genre that will surely have to multiply if political analysis is to gain in depth of investigation, range of application, and explanatory power. That is the conflation of method and substance. Political science has reached the point where virtually every new and challenging problem that presents itself requires its own custom-designed methodological technique for trying to solve it. In reporting on such work, the elaboration of the appropriate methodological approach can require as much or more attention than the description of the findings, for the validity of the latter depends upon the integrity of the former.

The models that are employed in this book were not created especially for application to decision making within the European Community. They can be and have been applied to other situations as well. But models of decision making based on rational choice theory are almost uniquely appropriate for trying to understand the EC, a constitutional system that rests ultimately on the equal sufferance of every member state.

Of course, the application of particular models sets limits to the range of questions that can be addressed at any one time about a constitutional system as complex as the European Community. We are primarily concerned here with which models work and, accordingly, with what they tell us about how the member states conduct their bargaining. That naturally requires us to direct our attention institutionally to the Council of Ministers and virtually to ignore the other EC institutions, such as the commission and the parliament. By concentrating almost exclusively on bargaining within the council, we have almost inevitably been forced to focus heavily on the strategic considerations of particular member states. Finally, our data requirements are sufficiently stringent that we have had to confine our analysis to a limited number of issues (however important and timely) that were decided more or less at the same time. We must know the initial position of each member state on any given issue, as well as how salient that issue is to each state. Such information is not generally available "in hard form" for the Council of Ministers, an institution that conducts its operations in secret. In the present state of affairs, there is no possibility of working with a sample of EC decisions. But the information is readily developed — even before the fact — with the help of individuals who specialize in the study of EC decision making.

We are well aware that what we have produced here is a first cut at understanding how the European Community works and not a definitive study of that unique constitutional system. But we are convinced that the modeling approach we have employed is the key to unlocking further secrets. One great virtue of the models is that they permit us to simulate decision making under different sets of conditions. This flexibility should permit future researchers to build on our foundation in order to produce a more complete picture of how the EC operates.

Once the most appropriate decision-making model has been determined, it can be applied to predict outcomes under different hypothetical conditions. For the models employed in this book, those elements of the situation that may be allowed to vary for purposes of simulation include: (1) the decision rules; (2) the actors participating in the decision; and (3) the issues on the agenda for decision. It is apparent that each of these three aspects of the overall constitutional context relates to one of the central issues that has confronted the European Community from its very inception.

The first issue is the allocation of decision-making authority, not simply in terms of voting rules within the Council of Ministers but throughout the EC generally, with special reference to the commission and the European Parliament (EP). The second major issue concerns the admission of new members, a question that has always been important but which took on added urgency with the liberation of Eastern Europe in 1989 and the collapse of the Soviet Union late in 1991. The third problem concerns determining those domains within which the EC may adopt common policies. This is, in terms familiar to students of the United States constitution, directly analogous to deciding on the "enumerated powers" of the central authorities, as opposed to those powers reserved to the separate (member) states. It should, of course, be quickly added that while these issues may be considered separately for analytical purposes, they are in fact linked to one another (especially the first and the second), and they will no doubt eventually be decided in the form of "packages."

In this book, we have begun to explore, via simulation, the probable effects of different rules, in the form of unanimity as opposed to qualified majority. This is a tricky business. As the rules change, so do the considerations of the actors, and these must somehow be taken into account in assessing variations in the expected outcomes. But it is apparent that the same technique of assuming different rules can be extended to include the probable effects of a European Parliament with various forms of legislative power on the ways in which decisions would be made and even on what those decisions might be.

We have also derived as much as we could in terms of the implications of size on EC decision making. It is obvious that the larger the number of independent actors the more complex the bargaining process becomes. It is less clear what kinds of specific effects enlargement of the EC would have in bargaining strategy and tactics. Would logrolling be resorted to more frequently in a larger EC than a smaller one? Would there be greater likelihood of the formation of more or less stable coalitions?

Variation by issue is a subject that we have not been able to pursue as far as we would have liked, mainly because data requirements reduced the number of issues we could examine. It is apparent, however, that there is considerable ore to be mined. We have investigated logrolling between aspects of a single issue. It is also possible that there is logrolling between issues, even some that are quite different in substance. Intuitively, one would think that such behavior is almost surely commonplace, yet to our knowledge it has not been established in any systematic manner.

Finally, there is the broad but critically important question of how representative in its decision making the European Community is of the populations of member states. Nowhere else in the democratically governed world is the issue of the overall representativeness of the constitutional structure debated so hotly as it is in the member states of the European Community with regard to the structure of the EC. Broadly speaking, the lines have been drawn between those groups (including governments) that insist that democratic accountability can only operate at the national level, and that EC decision making should therefore continue to be based on unanimity in the Council of Ministers, and those that argue that democratic accountability should be incorporated into the institutions of the EC itself by strengthening the European Parliament. No one, to our knowledge, has yet mounted an empirical study directed at determining whether the parliament would be more likely than the council to arrive at decisions congruent with mass opinion in the member states.

Yet such a test is possible within the framework of simulation based on models of the sort deployed in this book. Admittedly, the data-gathering task would be formidable, but it would not be impossible. The data requirements for such a study include:

1. sample survey data relating to mass opinion in the EC member states on issues likely to come before the EC for decision;
2. the positions of the EC member state governments on those same issues;
3. the salience of those issues to the EC member state governments;
4. estimates of the positions of the political groups within the European Parliament on those same issues; and, finally,
5. estimates of the salience of each of those issues to the political groups within the European Parliament.

With those data in hand, models of the kind employed in this book could be used to estimate which institution would be more likely to produce decisions congruent with public opinion in the member states.

We have no illusions about how soon such a research agenda might be implemented. The European Community was not built in a day, and it will also take time, energy, and resources to learn how such an evolving constitutional system operates. But we are happy enough to have had the opportunity to make a first exploration of the potentialities for getting to the heart of the matter. And we are happier still that the results look so promising.

I Policy Making in the European Community

The applied modeling approach advocated in this book combines deductive model building with a sparse amount of empirical data to explain and predict decision making in the European Community. The models are quite generic so that they can be applied to decision making in virtually any setting and with regard to almost any set of issues. The models tested here share some common requirements. In particular, it is necessary to specify the actors (decision makers) with the potential to influence decision making on the issues to be analyzed. For each actor, the models require estimates of only three variables for each issue that is investigated. These variables are the capability of the actor to influence the policy outcome; the salience of the issues for the actor; and the outcome preferred by the actor. The derivation of the required information depends on having access to extensive expert knowledge of the decision-making process and of the decisions at hand. Fortunately, area and issue experts almost always have the information required by our models so that one of the efficiencies of the approach advocated here is that it forges a useful and productive bridge between the strengths of issue or area expertise on the one hand and the strengths of a modeling approach on the other.

The capability of actors to influence policy outcomes needs to reflect both their formal decisional power and their informal weight in the decision-making process. The formal decisional power of the actors can be derived from their relative weight given the formal decision-making procedure in combination with the specific decision rules in force, whereas their informal weight is determined by many factors. The most important such factors include the degree to which each actor has timely access to decision making and the resources each actor can mobilize. These resources may include such features of decision making as access to exclusive or limited information and the mobilization of supportive forces to prevent certain outcomes.

The saliences of the decisions for the actors and the preferences of the actors with respect to the outcomes are often difficult to assess. Within the European Community, for example, the initial positions of the member states are not published. At most they are very broadly hinted at in public reports. To apply the models in the context of the European Community, therefore, a number of fundamental decisions have to be taken. Which actors should be considered? Which decisions will be included? How do we determine the values of the three basic variables for every actor with respect to each decision?

Our choices about these questions must be justified against a common background of information regarding the fundamentals of EC decision making. This background is given in chapter 2. The subsequent chapter makes our choices explicit with respect to the selection of issues, actors, and the estimation of values for our three basic variables of capabilities, preferences, and salience. We believe that these chapters also demonstrate more generally the type of knowledge that is required for the successful application of the models in other contexts.

Jan M. M. Van den Bos

2 The European Community, Decision Making, and Integration

Decision making in the European Community has fascinated scholars ever since the Community's inception some forty years ago. Granting the organization the power to make decisions that bind the residents of all member states without the prior consent of each member government added a new dimension to international relations. It is exactly this limiting of national sovereignty which makes the EC unique among international organizations.[1]

This chapter contains a brief description of the development of the EC up to the treaty of Maastricht, the institutions that make up the EC, and the Community decision-making process, as well as an analysis of European integration and its contribution to the understanding of EC policy-making. Finally, in an effort to reveal the mechanism that structures integration, we introduce our modeling approach to decision making. In describing the background of the analysis I hope to facilitate the appraisal of the contribution of our study to the understanding of EC policy-making.

Development of the European Community

Like other international organizations, the European Community was instituted as the result of the decision of a number of states to combine forces and collectively pursue common goals. In 1951, the initial step toward the EC was taken when

1. International organizations are normally based on three distinct principles: (1) decisions are taken by organs composed of government representatives, (2) unanimity is required to arrive at binding decisions, and (3) the implementation of decisions is reserved for the participating states themselves. Exceptions to each individual principle exist, but their abandonment as a starting point for international organization justifies the supranational label being given to the EC (Kapteyn and VerLoren van Themaat 1989, p. 2).

France, Germany, Italy, and the Benelux countries concluded the Treaty of Paris, which led to the establishment of the first of the three communities: the European Coal and Steel Community (ECSC). In contrast to other international organizations, where the founding treaty remains the constituting agreement under which the organization functions, cooperation among the member states of the EC has grown continuously. The initial successes have consistently stimulated the member states to expand the scope of activities. As a consequence, both the member states and a growing number of states wishing to join them have adopted new treaties extending cooperation, thereby making the organization more complex.

Early attempts to achieve a large degree of political union among the six member states with the establishment of a European Defence Community and a European Political Community failed in 1954 as a result of opposition in the French parliament. Following these difficulties, new initiatives focused on developing the economic relations among the member states. Important obstacles to economic development — such as trade barriers, convertibility of currencies, and balance of payments deficits — needed to be dealt with. In 1957, the six member states signed the Treaties of Rome establishing the European Atomic Energy Community (Euratom) and the European Economic Community (EEC), with the latter being the most important of the three European communities. The rapid economic growth of the 1950s and 1960s stimulated further expansion of cooperation. This was true despite attempts by Charles de Gaulle to bring the EC back into line with other intergovernmental organizations by subordinating the largely independent Community institutions to the member states. In 1967 the executive institutions of the three communities were fused into a single institutional structure, creating a single Council of Ministers and a single commission regulated on identical lines for all three treaties (the Merger Treaty).

Only after Pompidou took office in 1969 did the French attitude become more cooperative. This in turn led to rapid development of the EC in various directions. Whereas France had effectively blocked the British application for membership twice during the 1960s, the geographical area of the EC was greatly enlarged in 1973 with the admission of the United Kingdom, Ireland, and Denmark. The decision of principle taken then to allow other European countries to join the EC has led to a periodic enlargement of the Community. This enlargement has occurred under guidelines that insure that new members accept the constituting treaties and their political aims, the decisions taken in the framework of the treaties, and the choices made with regard to future development. In 1981 Greece became a member and in 1986 Spain and Portugal were also admitted, following protracted negotiations. In addition to the interest in membership shown by Eastern European countries since the disintegration of communism, the EC is dealing with formal applications from — among others — Austria, Finland, Norway, and Sweden.

In the 1970s new steps were taken to expand cooperation among the member states. With the institution of European political cooperation, a form of cooperation that was placed explicitly outside the framework of the EC, a pragmatic step was finally taken to extend cooperation into the political field. Given the increased involvement of the heads of state and government in European affairs and the role they acquired in settling disputes in the Council of Ministers, their summit meetings became institutionalized in 1974 in the European Council. In the Single European Act (SEA), which came into force in 1987, these meetings have been officially acknowledged as a part of the Council of Ministers insofar as they deal with EC matters.

In addition to the participation of heads of state and government in EC affairs and the increased political cooperation among the member states, agreement was reached in 1969 to develop an economic and monetary policy that would lead to an Economic and Monetary Union (EMU). Although the definitive realization of the goal met many setbacks after that, more modest objectives were carried through. These included the establishment of a European Monetary System and a European Currency Unit (the ECU). Only with the conclusion of the Maastricht Treaty on European Union have the members agreed to the establishment of the EMU, although the United Kingdom and Denmark are not obligated to participate in the final stage.

Following a period of relative stagnation, which is mirrored in the initiatives taken in the late 1970s and 1980s to create a European Union, cooperation in the EC regained momentum during the latter part of the 1980s. After years of difficult decision making in the council, otherwise stubborn member state ministers proved willing to cooperate. Confronted with international economic recession, the member states grew aware that their position in the world would be enhanced by a collective undertaking. The feeling that only a concentrated effort would enable the EC to beat the long existing stagnation and catch up with the United States and Japan spread quickly. Encouraged by industrial circles, the European Commission launched its white paper "Completing the Internal Market." As a result, the process of integration received an enormous impetus. On the basis of a strictly applied time schedule, the implementation of the unified internal market was largely carried out by 1 January 1993.

This changed frame of mind greatly stimulated European cooperation. The effect this had went far beyond the agreement of the Twelve to finally complete the internal market. Simultaneously, the European Parliament (EP) produced a draft treaty establishing the European Union, which in turn led the European Council to set up a committee to make suggestions for improving cooperation. The resulting intergovernmental conference held in Luxembourg in the autumn of 1985 led to the Single European Act (SEA). The SEA led, in 1987, to important changes in the involvement of the EP in various policy fields (the cooperation procedure), the implementation powers of the commission, the completion of the internal market, the administration of justice, and the system of financial resources of the EEC and Euratom. In addition, certain "new" fields of competence were explicitly drawn into the realm of Community decision making. These include economic and social cohesion, research and technological development, environmental policy, and consumer protection.

As a result of the development of European cooperation over the years, the EC has come to encompass a large number of policy fields, as summarized in table 2.1. In this respect EC policy-making has increasingly come to resemble the actions of a national government.

Following the unification of Germany and the disintegration of the Soviet Union, the EC is once again the focus of international attention. In the wake of the SEA and the pledge to complete the internal market by 1993, it became clear that EMU would have to be realized. A committee under the leadership of commission President Jacques Delors was set up in 1988 to study the matter. At the Strasbourg meeting of the European Council held in 1989 the decision was made to prepare for two intergovernmental conferences in 1991 to extend the scope of EC policy. The first would establish an EMU; the second would amend the treaties of the EC and lead to a European Political Union (EPU). With the signing of the Maastricht treaty, the EC reached a further stage of development. Both the steps toward and a timetable for the introduction of a common economic and monetary policy were clearly stipulated, while new fields of policy — such as defense, immigration, and justice — were (partially) brought into the realm of EC affairs. These latter fields of the political union are more or less based on the principle of intergovernmental cooperation. The end of development of the EC is still not in sight. The member states have already scheduled new initiatives for the EPU for 1996. Given the important changes that are taking place in Europe and the impact of the EC on their outcome, it is hardly surprising that interest in EC policy continues to increase.

The Community Institutions

The division of tasks and responsibilities among the institutions of the EC shapes the balance of power within the EC.[2] The most important institutions of the Community are the European Commission and the Council of Ministers. Together they almost exclusively exercise the power of deci-

2. For a more detailed discussion of the institutional structure of the EC, see Kapteyn and VerLoren van Themaat 1989, pp. 103–84.

Table 2.1

Meetings of the Council, 1980–88

	1980	1981	1982	1983	1984	1985	1986	1987	1988
Agriculture	14	11	15	14	16	14	11	16[a]	12
Budget	3	3	4	4	4	5	5	6	4
Civic Protection	—	—	—	—	—	—	—	1	1
Consumer Affairs	—	—	—	1	3	1	2[a]	3	1[a]
Cultural Affairs	—	—	—	—	2	—	1	—	1
Development Cooperation	1	3	2	2	2	2	2	3	2
Economic and Financial Affairs	10[b]	11[a,b]	10[a]	8	8	7	8	8[a]	7
Education	1	1	1	1[a]	1	1	2	1	2
Employment and Social Affairs	—	—	2	3[a]	4[a]	3[a]	3	2	2
Energy	2	3	3	3	2	3	3	2	2
Environment	2	2	2	3	3	3	3	4	3
Fisheries	7	8	7	9	5	3	5	3	5
General and Foreign Affairs	—	13	12	13	12	20	14	12	12
Health	—	—	—	—	—	—	1	1	2
Industry[c]	—	—	2	1	3	6	6	5	2
Internal Market	—	—	—	6	2	5	8[a]	6	8[a]
Iron and Steel[c]	—	4	—	6	2	1	—	—	—
Legal Affairs	1	—	1	—	—	—	—	1	—
Research	—	1	3	5	4	2	4	3	4
Telecommunication	—	—	—	—	—	1	—	—	1
Tourism	—	—	—	—	—	—	—	—	1
Transport	2	2	2	4	4	3	4	4	4
Other[d]	2	—	2	1	—	—	1	—	2
Adopted regulations	312	414	393	—	351	447	473	458	434
Adopted directives	51	45	42	—	53	59	74	40	63
Adopted decisions	136	150	128	—	99	109	184	125	131

Source: Data from the Twenty-Eighth–Thirty-Sixth Review of the Council's Work.
[a]Includes a joint meeting with another composition of the council.
[b]In 1980 EcoFin met once to deal with tax matters; in 1981, twice.
[c]Especially during the restructuring of the Community steel policy at the beginning of the 1980s, iron and steel policy was dealt with during special meetings of the Iron and Steel Council. In less precarious times, these matters are dealt with in the Industry Council.
[d]Includes specialized meetings of the General and Foreign Affairs Council to deal with associated states, negotiations in the framework of GATT, and so on.

sion. The European Parliament plays an increasing role in EC decision making. While the Court of Justice is also influential. The court determines where the national legal order ends and the scope of Community law commences. These four institutions play a central part in EC decision making.

The *European Commission* has the duty to serve the general interest of the EC as a whole. It consists of seventeen members, including two nationals from each of the five large member states (France, Germany, Italy, Spain, and the United Kingdom) and one from each of the smaller countries (Belgium, the Netherlands, Luxembourg, Ireland, Denmark, Greece, and Portugal). The members are appointed for a term of four years by common accord by the member state governments. The commission is a collegiate body, with a president and six vice-presidents who are appointed for two-year terms. Each commissioner appoints a cabinet (a personal staff) to assist in carrying out his or her duties as head of one or more directorate-generals of the commission and as a member of the commission. The commission presents itself and its program to the European Parliament. The initial debate and vote of censure that follows largely resembles the presentation of national governmental policy when a new cabinet is formed.

The role of the commission is similar to that of a national government. It cooperates with the Council of Ministers in exercising the legislative powers of the EC. The commission is responsible for administering EC policy and implementing decisions taken by the Community. Although this responsibility officially rests with the commission, it is often carried out in cooperation with intergovernmental officials and committees. Additionally, the commission ensures the observance of the treaties and EC decisions and, if necessary, brings cases to the attention of the Court of Justice for judicial settlement.

The most important task of the commission is, however, its duty to develop initiatives to obtain the objectives of the Community. This role in steering and stimulating initiatives is of great importance as the council, in almost all cases, can act only on the basis of a proposal from the commission. This exclusive right of initiative surpasses the right of national governments, but the commission is in truth only an embryonic European "government." Following the French reaction in the 1960s to the expansion of supranational powers of the EC, the commission has become more cautious in exercising its right of initiative. Before drafting a proposal, it is careful to take into account the wishes of the member states.

The Council of the European Community, or the *Council of Ministers* as it is better known, together with the commission, has the power to legally bind the EC's subjects. In contrast to most other international organizations, the delegates to the council are members of the governments of the member states. This reflects the wish of the founders of the EC that the institution that represents the member states be composed of politically responsible people. The delegates act under instructions from and under the authority of their governments.

In order to attain the objectives set out by the EC treaties, the council has been given the power to coordinate the general economic policies of the member states and the power to make decisions that bind (the residents of) those member states. Because EC treaties are best regarded as a framework for further cooperation, the way in which the treaties delegate this decision-making power and the manner in which it is exercised is of crucial importance.

The Council of Ministers exercises this policy-making function in co-operation with the commission. Decisions are made by the council on the basis of a proposal from the commission. Of course, the proposals are often amended during the deliberations. Since only member states have voting power, the brunt of authority in the exercise of policy-making rests with the council. As such it is the key institution of the Community. The proceedings in the council are chaired for a six-month period by each member state consecutively.

The presidency of the council has come to play an important role in decision making as the compromise proposals put forward by the council often determine the final outcome of an issue. Decisions in the council are made according to the decision rule that the EC treaties prescribe as applicable for the proposal at hand. As a result of French opposition to qualified majority voting, decision making in the 1960s and 1970s almost always took place on the basis of unanimity. Since the coming into force of the SEA in 1987, qualified majority voting has, however, become more generally applied.

The council is not a single fixed body. Its composition changes in accordance with the subject matter discussed, with the most senior official of each member state representing his or her government. With the activities of the EC expanding and becoming increasingly detailed, the council meets presently in more than twenty specialized compositions (see table 2.1), of which the General Affairs Council, the Agriculture Council, and the EcoFin Council are perhaps the best known. To prepare its deliberations and manage its daily functions, in 1958 the council established a Committee of Permanent Representatives (Coreper) (Lindberg 1963, pp. 77–87). Given the growth of EC policy, Coreper, in turn, has established numerous working groups and other technical committees made up of civil servants from all national administrations to discuss the technical merits of the proposals submitted by the commission.[3] In addition, much

3. As early as 1963, Lindberg noted the existence of some 127 expert groups and maintained that "the Committee of Permanent Representatives is serving more and more as

administrative decision making has been delegated to the commission and management committees. It should be stressed, however, that Coreper, working groups, and other technical committees have no independent powers. They only assist the council in the discharge of its duties. They have the legal status of a subsidiary body and cannot, therefore, make independent decisions.

The *European Parliament* consists of representatives of "the peoples of the states brought together in the EC." Whereas these representatives used to be appointed by their national parliaments, since 1979 they have been directly elected once every five years. Distributed roughly on the basis of population, each member state has a fixed number of the 567 seats in the EP: Germany has 99; the United Kingdom, France, and Italy, 87 each; Spain, 64; the Netherlands, 31; Belgium, Greece, and Portugal, 25; Denmark, 16; Ireland, 15; and Luxembourg, 6. In the EP the representatives organize themselves into groups according to party affiliation. The important groups such as the socialists, Christian democrats, and conservatives include representatives from all member states.

The EP exercises the advisory and supervisory powers conferred on it by the EC treaties. It has been given the power to discuss any matter concerning the Community and can adopt resolutions and invite the member states to act. Furthermore, it holds the power to make decisions with respect to the budget of the EC. The EP has a supervisory function with respect to the commission. By adopting a motion of censure it can dismiss the commission as a whole.

Before taking (important) decisions, the Council of Ministers is required to consult the EP. The influence of the European Parliament on EC decision making is, however, largely dependent on the willingness of the commission, which is politically accountable to the EP, to endorse its views. Given the limited influence of the commission on the outcome of EC decision making, the European Parliament has yet to exercise its authority. Furthermore, it can dismiss only the commission as a whole, which limits the applicability of the instrument.

In addition to the regular consultation procedure, the European Parliament has acquired a larger legislative role since SEA came into force. According to Article 149 of the amended European Economic Community treaty, the council is required, in specific fields which are important for the internal market, to give the EP three months to react to a common position it reaches. In this so-called cooperation procedure, the EP can either reject or amend such a position. In the case of a rejection, the council's position enters into force only by a unanimous vote of the council. In the case of an amendment, the commission decides whether or not

---

a clearinghouse for an expanding coterie of specialized committees, reserving for itself only matters of general, or essentially political importance" (idem., p. 60).

to adapt its proposal accordingly. This, in turn, can also be overridden by a unanimous council vote. This larger legislative role of the EP has been extended to more (economic) fields with the coming into force of the treaty of Maastricht on 1 November 1993.

Since the introduction of direct election, the EP has come to play a more active role in the functioning of the Community in a further respect. By bringing cases before the Court of Justice, it has been successful in stimulating the European Commission and the Council of Ministers to take action in certain fields (see chapter 3).

The *Court of Justice* of the European Community consists of thirteen judges and six advocates-general who are appointed by common accord by the governments of the member states for six-year terms. The judges choose from among themselves a president for a (renewable) term of three years. The advocates-general are assigned with the responsibility for drafting impartial "reasoned submissions" on cases brought before the Court of Justice. These submissions form the basis on which the court comes to its judgments.

The court has been given the power to settle disputes with regard to Community law, binding the residents of the member states without the prior consent of each national government. In contrast to most other international organizations, the judicial institution is widely accessible to private individuals. Through its interpretation and application of the EC treaties and their implementing rules, the court ensures the observance of EC law. As the Community legal order has no court of appeal, the decisions of the Court of Justice are final. Consequently it plays an important role in determining the direction in which the EC develops.

In addition to these four major institutions, the EC has created a few (minor) independent Community bodies and a large number of (advisory) committees to assist in the decision-making process. The most important of the independent bodies is the Court of Auditors, which examines the revenues and expenditures of the EC. The Economic and Social Committee, in which employers, workers, consumer interests, and experts are represented, is the advisory committee that is most often consulted. The council is specifically obliged to consult the Economic and Social Committee on socioeconomic proposals.

The Multilevel Community Decision-Making Process

As the EC developed and common policies became established, expanded, and adapted to new situations, the character of decision making became more technical. Ministers, given their predominantly national responsibilities, neither had the time nor the necessary expertise to deal with all matters (Lodge 1989). These developments have gradually resulted in the establishment of a multilevel Community decision-making structure in which national civil servants greatly assist their ministers, as indicated in figure 2.1.

At the first level a draft proposal is elaborated by the services of the commission. In general, this occurs in consultation with experts from the member states, who, acting in a personal capacity, furnish relevant information at working meetings. At this level the commission and its services are also frequently canvassed by interest groups. The commission remains, however, completely free to decide whether or not to act in accordance with this information when drafting a proposal. At the second level, the commission formally adopts the draft proposal during one of its weekly meetings and submits it to the council for a decision. At the third level, the commission's proposal is sent by the council to the European Parliament, the Economic and Social Committee, and other bodies required by treaties to be consulted. These in turn, after discussions with the commission, report to the council.

On the basis of the commission's proposal and the reports from the consultative bodies and technical committees, Coreper and council working groups prepare for the deliberations in the Council of Ministers by searching for preliminary agreement at the fourth level of the decision-making process.[4] At this level national governments submit amendments to the commission proposal, and these in turn are considered by the commission. If the presidency of the council regards the negotiations to have become deadlocked or in need of political guidelines, it refers them to the council. Upon receiving guidelines and further instructions from the council, deliberations at the preparatory level are continued — on occasion repeatedly — until the discussions are deemed to be well enough developed for final decision making at the level of the Council of Ministers.

At the fifth level of the process, the final decision is taken by the council. If full agreement has been reached at the preparatory level, the draft measure is adopted as a so-called A-item without deliberation, save in the extremely rare situation where a member state raises an objection.[5] If the negotiations held during the previous level have not led to agreement,

4. Deviations from this procedure do, however, exist. The most important of these arises with regard to the preparation of the discussion of technical agricultural proposals in the council. These proposals are dealt with in the Special Agricultural Committee. With respect to — among others — veterinary health proposals, the preparations take place in Coreper, where the agenda for all meetings of the council is determined. Among the other, less far-reaching, deviations are Committee 113 in the field of trade policy, the Monetary Committee, and the Budget Committee.

5. As a full agreement is deemed to have been reached with regard to these draft measures, they are considered as requiring only formal adoption and not debate by the council. As such they are, in contrast to B-items, placed on the agenda of the next scheduled council meeting, irrespective of the composition of the council that will then meet.

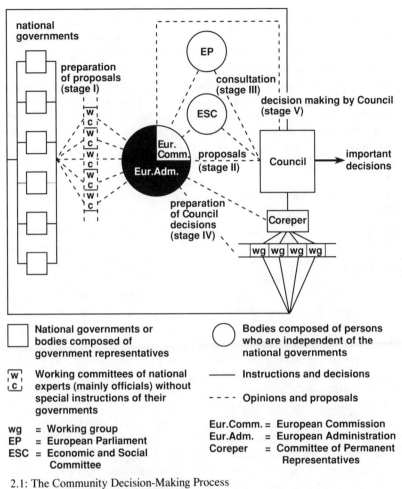

national governments

preparation
of proposals
(stage I)

EP

consultation
(stage III)

ESC

decision making by Council
(stage V)

Eur.
Comm.
Eur.Adm.

proposals
(stage II)

Council

important
decisions

preparation
of Council
decisions
(stage IV)

Coreper

wg | wg | wg | wg

National governments or
bodies composed of
government representatives

Bodies composed of persons
who are independent of the
national governments

w
c

Working committees of national
experts (mainly officials) without
special instructions of their
governments

———— Instructions and decisions

- - - - Opinions and proposals

wg = Working group
EP = European Parliament
ESC = Economic and Social
Committee

Eur.Comm. = European Commission
Eur.Adm. = European Administration
Coreper = Committee of Permanent
Representatives

2.1: The Community Decision-Making Process

Source: Jan M. M. Van den Bos, "Dutch EC Policy Making: A Model-Guided
Approach to Coordination and Negotiation" (Ph.D. diss., Interuniversity
Center for Sociological Theory and Methodology, Netherlands, 1991), p. 36.

these are continued in the council. On occasion this process can be very lengthy, requiring considerable diplomatic skill and negotiating technique in order to find a compromise acceptable to all parties.

The manner in which the decision-making process has evolved has not been without criticism. The process has been described as "so weighted down and compromised that coherence and comprehensibility are inevitably sacrificed" (Krislov et al. 1986, p. 32) and the decisions reached as "an amalgam of different national concerns rather than a clear policy instrument designed to achieve a particular policy objective as effectively as possible" (H. Wallace 1983, p. 63).

The Analysis of European Integration

The unexpectedly rapid economic progress in Western Europe during the early years of the Community — quickly outgrowing such initial goals as the establishment of a customs union — kindled the hopes and ideals that economic integration would not only lead to economic benefits for the member states individually, but would also create bonds and mutual interests. In the study of European integration, elements of both the unique supranational character of the EC and the political hopes and aspirations for Europe that followed the Second World War are clearly reflected (see Jansen and De Vree 1988).

Idealistically motivated conceptions have always played an important role in the analysis of European integration. As early as The Hague Congress of 1948, different conceptions of integration were advocated. Some of the same arguments and conceptions are still made today. In 1948, unionists proclaimed their desire to further the intergovernmental cooperation among European countries, while federalists went a step further and aimed at achieving a European federation as an ultimate goal. Unionists and federalists alike shared the conviction that the development of integration is fundamentally a consequence of political initiative.

The functionalist conception of European integration is less straightforward. In contrast to idealistically motivated federalists who focused primarily on political federation, functionalists were skeptical of the role of politicians in the development of international cooperation. They regarded the role played by ministers as being primarily motivated by power and politics. In their view, a more rational solution to the common economic and technical problems facing nations could be found by giving technical experts the authority to make decisions. In this way a spreading web of international cooperation was envisaged, a web that would develop as differing combinations of interested states emerged to fulfill different functions (see Mitrany 1933). Political integration was perceived in this conception as evolving indirectly, as a learning process of economic integration. The technical-economic imperative would generate the need for a unified decision-making structure.

As the course and practice of integration proved more complicated and irregular than the described theories had expected, a more encompassing, new conception was elaborated that fused both the dynamism of technical-economic cooperation with the need for political initiative. Progress toward economic and political integration is seen in this neo-functionalist conception as resulting from the explicit delegation of important and expanding tasks and the predicted, shifting loyalties of the political actors toward this new center (see Haas 1958, Lindberg 1963, and Scheingold 1965). Economic and political integration would develop gradually, reinforcing each other and ultimately leading to new forms of government.

European cooperation, however, suffered setbacks in the 1960s as a consequence of the French preference for intergovernmental cooperation rather than supranational organization. These setbacks precipitated a reform of neo-functionalist theory that stressed the need for a critical threshold of economic integration before the growth of international consciousness could set in. The critical threshold was believed to be a prerequisite for the predicted spillover of economic integration into political integration (Haas 1968). More pessimistic scholars went further, placing all but complete emphasis on the national dimension in EC affairs. They argued that the European Community was not fundamentally different from other international organizations: national interests remain the driving force behind integration in the Community. By directing their criticism at the shifting loyalty of governmental behavior as postulated by the neo-functionalists, the intergovernmentalists disavowed much of the European Community's presumed singularity. In their view, politicians should be seen as gatekeepers guarding their domestic political systems rather than as advocates of greater integration (see Hoffmann 1966, 1982). The experiences of the EC during the 1960s, 1970s, and early 1980s seemed to legitimate this conception.

Since the early 1980s, however, changes indicate that the development of the EC is less of an unfolding process than any of the conceptions of integration had forecast. Confronted with serious international economic recession, awareness grew among the member states that many of the problems they faced could be solved only through mutual cooperation. Following the coming into force of the SEA and the Treaty on European Union, EC policy-making has reached a new threshold of expansion, by first deepening and then broadening its scope of activity. Recently the pace of the integration process has once more slowed, however, with civil strife occurring in eastern Europe and economic stagnation confronting the member states.

In retrospect, one is struck by the trend that can be found in the theory of European integration. The idealistically motivated conceptions of integration that originated following the Second World War were based on the conviction that the political initiative necessary for greater European integration would emerge. Pessimism with regard to the willingness of politicians to relinquish national sovereignty has increased in later years. Functionalists were wary of politicians and so placed emphasis on the dynamics of economic integration. They granted politicians only a more or less passive role in the process of integration. Neo-functionalists not only recognized that politicians often do not actively support integration, but asserted that they are detrimental to the process. This growing, pessimistic attitude toward the role of politicians in the promotion of European integration culminated in intergovernmentalism, where the unique elements of the European Community were largely ignored. In this conception of integration, the European Community was not considered fundamentally different from other international organizations.

Notwithstanding the growing "realism" — or, if preferred, "pessimism" — that has characterized the theory of integration, it cannot be denied that European cooperation evolved gradually, drawing the economies of the member states closer together, solidifying economic and political relations among the Twelve. During the initial phase of its development, the EC could still be regarded as an international organization in which the member states were engaged in the achievement of goals and the development of common policies set out in the framework of a treaty. The revolutionary manner in which the member states had delegated powers to the institutions of the Community, however, inevitably generated its own dynamic process.

Given the legislative nature of the decisions taken by the Community — directly binding the residents of the member states — and the continuous development of the policy dealt with by the EC, Community decision making has increasingly acquired the character of a unified government. The scope of decisions, together with their importance for the economies of the member states, suggests that government in the Twelve has acquired an international level of administration that goes hand in hand with traditional municipal, regional-provincial, and national administration. In light of such developments, scholars have been tempted to classify the European Community as a federal entity (see, e.g., W. Wallace 1983). This, however, does as little justice to the character of Community decision making as would classifying it as a mere international organization. The EC frankly defies simple categorization. The complexity lies precisely in the fact that the major decision-making institutions of the EC (the Council of Ministers and the European Commission) are only indirectly linked to the subjects of Community legislation (the residents of the twelve member states). In contrast to federal constitutions, where provisions are contained ensuring government by and for the people, the constituting treaties of the European Community — or the European Union, as it is now officially called — can at best be regarded as a framework for the pursuit of common interests by the member states.

All in all, the development of European integration has become a step-wise process, with new stages of development occurring in the wake of major international events — either economic or political. Only under such circumstances do all member states prove willing to agree to the collective pursuit of their interests above continued national authority. The final outcome of the process of integration has, therefore, not yet been determined. Much will depend on the member states and their continued willingness to participate constructively in the process.

The Modeling Approach

The key to understanding European cooperation does not lie in the description of the developmental consequences of integration, but rather in the dynamics that structure the process of integration: its decision-making process. In the course of the 1970s and 1980s research on policy-making has come to regard policy as a body of collective decisions made by a network of actors interacting in the multilayered institutional framework of a policy domain (see, e.g., Bueno de Mesquita, Newman, and Rabushka 1985, Kenis and Schneider 1989, Laumann and Knoke 1987, and Stokman and Van den Bos 1992). In our view European cooperation, too, can best be analyzed in such a context.

Research on the manner in which Community decisions are actually made has yet to develop. To a large extent this can be explained by the confidential character of council deliberations. With the exception of a few case-study descriptions in the framework of broad academic analyses and some background newspaper articles on controversial issues, little is known of the way in which decision making occurs in the Council of Ministers. Comparative analysis of the aspects that structure Community decision making in practice has still to be conducted. With this book, we hope to contribute to this new field of research.

The European Community was never intended to become a level of government superior to and independent from national government. Both the institutional structure and the history of the development of the EC have proven that the critical actors in the decision-making process are the member states themselves. Regardless of the large degree of authority delegated by the members to the EC, the governments of the member states were careful to retain legislative power for themselves in the Community (see Axline 1968). The substance of the Community's own legal order — in other words, the decisions it makes — is largely determined in the Council of Ministers, where representatives of the member states negotiate with the European Commission on the basis of a proposal drafted by the commission. Finally, only the member states have the power to decide whether the proposed legislation — which is often greatly amended in the process — will be adopted. Given the controversial character of this process of decision making, we feel justified in directing our attention exclusively at the phase of final decision making in the council. One of our hopes is to elucidate the manner in which the member states, in consultation with the commission, reach agreement.

In this book the more or less metaphorical concept of policy networks is elaborated into alternative models of policy-making — the basic expected utility model and its strategic behavior counterpart, as well as alternative logrolling models — in an effort to reveal the mechanism that structures decision making in the council (see Bueno de Mesquita 1985 and Stokman and Van Oosten 1990). An important advantage of such an approach for the study of policy-making is that it enables us to judge the assumptions behind each model on the basis of the ability to predict correctly the outcome of the decisions at hand. In the models presented here, this is done with the help of relatively easy-to-acquire data — on the capabilities and resources of the actors concerned and their saliences and policy positions for decisions — from an expert in the policy field. By comparing the results of the different models, it then becomes possible to derive a more justified specification of the conditions that structure decision making. Consequently, we expect that the modeling approach will enable us to better understand the sparks and setbacks that accompany the development of the European Community and thereby will contribute to the development of a new field of research.

Jan M. M. Van den Bos

3 The Policy Issues Analyzed

In order to test the models presented in this book, data have been collected with regard to four important policy dimensions in the EC. These concern the determination of the maximum permissible levels of radioactive contamination in foodstuffs, the setting of emission levels for exhaust gases of motor vehicles, the liberalization of intra-EC civil aviation during an experimental three-year period, and the development and character of the Community banking system leading to the establishment of an Economic and Monetary Union. These issues all had important ramifications for the development of their respective policy fields and were only settled after protracted deliberations at the level of the Council of Ministers itself. By analyzing these four different policy fields, the broad scope of Community policy is also illustrated.

Such an analysis, moreover, enables us to address the question of whether the manner in which policy is made depends on the type of policy discussed. Each of the issues was dealt with by a different group within the Council of Ministers: the General Affairs Council, the Environment Council, the Transport Council, and the Economic and Financial Council. Although only four of the twenty-three composi-

The data described on the exhaust emissions, the air transport liberalization, and the radioactive contamination issues were collected by the author in the framework of the research project on Dutch EC policy-making and the contribution of national civil servants. This project was conducted in 1986–91 and was supported in part by the Netherlands Foundation for Scientific Research in Politics and Public Administration, subsidized by the Netherlands Organization for Scientific Research, and by the Commission of the European Communities. The data on the EC banking system, along with the material on which the descriptions of the issues are based, were furnished by John H. P. Williams (see chapter 8; Kugler and Williams 1990; Williams 1991).

tions of the Council of Ministers are analyzed here, we feel this represents a broad cross-section of the Community policy domain. It stretches from general policy fields (monetary policy) to sectoral fields (environmental protection, nuclear affairs, and civil aviation), from more or less political fields (nuclear affairs and monetary policy) to largely economic fields (civil aviation and — at least for the period under consideration — environmental policy), from policy fields nationally dealt with by a single ministry (civil aviation) to inter-ministerial fields (environmental protection, nuclear affairs, and monetary policy), and from policy fields whose ministers regularly participate in EC affairs (monetary policy and for many member states nuclear affairs) to fields involving ministers who less often take part in the Council of Ministers (civil aviation and environmental protection).

Given the controversial nature of decision making in the four issue areas studied, our analysis will be based on data concerning the deliberations held in the council itself. All aspects of the issues that are analyzed here concerned critical national interests and were decided upon by the ministers or by the heads of state or government themselves. While outside pressure was instrumental in persuading the member states to settle their disagreements over each issue, only the member states had the power to decide. We therefore focus our attention exclusively on this final phase of negotiation and on the way in which the member states reconcile their differences.[1] Discussions were protracted in all cases; multiple meetings were needed to bring about the desired consensus.

Emission Limits For Exhaust Gases of Motor Vehicles

As a result of an initiative taken by the German delegation during a meeting of the Environment Council in June 1983, and reiterated during the European Council held in Stuttgart later the same month, the European Commission presented a proposal in May 1984 to reduce motor vehicle emissions of carbon monoxide, unburned hydrocarbons, and nitrous oxides. In an effort to protect public health, combat deforestation, and to stimulate efforts by the European automobile industry to improve its competitiveness in the world market, the commission proposed setting limit values that would achieve, by 1995 at the latest, results similar to those realized by American and Japanese emission standards.[2]

The proposals envisaged carrying this out in two stages irrespective of the weight or capacity of the vehicle. In the first stage, which would apply to new models from 1989 and for all new vehicles as of 1991, exhaust gases would be allowed to contain only up to 45 grams of carbon monoxide

1. It should be recognized, however, that the models themselves are capable of dealing with the internal political processes in each member state, or in the dynamic interchanges between constituencies within each member state and the EC as a whole.
2. See also Van den Bos 1991, p. 165–71.

(CO), 15 grams of combined unburned hydrocarbon (HC) and nitrous oxide (NOx) content, and 6 grams of isolated NOx content per test. By 1995, the latest date for enforcing the second stage, similar results as achieved in Japan and the United States were to be reached. The commission left the choice of technology by which these results were to be achieved to the discretion of the industry (*Agence Europe* 3852, pp. 5–6).

From the onset of discussion in the Council of Ministers in May 1984, the member states displayed different interests. Germany welcomed the commission's proposals. Given the grave condition of forests in the Federal Republic, the resulting strong public pressure to take measures, and the fact that the German automobile industry regarded the installation of catalytic converters as a necessary step to remain competitive in markets outside Europe, it is hardly surprising that the Germans took the initiative to request a proposal from the commission. As an advocate of firm and swift action, however, Germany considered that the proposed timetable involved too much delay; the requisite technology was already available.

Although not specifically regulated in the proposal, the possibility that a member state would implement the chosen emission standards preemptively created a controversy. Since Germany was anxious to achieve results, from the beginning it contemplated awarding fiscal incentives in the form of tax concessions to owners of cars meeting these stricter emission levels. The German position quickly received support from traditionally pro-environmental member states, such as Denmark and the Netherlands.

Among the other large European automobile producers — that is, France, the United Kingdom, and Italy — interests were different. In contrast to Germany, where the automobile industry prospered, the French, British, and Italian industries faced large problems. The extra cost of introducing devices to limit emissions would affect their market position still further. Especially with respect to smaller cars, where the cost would be relatively high, Japanese and to a lesser extent American competitors would have a good chance of benefiting.

An extended timetable, such as the one proposed by the commission, would, therefore, be an essential element in any agreement acceptable to these member states. It would also give alternative technologies, such as the lean burn engine, which was still in the laboratory stage of development in the United Kingdom, the chance to develop. As a result, France, the United Kingdom, and Italy staunchly opposed the German plans to introduce fiscal incentives. Publicly they based their opposition on the fear that the free movement of motor vehicles would be endangered and on their concern to preserve the unity of the internal market. Fear of a deterioration of their market position inside the Community, however, seems to have been as strong a motivation.

Ordinarily, given the interests at stake and the polarized positions held by the large member states, such a conflict would make the required unanimous agreement virtually unattainable. Yet the pledged commitment to the environment was translated into an agreement only a year following the presentation of the commission proposal. This had everything to do with the interest Germany had in the issue and the subsequent pressure applied by the Germans. Furthermore, France, Italy, and the United Kingdom were, given the weakness of their industries, especially eager to ensure the integrity of the internal market. Unilateral German measures could spark others to do the same and thus jeopardize their European markets. In addition, general public opinion in Europe would make unilateral steps taken by Germany and not followed by the others difficult to justify politically.

On 19 September 1984 the German cabinet, following a disappointing discussion held in the council in June, approved tax-exemption plans to stimulate the introduction of nonpollutant motor vehicles on the national market. The German plan called for compensating the purchasers of these vehicles with a tax-exemption of DM 3,000 for additional costs and servicing. The measure would be voluntary and come into effect as of 1985. Plans to make the measure compulsory for large cars (with a cubic capacity of 2.0 liters or more) as of 1988 and for other cars as of 1989 were being drafted. If brought before the Court of Justice by the commission, the German government made it clear that it would resort to Article 36 EEC, which foresees the possibility of member states taking measures to protect, among other things, the health and life of persons, animals, or plants.[3]

Having thus made very clear the importance Germany attached to this decision and their intent to take unilateral measures if necessary, discussions in the council focused on finding a solution acceptable to all. After a group of senior-ranking national civil servants had discussed the issue a number of times, agreement was reached on the principle of differentiating between cars according to cylinder capacity. The fact that the structure of the car markets in the member states differed, as did the market segments upon which various national automobile industries were oriented, facilitated reaching agreement on this matter.

Germany, with a national market in which cars with a large cylinder capacity are prominent, was focused primarily on the large car market segment. Priority was placed on reducing emission norms in this segment as soon as possible, as national political opinion demanded concrete results and this segment had the most to offer. German automobile producers were not opposed to the position of their government. Given the price of automobiles in this segment, the extra cost of installing a catalytic

---

3. Minister Bangemann noted in the Internal Market Council that the measure "is a national objective which, of course, the FRG hopes will be accepted at Community level, but which, whatever the circumstances, will be achieved separately if the next negotiations at Council level do not lead to any agreement" (Agence Europe 3950, p. 6).

converter would not translate into a competitive edge for automobile manufacturers from outside Europe. As the German industry forms the most internationally oriented automobile industry in Europe, the pressure to comply with American and Japanese standards was most quickly felt in Germany (Ruigrok 1990).

A different picture emerges for the other important automobile-producing member states. Having a national market made up almost entirely of cars with a small cylinder capacity and an industry focused primarily on the European smaller car segment (less than 1.4 liters), France and Italy were particularly interested in extending the timetable for small cars. The member states without an important automobile industry also shared the French and Italian perspective. Given the high price of three-track catalytic converters in relation to the price of this car category, an extended timetable would provide time to seek alternative technologies and to allow the small car producers to adapt and become more competitive. In the United Kingdom, the national market was less skewed toward the small car segment, with relatively more cars in the intermediate range (between 1.4 and 2.0 liters). In contrast to France and Italy, with respectively 61 and 73 percent of new car sales in the small car category in 1983, less than half of new car sales in the United Kingdom (48 percent) were in this category (*Agence Europe* 4045, p. 6).

With these differing interests in mind, a preliminary agreement about the classification of cars, the definition of emission standards, and the date of introduction of the new emission standards was reached on 21 March 1985. This agreement was made possible by mutual concessions regarding the date of the compulsory introduction of European standards and the implementation of financial incentives. The Germans agreed that financial incentives would be tied to the European standards; they would apply only to cars that would perform 15 percent better than the standards that were to be decided upon; they would not commence before 1 July 1985; they would amount to considerably less than the additional costs (DM 750 for small cars during the first stage, and DM 2,200 for large and medium cars); and they would be spread over a number of years. As a result of this preliminary agreement the commission announced that it would no longer oppose German tax incentives.

Although the magnitude of the emission standards had always been an aspect of the negotiations, the discussion did not focus on this precise issue. Given the difficulty of solving the controversies with respect to the differentiation of cylinder capacity, the date of introduction, and the application of tax incentives, the preliminary agreement reached in March only stipulated that European standards based on the American norm were to apply.

Between March and June 1985 the commission drafted a proposal transposing the standards based on American norms into European standards.

Table 3.1
Proposed Emission Standards

Category of Vehicles	Date of Implementation (new model/new cars)	Emission Norms (grams test)
More than 2.0 liters	1 October 1988/1 October 1989	CO 25; HC + NOx 6.5; NOx 3.5
1.4 to 2.0 liters	1 October 1991/1 October 1993	CO 30; HC + NOx 8
Less than 1.4 liters		
Stage A	1 October 1990/1 October 1991	At least CO 45; HC + NOx 15; NOx 6
Stage B	To be fixed by 1987 and implemented no later than 1 October 1992/1 October 1993	European Standard

This matter formed the core of the discussions in the subsidiary bodies of the council to transform the political agreement of March into an operational directive. Some delegations found the proposals put forward "not at all satisfactory and could not have an environmental effect equivalent to the American standards," while others considered the limits "too restrictive in comparison with the second objective provided for by the March council general decision, namely the use of technologies other than the three-way catalytic converter." Given the profound divergence of opinion, the only possible solution was to accept the levels proposed by the commission, which are summarized in table 3.1 (*Agence Europe* 4114, p. 9).

Only with respect to the separate NOx limit for medium cars did the final decision deviate from the proposal. By lowering this limit, the further development of lean burn technology for medium cars became possible for the United Kingdom. By linking the NOx limit to other issues, a compromise was produced that satisfied the demands for environmental protection and for industrial opportunities. The linkage included agreements on making lead-free gasoline available, an earlier introduction of the second stage of regulations for small cars, and the withdrawal of French and British opposition to the proposed German fiscal measures. In addition, given that an agreement of principle on introduction dates and tax incentives had been reached in March, important decisions for Germany had already been made. It was of domestic political importance for the Germans to apply the tax incentives as of 1 July 1985. To permit Germany to do so, the commission would have to drop court proceedings; a contingency the court was willing to undertake only in the case of a final agreement. This helps explain the willingness of Germany to accommodate the wishes of other member states in order to achieve a settlement.

The agreement reached on 27 June 1985 was, however, subject to a general reservation from Denmark. The Danish delegation, due to the position taken by the Folketing, its national parliament, had wanted significantly stricter limit values and introduction schedules for all types of cars than the commission proposed or which could realistically be expected from a greatly divided council. Given the staunch pro-environmental position taken by the Folketing, the Danish government was not prepared to withdraw its reservation. After joining the Community in 1986, Spain and Portugal quickly accepted the agreement. In the end, with the coming into force of the Single European Act in July 1987, it became possible to set the Danish reservation aside. By placing the proposed directive in the framework of the harmonization of national legislation in order to complete the internal market, the legal basis on which the commission proposal was based shifted from Article 100 to Article 100A EEC. As a consequence, unanimity was no longer required. On the basis of a qualified majority, with the Danes voting against, the directive was finally adopted on 3 December 1987.

The commissioner responsible for the protection of the environment, Clinton Davis, noted in March 1985:

> The Ten have shown the "Environment" Council's capability to solve problems initially surrounded by a great deal of controversy. A balanced solution has been found between, on the one hand, the imperative requirements of protection of the environment, and, on the other, the need to give the European motor manufacturing industry sufficient time to enable it to adapt to the new emission values, which are considerably stricter than those currently in force. This agreement constitutes an important step forward for European environmental policy. (*Agence Europe* 4054, p. 5)

Maximum Permissible Radioactive Contamination

Following the nuclear accident at Chernobyl in April 1986, safeguarding public health against the effects of radioactive contamination became an extremely important political issue. The risk that the EC would be flooded with contaminated agricultural products from the Soviet Union and Eastern Europe if restrictions were not decided upon quickly seemed extremely threatening. Given the need for reaching a solution as soon as possible, the Twelve, notwithstanding great differences of opinion as to which standards should be applied, arrived in the following month at a purely political compromise on the levels of radioactive contamination that were to be permissible in imported agricultural products. The provisional levels that came into force were 370 becquerels of caesium radioactive contamination for a liter of milk or kilogram of children's foods and 600 becquerels for a kilogram of other foods. The agreed-upon regulation — the so-called 1707 regulation or post-Chernobyl regime — was to have a temporary character: it would apply until the end of November 1986, by which time a proposal setting up permanent standards based on scientific analysis was to have been decided on.

It required another nineteen months of intense deliberations to arrive at a permanent set of radiation standards. In November 1986 and February 1987 the temporary regime had to be extended. A commission proposal had not yet been formulated due to a lack of sufficient scientific data on which to base the definitive levels. The decisions to extend the 1707 regime, however, were not simple. A few member states — particularly France — considered some aspects of the temporary regime excessively demanding and without valid scientific justification. Others — most notably the Netherlands — were anxious to prolong the temporary regime and in fact set up a permanent system of maximum permissible levels (*Agence Europe* 4488, p. 5). In the light of the feeling of the general public following the Chernobyl accident, however, France — though opposed to the temporary regime — abstained from voting when the extension decisions were brought to a vote, thereby not endangering the required unanimity.

During the entire period of decision making the attention of the council focused repeatedly on the question of whether a permanent system of maximum permissible levels should be set up in normal circumstances, or whether such a system should only be introduced in the case of a nuclear accident or abnormal radioactivity. The Netherlands was the most important protagonist of the former position, a position that corresponds with the great interest the Dutch have in exporting agricultural products. If the EC were to apply the system of maximum permissible levels only in the case of an emergency, then confidence in the quality of Dutch agricultural exports could be undermined. A less stringent position was upheld by France and the United Kingdom, countries with important nuclear (defense) industries over which they did not wish to compromise their national control. As the council remained divided on this question, the commission proved instrumental in arbitrating this conflict. On the basis of the results of an international scientific symposium, organized by the commission and held in Luxembourg on April 27–29, and after hearing the latest advice of the Article 31 Committee of Euratom, the commission proposed the maximum permissible levels of radioactive contamination shown in table 3.2.

In this proposal the commission accepted the levels for iodine, strontium, and plutonium isotopes advised by the Article 31 Committee. In the

Table 3.2
Maximum Permissible Levels of Radioactive Contamination — Proposed

Isotope	Dairy Products	Other Foods	Drinking Water	Foodstuffs
Iodine and strontium	500	3,000	400	
Plutonium	20	80	10	
Caesium	1,000	1,250	800	2,500

case of caesium, the proposed standard was four times stricter for dairy products and other foodstuffs — in correspondence with strict standards abroad and in order to receive the confidence of the general public (*Agence Europe* 4554, p. 5). These levels would be established on a permanent basis, although the commission would introduce maximum levels and appropriate control measures only in the event of a nuclear accident or any incident that could bring about abnormal levels of radioactivity. By means of a semi-automatic procedure applied by a management committee set up to administer the regime, different levels could be brought into force under certain circumstances. After the commission chose the side of the majority of the member states by proposing a definitive regulation for permissible levels only in the event of a nuclear accident or incident, the advocates of a permanent system were gradually isolated.

Notwithstanding continuous attempts to salvage as much as possible, many advocates of a permanent system felt forced to give up their position following the failure to extend the 1707 regime in November 1987. The extension proposal had not succeeded in reaching the required unanimity. An opposing vote was cast by the Greeks, who were frustrated over the unwillingness of the other member states to permit the marketing of Greece's stock of contaminated durum wheat. By linking the reestablishment of the post-Chernobyl regime to the acceptance of a permanent system triggered only in the case of an emergency, the crux of the debate shifted. Discussions became focused on the height of the levels permissible and on the extent of contamination in the case of an accident. With regard to the latter matter, the Germans and Dutch led the opposition by objecting to this part of the commission proposal based on the conviction that all food supplies might be contaminated following a nuclear accident, and not just the 10 percent of supplies, as assumed in the Article 31 Committee. Following several compromise proposals put forward by the presidency of the council and an amended commission proposal, a number of member states — most notably the Netherlands — succumbed to the pressure to reach a qualified majority. Given the wish, on the one side, to

Table 3.3
Maximum Permissible Levels of Radioactive Contamination,
Adopted 22 December 1987

Isotope	Dairy Products	Other Foodstuffs
Iodine	500	2,000
Strontium	125	750
Plutonium	20	80
Caesium	1,000	1,250

quickly reestablish the integrity of the internal market by renewing the 1707 regime, and, on the other side, to limit finally the levels permissible to cases of emergency, various complicating aspects of the original commission proposal were omitted from the proposal and delegated to future consideration. As a result the determination of the radioactivity limits for baby foods, liquids, and other foods was postponed.

In the end four member states voted against the regulation determining the maximum levels permissible, namely, the Federal Republic of Germany (FRG), Luxembourg, Greece, and Denmark. Together with the Netherlands, Ireland accepted the proposal. This enabled the Danish presidency to vote against the measure and thus save its pro-environment face at home — where the Danish government has to account to its national parliament to a much greater extent than other member state governments. In total twenty votes were cast against the proposal; three short of a blocking minority. In addition a proposal renewing the post-Chernobyl regime for an additional two years was accepted. By basing this proposal on Article 113 EEC (trade policy), the problem of acquiring a unanimous vote was avoided: as was the case with the emergency system regulation, only a qualified majority was required. In the end, only Greece voted against the renewal of the 1707 regime.

As the European Parliament had failed to convince the commission to base its proposal on Article 100A EEC, which calls for the cooperative decision-making procedure brought into being by the Single European Act, the stricter limit values propagated by parliament could be neglected. Following the consultative opinion of the European Parliament, the two draft regulations proposed by the council were formally adopted on 22 December 1987. The occasion marked "a major step forward in Community policy on nuclear safety" according to Commissioner Clinton Davis (*Agence Europe* 4690, p. 6).The emergency limits of radioactive contamination in becquerels per liter or kilogram adopted by the EC are indicated in table 3.3.

The First Liberalization of Civil Aviation

After eight years of discussion, the Council of Ministers took the first step toward establishing a common policy in the field of civil aviation in December 1987. In this issue, too, pressure from outside the council was necessary to persuade the ministers of transport to reach a decision. In this case, however, the impulse to liberalize came from the European Parliament. By charging the Council of Ministers with not fulfilling its obligation under the Treaty of Rome to establish a common policy in the field of transport and by having the Court of Justice rule in its favor, the EP compelled the member states to take steps that they would otherwise not have been willing to take.

In the past, civil aviation in Europe was based completely on the traditional system of bilateral agreements between governments. In these agreements the right to conduct air services between two countries was exclusively granted to specified (national) airlines on the basis of parity between countries. The first discussion in the Transport Council of a common policy in the field of civil aviation dates from 1979. In its first memorandum on civil aviation, the European Commission proposed developing a policy that greatly resembled the American system of deregulation, in which airlines engaged in direct competition for market share.

This memorandum, which proposed the abolition of the traditional system, met widespread opposition in the council. This was not surprising given the direct interest held by the member governments in their respective national airlines and the general public's identification with their national airline. In 1981 the commission took the next step by submitting its first two legislative proposals to the council. One proposal concerned the application of the rules of competition to air carriers. The other focused on the fares for scheduled air services between member states. These proposals were strongly opposed by a majority of the council, which regarded the envisaged degree of competition between air carriers and the proposed freedom to determine fares as much too great.

In 1984 the situation changed. The European Commission adapted its approach in an effort to find a solution to the existing stalemate. In February, the commission presented a new memorandum and revised its proposals to take the positions of the majority of the member states into account. Instead of attempting to establish a new system for intra-EEC air transport, the commission based its revised proposals on the existing system. This structure of agreements and arrangements between the member states would have to be considerably relaxed, however, in order to make it more flexible and to introduce greater competition (*Agence Europe* 3798, pp. 14–15). This less radical approach, together with the court procedure initiated by the EP to rectify the failure of the council to act in the field of transport, produced a more favorable response to the new proposals.

On 10 May 1984 the council held its first meeting on the second memorandum and the four proposals submitted by the commission regarding the fares for scheduled air services, sharing of passenger capacity between air carriers and access to scheduled routes, the application of rules of competition to the field of air transport, and the exemption of certain categories of agreements and prices from these rules. During this meeting the council set up a special high-level group, comprised of senior-ranking civil servants from the member states and the commission, to draw up guidelines for the discussion by the ministers in the Transport Council.

Following numerous meetings in the summer and autumn of 1984, this group drafted a report for the council. On the basis of this report, in its meeting of December 11–12 the Transport Council adopted a resolution stressing the need for a flexible approach on behalf of all delegations with respect to all four proposals. Although member states such as the United Kingdom felt that the guidelines did not go far enough, most considered the package "a sensible initial step" (*Agence Europe* 4012, p. 13).

In light of the many interpretations the guidelines gave rise to, it is not surprising that there was strong opposition to the proposals. Discussions on each of the four proposals became protracted, with conditions being attached to almost every article of the draft legislation. The discussions held in the council on these proposals, however, all reflect one basic dimension; each member state's willingness to liberalize air transport. This fundamental view was, in turn, based on the competitive strength and specific weaknesses of the respective national airlines.[4]

In the meantime, the pressure to establish a more liberal air transport policy mounted. The United Kingdom started concluding agreements for specific air routes with other liberal member states. The agreements reached with the Netherlands, Luxembourg, Germany, and France contained provisions with respect to the setting of fares or the distribution of seating capacity between the two parties. In addition, various lobbying groups, such as the European Bureau of Consumers' Unions (BEUC) and the Independent Air Carriers (IAC), became active protagonists of liberalization. Moreover, the decision of the commission in April 1985 to open proceedings against agreements that erected excessive barriers to com-

4. With respect to this underlying dimension, Agence Europe — in a report of a council meeting held under the presidency of the United Kingdom in November 1986 — categorized the member states in four groups of three each: "the 'great liberalizers' (the Netherlands above all, followed by the United Kingdom and Ireland); those who would accept fairly substantial liberalization but show more readiness to compromise later (Germany, France and Luxembourg); those who want fairly tough regulations but seem prepared to move towards the 'liberalizers' (Belgium, Italy and Portugal) and the champions of a restrictive regime (Denmark, Spain and Greece)" (Agence Europe 4427, p. 8).

petition, as well as the judgment of the Court of Justice of May 1985 that the development of a common transport policy was an obligation laid down by the Treaty of Rome, made the Council of Ministers aware that the time had come to act.

Regardless of the increased pressure, the restrictive member states tenaciously held ground. The progress made during the council session held on 23 May 1985 was described as disappointing. In October the commission decided that it would go ahead with further action against excessively restrictive bilateral agreements and practices unless liberalization measures were taken by the council by June 1986. By November 1985, however, consensus had not yet been found, with a "rift between the countries in favour of deregulation . . . and the cautious and reluctant countries" being reported (*Agence Europe* 4205, p. 5).

In view of the May judgment of the Court of Justice, the Transport Council decided during its November meeting to achieve a free transport market by 1992 at the latest and gradually to abolish distortions to competition. No specific measures were reported for the field of civil aviation. During its March 1986 meeting no detailed debate of the air transport proposals took place. At this meeting the ministers merely took note of the slow progress and authorized the permanent representatives to draw up a "coherent set of proposals concerning tariffs, capacities and rule for competition, allowing for more flexibility" (*Agence Europe* 4282, p. 5).

During the second half of the Dutch presidency, however, the negotiations evolved rapidly. On April 30, the Court of Justice confirmed in the Nouvelles Frontieres case — a case in which an air carrier claimed access to a scheduled route on the basis of a competitive fare — that EEC competition rules apply to air transport. In light of this ruling, the commission redrafted its proposals to strengthen competition with regard to fares and to increase the flexibility of capacity sharing. The new draft proposals were submitted to the council on the day before its June session. Given the lack of time for the member states to study the redrafted proposals, and the submission of a Franco-German compromise solution on the day of the council session, the Transport Council decided to postpone its discussion of the matter until the end of June.

At the June 30 Transport Council meeting, positions were taken that would greatly influence the final outcome of the first liberalization package. In both the commission proposals and the Franco-German compromise the establishment of a zoning system of differentiated air fares, consisting of conditions and time slots for a normal fare, a discount fare, and a deep discount fare, were agreed upon. Within each zone, the airline would fix its fare unilaterally. The two proposed systems, however, did not agree on the conditions required for passengers to become eligible for a discount or deep discount fare. Moreover, they differed with respect to the discount rate that could be applied. While the commission proposed a range of 90 to 60 percent of the normal fare as the discount zone and 60 to 40 percent as the deep discount zone, France and Germany proposed a 90- to 65-percent zone and a 65- to 45-percent zone, respectively.

Both systems agreed on the possibility of an increase in seating capacity within certain limits. Whereas the European Commission proposed authorizing government intervention in normal situations only when the share of capacity fell below 25 percent, France and Germany were willing to go only as far as a 45/55 percent distribution after two years, with the possibility of further improvement in the third year of a three-year experimental period.

Four days before the final Transport Council meeting under the Dutch presidency was held, a meeting of the European Civil Aviation Conference (ECAC) — in which the airlines of twenty-two West European countries are represented — greatly influenced decision making in the council by authorizing lower fares and more flexible capacity-sharing arrangements for a two-year period. By agreeing to a 90- to 65-percent discount zone and a 65- to 45-percent deep discount zone, as well as to a 45/55 percent distribution after two years, the European civil aviation industry firmly endorsed the Franco-German compromise. During the following Transport Council meeting the United Kingdom, the Netherlands, and Ireland were confronted with nine other member states willing to accept the Franco-German compromise. For the three most liberal member states, however, this compromise did not go far enough. Given the voting requirement of unanimity, the council could only conclude its meeting with the reaffirmation of the desire of the member states to establish a more liberal system than the present one and the intention to do so in stages beginning with a three-year period.

Considering that it had not been able to produce a revised proposal regarding access to the market on time, that the negotiations had faced serious differences of opinion, and that a compromise had been blocked by the liberal member states, the commission decided to refrain temporarily from legal proceedings against excessively restrictive bilateral agreements. In October, the council — under the presidency of the United Kingdom — met informally in London to discuss a compromise proposal for the gradual liberalization of air transport. The British proposal reflected the Franco-German compromise with regard to fares and capacity, although it proposed a 40/60 percent distribution in the third year of the experimental stage. Other aspects of the commission proposals, however, now became controversial, with discussion focusing on access to the market.

The presidency proposed substantial liberalization of air transport between hub airports in one member state and regional destinations in others. For many liberal and restrictive countries this turned out to be a critical aspect of the liberalization proposals. Whereas the more liberal member states wished to have hub-regional traffic liberalized and not accounted for in the capacity balance between countries, the restrictive member states such as Denmark, Spain, and Greece — with many regional (tourist) airports and less competitive national airlines — were set upon blocking these proposals. Given the shared intensity, albeit opposite direction, of interest, access to the market aspects of the commission proposals became highly contentious.

For the Netherlands and Ireland the greater flexibility displayed by the United Kingdom was considered a betrayal. Denmark, Spain, and Greece regarded the manner in which access to the market was dealt with in the British compromise proposal as unacceptable. Only France and Germany were willing to accept the overall compromise.

During the two regular meetings of the Transport Council held during the remainder of the British presidency, discussions continued with regard to all proposals, but without great progress being made. At the November 10–11 meeting, the debate focused on access to the market. During this meeting the restrictive countries hardened their positions (*Agence Europe* 4427, p. 8). In addition, the conditions and time slots under which discount and deep discount fares could be offered remained controversial. These latter matters have been reported to be the principal reason why the British presidency was not able to reach a compromise during the meeting of December 15. With regard to the exemption from the ban on agreements and concerted practices, an aspect of interest to the restrictive countries, "Ireland, the United Kingdom and the Netherlands imposed reserves, on the grounds that the progress made on other issues [was] insufficient to justify such exemptions" (*Agence Europe* 4428, p. 6).

It was not until Belgium occupied the presidency during the first half of 1987 that a compromise among the Twelve was finally reached. It took three regular council sessions and one informal meeting, however, to bring the member states together. During the informal meeting held in Brussels on February 17, no major shifts in national positions occurred. This caused Commissioner Sutherland, who was responsible for competition, to indicate that the commission was seriously considering withdrawing its proposals and would implement legal proceedings against excessive agreements if no headway were made (*Agence Europe* 4491, p. 6). In addition, the commission reiterated its intention of withdrawing its proposal on exemptions if the results reached by the council proved unsatisfactory.

Under the applied pressure, the Transport Council made unexpected progress during its March 23–24 meeting. Indeed, a wide consensus was reached regarding fares and capacity shares. The margins decided upon were in correspondence with the Franco-German compromise of June 1986, and most conditions pertaining to these matters were settled. Grave problems, however, remained with respect to access to the market and the extent to which exemptions to competition rules were to be applied.

The Transport Council meeting of June 9 — solely convened to deal with the air transport liberalization package — did not lead to the hoped for consensus. Instead, a polarization of positions evolved concerning the number of exemptions permissible from the proposed liberalization of hub-regional traffic. While the liberal member states felt that they had greatly compromised on other aspects of the proposals and regarded concessions by the restrictive countries as essential, Greece, Denmark, Italy, and Spain refused to give in. They submitted demands to the council that were classified as tough and excessive by the liberal countries. These included exemptions for ten of the twelve Danish airports, all Greek airports on the islands as well as Athens and Salonika (in other words, most of the country's air traffic), eight Spanish airports, and eight Italian airports in the Milan region.

The compromise proposals did not lead to a solution. The meeting broke up deadlocked, with the liberal countries complaining of a total lack of balance in the package. While Commissioner Clinton Davis regarded the discussions as reflecting a sufficient step forward on the road to liberalization, he also stressed that the council would have to reach a compromise at its June 24–25 meeting to avert the withdrawal of the proposal allowing exemption by the commission.

During the following meeting the Transport Council did reach a compromise. In a final attempt to find a consensus, the presidency tabled a proposal that granted the restrictive countries almost all the demanded derogations from the proposed liberalization of hub-regional traffic, albeit some temporarily. In addition, it foresaw only a partial accounting of this traffic in the capacity balances (the capacity of planes with a capacity of more than seventy seats). Although this proposal could hardly be judged a victory for the liberal member states — as 80 percent of the hub-regional flights were carried out by large planes — the alternative to accepting the proposal was even less favorable. Given that the coming into force of the Single European Act would lead to qualified majority voting after July 1, together with the expectation that the upcoming Danish presidency would not ensure a better preparation of access to the market, the liberal member states were more or less forced to accept. Following the acceptance of the presidency's compromise by eleven delegations, the Netherlands, after initially refusing, finally accepted the compromise. Spain, however, made a reservation with regard to Gibraltar, where a British airport could divert many tourists en route for Spain. Only when this problem was solved would it accept the final compromise.

In the end, however, the Spanish problem over Gibraltar proved more difficult to resolve than was expected. Given the matters of sovereignty and international law that were involved, various rounds of negotiations between the ministers of foreign affairs of the United Kingdom and Spain proved necessary. As a result, the first liberalization package had to be officially decided upon under the new regime of decision making in the council, with a second reading occurring in the EP during the autumn. To preclude a disintegration of the package, the French proposed in September that the Twelve apply the decided-upon measures while awaiting the outcome of the Spanish-British negotiations. This was accepted by the other member states. Finally, on 3 December 1987 an agreement was reached in London on the use by both the United Kingdom and Spain of the Gibraltar airport. At their December 7 meeting, the ministers of transport officially adopted the liberalization package, which entered into force on 1 January 1988 and was set to be revised by 30 June 1990.

The EC Banking System

The ongoing debate regarding the economic and monetary confines of European integration reached a decisive stage as 1993 — the target date for the completion of the internal market — approached. In order to bring about a genuine single market, a large measure of convergence in the national fiscal, monetary, and economic policies of the member states would be necessary. In the past, however, the vital interest of all member states in such matters, together with the desire of each to protect delicate socioeconomic structures and uncompetitive older industries, had proven a too formidable barrier for the delegation of sovereignty to the EC.

Ever since the Hague summit in 1969 when the — then six — heads of state or government agreed to establish an Economic and Monetary Union (EMU), the need to harmonize economic and monetary policy of the member states had been repeatedly expressed. The character of a Community banking system and the degree to which it should develop into an EMU, however, remained a major controversy among the member states. The objectives developed in the early 1970s proved too ambitious. They had to be limited in 1978 to the establishment of a more modest European Monetary System (EMS) and the subsequent introduction of the European Currency Unit (ECU). Given the interests involved, it is not surprising that a decision as to the character and powers of the banking system only recently became possible, and then only following greatly protracted and extremely controversial negotiations.

The commission's white paper "Completing the Internal Market, which appeared during the mid-1980s, was the watershed. In endorsing Lord Cockfield's white paper the member governments signified their pledge to transfer a degree of individual sovereignty in the field of monetary policy to the Community. With regard to the character of the banking system that would be established, opinions still were far apart, but the necessity of developing a common policy in the monetary field was accepted.

With the establishment of the Delors Committee to define the economic and monetary cooperation necessary to complete the single market, decision making about monetary policy entered its seemingly conclusive stage in 1988. The most important aspect of policy to be decided on concerned the character of the Community central bank. Should the bank be granted the power to direct the economic and monetary policy of individual member governments independently and to impose sanctions for noncompliance? The answer to this question not only posed a serious challenge to existing monetary policy, but it also had great potential influence over other areas of domestic policy.

In its report, the Delors Committee proposed three stages of increasing cooperation that would lead to the establishment of an EMU with a supranational central bank and a single currency. During the first stage, a program would be carried out that would permit the development of a single market. The less developed member states would be brought into line with the others during this stage. For the more developed members, only some minor adjustments would be necessary. During the second stage, more radical measures would be taken to solve some of the controversies surrounding the institution of a common currency, and to make the creation of a supranational bank possible. Finally, in the third stage, the constituent treaties would be amended, formalizing the establishment of an Economic and Monetary Union.

The deliberations of the Delors Committee were held during the fall and spring of 1988–89. These served as a catalyst for discussions in the Community. The committee had been asked to draft a report for the meeting of the European Council in Madrid in June of 1989. All members were aware that the meeting was expected to be decisive. Still the positions taken by the individual member states remained far apart. Some favored a supranational bank, some preferred to keep the control of policy in the hands of the individual member states, while others were somewhere in between.

Most important in the debate were the United Kingdom, Germany, and France. These countries all held different positions. Germany initially favored a supranational institution that — given German economic dominance — it would largely control. France was more skeptical of such an institution and so favored a central bank in which the governments of member states would continue to play an important role in determining policy. The United Kingdom, led by Margaret Thatcher who placed great significance on retaining British independence and sovereignty, did not favor the establishment of a supranational institution at all. From her perspective, national control of the bank was preferable. The other member states were comparably divided as to which course to take.

The large diversity of opinion, together with the fact that both the German chancellor and the British prime minister faced growing internal opposition to their policy position, did not make the negotiations easier. As the Madrid summit approached, positions shifted in light of the findings of the Delors Committee. Most clearly influenced by the report was French President François Mitterrand. He became an adamant supporter of radical reform and the prompt creation of a supranational bank to serve the Community. France adopted the Delors Committee report as its own policy position. Germany, in contrast, moderated its position as a result of Bundesbank President Karl-Otto Poehl's advice to the German government. While the Germans had originally wanted an independent supranational bank, they came to fear that the bank would not be truly independent and decided to back a Bundesbank-type arrangement.

The United Kingdom continued its opposition to a supranational central bank. Prime Minister Thatcher wished to retain the current banking environment. Her unrelenting endorsement of this conservative position met with increasing opposition in the United Kingdom, where even the chancellor of the exchequer, Nigel Lawson, entered into open conflict with her over the issue. As a result, the determination of the British position for the negotiations in Madrid became extremely controversial within the United Kingdom.

Given the wide disagreement among the member states with regard to the character of the banking structure to be adopted, along with the increasing opposition and recent shifting of policy positions before the Madrid summit, it is not surprising that the Twelve were not able to reach a compromise in June 1989. The behavior of Prime Minister Thatcher was critical; her uncompromising position left little room for negotiation. The member states, therefore, decided to explore the matter further and empowered a new group with the task of searching for a political compromise acceptable to all.

With France occupying the presidency of the Council of Ministers during the latter half of 1989, the reform-minded elements retained the initiative. As the iron curtain rapidly melted, however, attention was involuntarily focused on other issues. President Mitterrand, nonetheless, kept the pressure as high as possible on the Twelve to arrive at a decision of principle with regard to the character of the central bank of the EMU. By scheduling a separate summit to deal with the developments in Eastern Europe at the end of November in Paris, France, set favorable conditions for a successful conclusion of the EMU discussions during the Strasbourg summit in December.

During the six months leading up to the Strasbourg summit, the positions of a number of member states evolved. As opposition from the British business community to Prime Minister Thatcher's position grew, so did her conflict with Chancellor Lawson. In October, this conflict led to the resignation of Lawson, who was succeeded by John Major. Chancellor Major in turn developed a compromise position that received endorsement from the British cabinet and the Conservative party. In the meantime, Germany moderated its position further. Self-evidently, this adaptation of its policy position was greatly influenced by the disintegration of Eastern Germany and the rest of Eastern Europe. The shift of German support from an independent supranational bank to an international bank that would allow for government-led economic and monetary convergence, however, should be seen from a strategic perspective. By modifying their position, it seems that the Germans hoped to have staked out the key position that would lead to a compromise during the Strasbourg summit.

Once again, however, the behavior of Prime Minister Thatcher determined the outcome of the summit. Having received support from the Bruges Group — a prestigious group of European scholars and economists — only two days before the Strasbourg summit, Mrs. Thatcher decided to stick to her position during the negotiations. Instead of putting forward the compromise position that had been developed by Chancellor Major at the onset of the deliberations, Mrs. Thatcher used the compromise proposal only as a fallback position. The result of this tactic was to keep the United Kingdom isolated and to convince Germany, France, and the other member states that the solution would have to be sought in a compromise of their respective positions.

At Strasbourg the European Council agreed in principle to the establishment of a European central bank. In addition, it decided that the United Kingdom should bring its currency into the parity grid of the European Monetary System by July 1990. The council further agreed to establish two committees: one to study the amendment of the treaties of the Community and the other, comprised of the central bank governors, to discuss the structure for the (supranational) bank. These committees were to report to the European Council in December 1990, following which their work would be taken up by the intergovernmental conferences (IGCs) to establish an EMU and a European Political Union (EPU). While the ultimate shape of the European central bank was not yet clear, the outcome of the Strasbourg summit can only be seen as a painful defeat for Prime Minister Thatcher. The plans that emerged, however, fell short of producing a clearly defined central bank.

During 1990 the discussions were further influenced by the unification of Germany and the growing opposition Prime Minister Thatcher's views met in the United Kingdom. The committees established to prepare the IGCs were not to report until December, and so not much progress on the EMU plans was recorded during the Irish presidency. At the end of June, the European Council met in Dublin. There the existing problems, such as the length of the second stage and the precise structure of the bank, were left unresolved. This time Mrs. Thatcher did moderate her position. The United Kingdom did not attempt to block the plan for the IGCs at Dublin. In fact she put forward a plan — developed by Chancellor Major — to manage the second stage. In this plan the creation of a fund to manage the EMU was proposed. The fund would function under a system in which a hard ECU would parallel the national currencies. The other member states, however, felt that this plan had come too late and that the discussions on this matter had largely been completed.

At the same time the linkage between the discussions on the EMU to those on the EPU became more and more apparent. While France wished to complete the internal market as quickly as possible and, therefore, placed priority on the conclusion of the EMU, Germany felt that economic union should be preceded by political union. This created possibilities for Britain. Although she had isolated herself in the EMU negotiations, Prime Minister Thatcher found allies in Denmark and some other member states. As a result of the simultaneous consideration of both matters by the European Council, the United Kingdom might still be able to influence the plans on economic and monetary union.

At home, however, Prime Minister Thatcher's credibility was damaged by the way she conducted the negotiations in Strasbourg. While the Conservative government was united in its wish to constrain the ability of the Community to interfere in national governmental policy, opinions diverged with respect to many aspects of the issue. Confidence in Mrs. Thatcher's judgment declined. At Dublin, the prime minister had moderated her position. Had this been a tactical decision? What were her real intentions for the discussions in Rome at the end of the year?

In October and November 1990 disagreement grew within the British cabinet. During a preparatory meeting of ministers of finance held in Rome in October, policy proposals tabled by the United Kingdom were not received favorably. During the same month Deputy Prime Minister Geoffrey Howe resigned as a consequence of his growing disagreement with Mrs. Thatcher on European policy. A few days later Conservative MP Michael Heseltine decided to challenge the prime minister for the leadership of the Conservative party. Her inability to win the leadership election on the first ballot led Mrs. Thatcher to resign in favor of Chancellor Major.

At the October preparatory meeting of the ministers of finance, the major results of the discussions of the committees established in Strasbourg were presented: the so-called Delors plan and a draft statute for the European central bank drawn up by the national bank governors. In the Delors plan, which built on the three-stage approach that the Delors Committee had developed in 1988–89, a further specification of conditions pertaining to each of the stages and a timetable for its implementation was given.

During the first stage, which officially began in July of 1990, the universal membership of all member states in the Exchange Rate Mechanism (ERM) and the abolition of exchange controls would be established and effectuated, thereby enabling the completion of the internal market. During the second stage which, subject to certain conditions, was to take effect in January 1994, a new EMU treaty would be adopted and a European system of central banks would be established. During the final stage, full monetary and economic competencies would be transferred to the Community institutions. In addition, the exchange rates of currencies would become irrevocably locked and a single currency would be adopted. This final stage would commence within three years of the beginning of the second stage. A date for its realization, however, was not set.

While the impetus to achieve a supranational central bank was strong, the timetable and the balance of national and supranational power had not been settled. Opinions varied, for instance, as to the time necessary to implement the different stages. Bundesbank President Poehl emphasized that the second stage need not span a long time if the first stage were completely carried out. The British, however, did not want to rush into the third stage and stressed that the second stage could have a substantial duration.

The European Council summit held in Rome in December 1990 accepted the overall goals put forward in the Delors draft treaty. Nevertheless, significant disagreements still existed and these had been reinforced rather than resolved. In contrast to the proposals put forward in the so-called Delors Plan, the European Council accepted that Prime Minister Major further develop his plan for the management of the second stage. Furthermore, once the monetary IGCs began meeting, differences among the member states became clearer. A substantial number of questions remained unanswered.

The presidency of Luxembourg during the first six months of 1991 focused its attention on the discussion of the EMU and EPU proposals in the IGCs. During the latter half of the year the discussions concerning both proposals became more and more entwined. In the end, the United Kingdom proved to be the central actor with regard to many aspects of the Treaty on European Union, which was concluded at the Maastricht summit in December 1991. A description of the decision-making process during this final crucial year is given in chapter 8.

Method of Data Collection and Measurement

Our analysis of decision making focuses on the ability of different models to predict the outcome of controversial decisions. This is the only straightforward manner available to test the accuracy of each specified model. In order to apply our models, data on three variables are required: information regarding the capabilities and resources of the actors concerned, their saliences, and policy position each supported at the outset. The data presented here have been collected from official sources and from an expert who — in three of the four issues — personally participated in the negotiations.

Table 3.4
Actor Capabilities

Actor	Capabilities
France	10
Germany	10
Italy	10
United Kingdom	10
Spain	8
Belgium	5
Greece	5
Netherlands	5
Portugal	5
Denmark	3
Ireland	3
Luxembourg	2

In this book we have defined as *actors* only the member states participating during the negotiations in the council. This may be a limitation,
but it does help to ensure comparability.[5] The *capability* of the actors to
influence the outcome of a decision has been simply defined according to
the number of votes they may cast in cases of qualified majority voting.
We regard the assignment of these voting weights to be the codification
of the capabilities an actor can successfully exercise during negotiations
(Bueno de Mesquita and Lalman 1992; Van den Bos 1991). These apply
for the entire Community policy domain and are given in table 3.4.

In a number of cases it has been appropriate to use alternative definitions, either of the actors participating (see chapter 8), or their capabilities
(see chapters 5, 7, and 8). When alternative specifications are used, these
will be clearly indicated.

We measured the *salience* of an actor for a given decision on the basis
of data collected from a relevant expert in the field. The expert was asked
to indicate on a scale of 0 to 100 how great the interest of each participating
actor was in the particular decision. On this scale 0 corresponded with "of

5. It should be noted that this may be a limitation of the specific analyses conducted here,
but it is *not* a limitation of the models. They are perfectly capable of assessing behavior
of individuals, interest groups, or national delegations. They are also capable of assessing interactions between actors or stake holders within a country and decision
makers or influential parties in another country. The models are not limited by national
or international boundaries.

no importance," 50 with "neither important nor unimportant," and 100 with "of vital importance."

With regard to the *policy position* of actors, we have based our analysis of the nuclear radiation levels issue and of the exhaust emissions issue on data published in *Agence Europe* by the leading press agency in the field.[6] In this way distortions in the data collection due to hindsight were avoided. The daily news reports of Agence cover the entire scope of current Community events and the negotiations in the council in particular. As a result of its well-developed network of contacts in the Community institutions as well as in the member states, *Agence Europe* is considered authoritative; it forms an important source of information for participants in negotiations. In most cases the policy position of the member states was specifically mentioned. In a small number of cases, however, the position of a country was referred to only in relative terms — such as "more liberal than." In such a case, the policy position was assumed to be precisely halfway between the positions of the nearest member states with a specifically mentioned policy position. If no indication of the policy position of a member state was given in *Agence Europe,* then the country was not given a policy position and, consequently, was excluded from the analysis for the respective decision.

In the case of the air transport liberalization issue and the Community banking system issue the procedure just described could not be utilized. Either sufficient published data could not be found (air transport liberalization), or the amount of material that would have had to be researched was too time-consuming (Community banking system). In these two cases, our experts were once again asked to rank each actor on a scale from 0 to 100, where 0 and 100 represent the most extreme positions held and the numerical differences between actors reflects the distance in preference between alternatives. By relating the actual outcome to these extremes, the outcome could also be numerically defined.

The Data Matrices

Emission Limits for the Exhaust Gases of Motor Vehicles

In the analysis of the exhaust emissions we divide the directive into three issues, each of which has a clear outcome: the date of introduction of the

6.   With respect to a number of aspects of the car emissions issue, we have not been able to award all member states a policy position. These countries, however, may be assumed not to have played a predominant role during the debate of these issues. In the derivation of the predicted outcome for these aspects, these member states were consequently omitted. In the case of the small car emission standards, we have had to base our policy positions on the publicized initial positions taken when the council dealt with the introduction and implementation of the second stage.

Table 3.5
Salience for Emission Standards

	Delay of Introduction Date			Tax Incentives			Emission Standards		
	S	M	L	S	M	L	S	M	L
France	100	60	60	100	100	50	100	70	60
Germany	30	80	100	50	70	100	40	80	100
Italy	100	60	60	80	60	50	100	70	50
United Kingdom	60	90	60	70	100	60	80	100	60
Belgium	40	40	40	25	25	25	40	40	40
Greece	100	70	40	0	0	0	100	70	40
Netherlands	100	80	100	100	100	100	100	100	100
Denmark	100	100	100	0	0	0	100	100	100
Ireland	10	10	10	0	0	0	10	10	10
Luxembourg	20	20	20	20	20	20	20	20	20

European standards, the amount of financial incentive given to purchasers, and the European standard levels for emission control. Given the fact that these aspects were decided on according to cylinder capacity, each issue is further divided into three separate decisions. The introduction date decisions and the fiscal measure decisions were decided upon first, the emission standard decisions later.

With respect to the introduction date decisions, policy positions varied from delaying for four to ten years after 1985. On the tax incentives, positions ranged from no financial incentives at all to DM 3,000. With regard to the emission standards, the most tolerant position was taken as a standard measure and weighted so that each category distinguished in the final decision (CO, HC + NOx, and in two of three cases NOx) received equal emphasis. In the case of the large car emission standards, the United Kingdom was the most tolerant member state for all three emission criteria: 30 grams of CO, 8 grams of HC + NOx, and 5 grams of isolated NOx per test. As such it has received a score of 1 as its policy position. The most pro-environmental position in the large car emission standard aspect of the issue was taken by the Danish with 20, 2.5, and 2.5 grams per test. It, therefore, received a score of .493 [(.667 + .313 + .500)/3].

In tables 3.5 and 3.6 the saliences and policy positions of the member states are provided for the nine automobile emission decisions.

Table 3.6
Policy Positions for Emission Standards

	Delay of Introduction Date (in years)			Tax Incentives (in DM)			Emission Standards		
	S	M	L	S	M	L	S	M	L
France	10	10	10	0	0	0	1.00	1.00	.933
Germany	4	4	4	3,000	3,000	3,000	.494	.448	.549
Italy	10	10	10	0	0	0	1.00	1.00	.782
United Kingdom	10	10	10	0	0	0	1.00	1.00	1.00
Belgium	7	7	7	—	—	—	.762	1.00	.933
Greece	7	7	7	—	—	—	.494	—	—
Netherlands	4	4	4	3,000	3,000	3,000	.494	.533	.500
Denmark	4	4	4	3,000	3,000	3,000	.494	.448	.493
Ireland	7	7	7	0	0	0	.762	—	—
Luxembourg	4	4	4	3,000	3,000	3,000	.762	.533	.500
Actual Outcome	8.833	8.833	4.833	750	2,200	2,200	.762	.792	.782

Note: Emission standards are scaled so that 1.00 reflects the greatest tolerance for pollutants and 0 indicates no tolerance.

Maximum Permissible Levels of Radioactive Contamination

Our analysis of the nuclear radiation levels issue focuses on the two most controversial decisions of the council deliberations: the height of the levels of the emergency system and the decision to renew the post-Chernobyl regime. Another crucial dimension of this issue concerned the character of the system: should it be a permanent system or an emergency system? We have, however, not analyzed this aspect as it was not decided on by the council. The commission actually took the decision when it proposed an emergency system. Furthermore, the crux of the issue shifted to the aspect of the height of the levels after the failure to extend the 1707 regime.

The two decisions that will be analyzed represent the core of the ultimate choices taken by the council on the issue. With respect to the height of the radioactive contamination levels, the most tolerant policy position supported by any member — weighted so that each category of radioactive contamination distinguished in the final decision (iodine, strontium, plutonium, and caesium) received equal emphasis in the composite score — was taken as standard. The French, Spanish, and British held the most extreme position of the member states. They endorsed the initial recommendation of the Article 31 Committee which described as permissible 3,500 becquerels iodine radiation, 3,500 becquerels strontium radiation, 100 becquerels plutonium radiation, and 9,000 becquerels caesium radiation contamination per liter or kilogram. As these were the largest levels propagated for each type of contamination, France, Spain, and the United Kingdom received a score of 1. The Greeks and Italians endorsed the commission proposal, which advocated the same levels for the first three types of contamination but which also called for a much more stringent level for caesium (2,250 becquerels). As a result they have received a score of .813 $[= (1 + 1 + 1 + .25)/4]$. The policy positions for this aspect of the issue ranges from 0 to 1. The outcome of this dimension of the issue was equivalent to a score of .356.

The second decision on radiation, involving the renewal of the post-Chernobyl regime was a simple dichotomous vote (yes = 1 and no = −1). As the regime was finally renewed, the outcome is coded as 1. It should be recalled that the two radiation questions did not require unanimous decision making as both aspects of the issue were based on articles of the EC treaty that call for qualified majority decisions (in other words, 54 of 76 votes).

In table 3.7 the saliences and policy positions of the member states are given.

The First Liberalization of Civil Aviation

In the case of the air transport liberalization issue, data were collected for five decisions: the lowest possible deep discount fare, the fluctuation mar-

Table 3.7
Salience and Policy Positions for the Maximum Permissible Levels of
Radioactive Contamination

	Salience		Policy Position	
	Height Levels	Renewal of Post-Chernobyl Regime	Height Levels (weighted score)	Renewal of Post-Chernobyl Regime
France	100	25	1.00	opposed
Germany	100	100	.100	in favor
Italy	60	75	.813	opposed
United Kingdom	75	50	1.00	opposed
Spain	50	40	1.00	opposed
Greece	10	100	.813	opposed
Netherlands	80	100	.108	in favor
Portugal	25	20	.108	in favor
Denmark	100	60	.250	in favor
Ireland	70	50	.108	in favor
Luxembourg	80	100	.108	in favor
Actual Outcome			.356	in favor

Note: A height level of 1.00 indicates support for the maximum recommended
level of radioactive contaminants. As the height level falls, so does the
acceptable amount of radiation in foodstuffs.

gin in the capacity distribution, the number of discretionary exemptions
to the inclusion of hub-regional traffic in the liberalization measures, the
degree to which hub-regional traffic would be taken into account in the
capacity balance, and the duration of the first liberalization package. In
an extensive interview that was held with a senior Dutch official who had
personally participated in many of the preparatory meetings, both the
saliences of the member states and the positions they held with regard to
these controversial issues were ascertained.

The policy position with regard to the deep discount reduction decision
has been measured as the percentage of the normal fare a member state
supported initially as a deep discount fare. Liberal member states, such
as the United Kingdom and the Netherlands, were willing to accept 30
percent of the normal fare as an acceptable deep discount fare. They,
therefore, received a score of 30.

Regarding seating-capacity distribution, the policy positions are measured as the marginal percentage member states were willing to accept in the distribution of capacity between two parties to a bilateral agreement. Here too, the British and the Dutch were most liberal. As they preferred no regulation of the matter, they have been given a score of 100. In other words, each party to an agreement could claim anywhere between 0 and 100 percent of the seating capacity. At the other end of the spectrum, France, Italy, Greece, and Spain wished to continue the traditional arrangement in which each party participated on the basis of an equal share of the seating capacity. In this case a margin of fluctuation is nonexistent and these member states were, therefore, awarded a policy position of 0. The outcome of this event has been scored as 13.333. This is due to the fact that the council decided that during the first two years of the experimental period a margin of 10 percent would apply and in the third year a margin of 20 percent.

Another controversial decision concerned the liberalization of air transport between hub airports in one member state and regional airports in another and the number of exemptions allowed. In measuring the policy position of member states we have used the following scale: If a member state did not wish to accept exemptions (e.g., the United Kingdom, the Netherlands, and Ireland), it was given a score of 0; if it accepted one or two exemptions, a score of 1; if it accepted some exemptions, a score of 2; if it accepted many exemptions, a score of 3; and if it accepted all exemptions, a score of 4.

A further hub-regional traffic decision has also been considered: the percentage of this traffic that would fall under the capacity-sharing arrangement. Liberal member states did not wish to include hub-regional traffic in the capacity balances. Other members, such as France, Italy, Greece, and Spain, preferred complete incorporation. In our analysis France has, therefore, been given a score of 100 and the United Kingdom a score of 0. In the end the space on planes with a seating capacity of seventy seats or fewer was not included in the balance. This, however, only accounts for 20 percent of hub-regional flights. The outcome has, therefore, been scored as 80.

Finally, with regard to the duration of the first liberalization package, the discussion focused on whether the package would continue if the member states could not agree on further steps. Liberal members wished that the package would then terminate, thereby forcing the council to take further steps. This position has been given the score of 1. Members that preferred the continuation of the package in the case of nondecision on future steps have been awarded a score of −1.

In tables 3.8 and 3.9 the saliences and policy positions of the member states are summarized.

Table 3.8
Salience for the Air Transport Liberalization Issue

	Deep Discount Fare (percentage of normal fare)	Capacity Margin (percentage of seating capacity)	Exemption of Hub-Regional Traffic from Competition (0 = no exemption)	Inclusion of Hub-Regional Traffic (percentage included in reforms)	Duration Extended (opposed or in favor)
France	85	90	50	90	65
Germany	80	87	50	75	65
Italy	100	100	100	90	90
United Kingdom	100	75	85	85	90
Spain	85	90	85	90	80
Belgium	65	70	50	80	70
Greece	80	80	100	100	90
Netherlands	80	100	90	100	90
Portugal	85	90	90	80	75
Denmark	80	70	100	85	90
Ireland	75	90	85	90	85
Luxembourg	40	40	50	50	55

The EC Banking System

Six aspects of the Community banking system issue have been analyzed, including one key question and five controversial decisions. The key question concerns the kind of banking arrangement that should be adopted. The parts of the issue that became especially controversial include the period within which the central bank should be institutionalized, the allocation of power to determine policies, the scope of responsibilities of the bank, the harmonization of economies, and the relationship between the ECU and national currencies.

The key focus of the Community banking system issue is the kind of banking arrangement the EC should adopt. The policy positions of the member states are placed on a scale from 1 to 100 that runs from a national bank in each member state (the status quo), via the establishment of an international bank after market-led convergence among the European economies (20) and the establishment of an international bank during government-led convergence (80), to the establishment of a supranational bank during government-led convergence. In 1991 the United Kingdom had come to favor the establishment of an international bank somewhere during the process of convergence, and has, therefore, been given a score

Table 3.9
Policy Positions for the Air Transport Liberalization Package

	Deep Discount Fare (percentage of normal fare)	Capacity Margin (percentage of seating capacity)	Exemption of Hub-Regional Traffic from Competition (0 = no exemption)	Inclusion of Hub-Regional Traffic (percentage included in reforms)	Duration Extended (opposed or in favor)
France	50	0	2	100	opposed
Germany	50	20	2	60	in favor
Italy	55	0	4	100	opposed
United Kingdom	30	100	0	0	in favor
Spain	60	0	2	100	in favor
Belgium	50	20	1	40	opposed
Greece	60	0	4	100	opposed
Netherlands	30	100	0	0	in favor
Portugal	50	20	3	70	in favor
Denmark	55	20	4	50	opposed
Ireland	45	30	0	0	in favor
Luxembourg	50	20	1	50	opposed
Actual Outcome	45	13.333	4	80	

of 50. Given the French and Spanish preference for a supranational bank, these member states have been given a score of 100.

Other controversial decisions of the Community banking system deal with the time of institutionalization of the central bank. In this case, policy positions can range on a scale of 1 to 100, with 1 meaning never, so that the status quo is maintained; via a delayed institutionalization until the changes accompanying monetary convergence have occurred (30); the arrangement formulated in the compromise of the Luxembourg summit (50); and the institutionalization once the single market has come into effect (80); to the earliest possible moment — in other words, 1992 (100).

On a similar scale of 1 to 100 the policy positions have been measured with respect to who will direct and execute the European central bank policy. The policy positions could range from the ministers of finance (1); via a council of national central bank governors that sets and executes policy alone (40); a council of national central bank governors that directs policy while a European bank board executes the policy (60); and a situation in which both the council of national central bank governors and the

Table 3.10
Salience for the Community Banking System

	Kind of Banking Arrange-ment	Time of Institutional-ization	Power over Policies	Scope of Responsi-bilities	Harmon-ization	ECU/National Economic Currency
France	75	90	90	80	70	80
Germany	100	100	100	100	70	90
Italy	60	70	50	60	30	60
United Kingdom	90	60	90	90	90	50
Spain	50	60	70	50	50	60
Belgium	50	50	90	50	50	50
Greece	60	30	40	60	50	40
Netherlands	90	50	60	60	50	50
Portugal	25	30	50	70	40	30
Denmark	60	70	75	80	50	50
Ireland	50	25	40	50	20	40
Luxembourg	40	70	40	50	40	40

Table 3.11
Policy Positions for the Community Banking System

	Kind of Banking Arrange-ment	Time of Institution-alization	Power over Policies	Scope of Responsi-bilities	Harmoni-zation	ECU/National Economic Currency
France	100	100	70	90	100	40
Germany	80	30	100	65	50	90
Italy	85	80	60	75	30	70
United Kingdom	50	30	60	40	30	100
Spain	100	80	60	80	30	70
Belgium	80	50	70	65	60	70
Greece	80	50	60	100	30	70
Netherlands	80	50	70	65	60	60
Portugal	80	30	60	30	30	70
Denmark	50	30	60	30	25	40
Ireland	60	30	60	80	30	70
Luxembourg	80	50	40	50	60	60

European bank board share policy powers (70); to a situation where an independent European bank board sets and executes policy.

With respect to the scope of the responsibilities of the central bank, policy positions vary from the status quo, where there is no authority for the bank to intervene in policy — the only responsibility of the bank is the management of accounts — (1); via the authority to advise on inflation (65) and the authority to control inflation with the help of the ECU rates (85); to the authority to intervene in domestic economies (100).

With respect to the harmonization of national economies, positions have once again been measured on a 1 to 100 scale. In this case policy positions can vary from letting the harmonization of the economies be market led (1); via a government directed harmonization (30) and linking the major economies and letting the others catch up (60); to a managed convergence by first linking the major economies and then managing the merger of the minor economies (100).

Finally, policy positions with regard to the relationship between the ECU and the national currencies have been scaled from the EMS approach — a united basket for all assenting members (1); via a united basket of all member states currencies (40) and the deutsche mark for all member states; to a hard ECU — in other words, an ECU based on a fixed exchange with other currencies (100).

In tables 3.10 and 3.11 the saliences and policy positions of the member states are once again summarized.

II The Models

We shall present two classes of models and illustrate their use with some simple examples. Before doing so, however, we want to stress some basic features that underlie the applied modeling approach in this book.

The models are not intended to reflect all of the nuances in the decision-making process. Almost to the contrary, the models aim to represent only the most basic underlying principles in decision making. They do so by starting with a small number of simplifying assumptions that render the analysis of decision making tractable from a modeling perspective. The intention is not to make the models as realistic as possible, but to make them as simple as possible and as complex as necessary. This is a point emphasized in Roy Pierce's introductory chapter, and one which now bears re-emphasizing.

Reality is infinitely complex. There is no hope of capturing reality by trying to replicate it, but there is hope of capturing its essence with a quite limited and parsimonious set of assumptions. This means that we are content to emphasize simple models so long as more complex models do not do appreciably better than our simple representation when applied to concrete decision-making situations. The issue of how much complexity is the right amount of complexity should be resolved, we think, on practical grounds.

The models presented in the next few chapters share the most basic assumptions, namely, unidimensionality of decisions and single-peaked preference functions for the actors. Unidimensionality means that the possible outcomes of a decision can be represented as points on a line, as values on an underlying continuum. Some issues, like the size of a budget, seem to fulfill this criterion easily, but for others special interviewing techniques are required to transform the different alternatives into such a scale. We will demonstrate that this is feasible even for such complex issues as are involved in the debates over a European banking system.

Collective outcomes can not be explained without reference to the choices made by the actors in the relevant social system. At the highest level of abstraction, actors are assumed to have monotonically increasing utility functions related to universal goals, like physical well-being and social approval, but they have different instrumental preferences for the means that lead to these ultimate goals (Lindenberg 1990, 741). In this perspective, outcomes of collective decision making can be perceived as instrumental goals: whereas one outcome can produce physical well-being or social approval for one set of people, another outcome can be better for others. Within a collective decision-making setting, differences of instrumental goals among actors result in two types of relations between actors and issues.

First, what is an important issue for one actor might well be irrelevant for the realization of the ultimate goals of another actor. Second, differences in instrumental goals result in diverging political stances of actors on issues. Consequently, people can be expected to behave quite differently despite the assumption that they are all rational in the sense that they are interested in maximizing their welfare. Even people in possession of the same information and, of course, holding the same universal goals, may nevertheless have radically different instrumental objectives.

The importance of an issue for an actor is denoted by the salience the actor attaches to the issue. The outcome on an issue that an actor desires is denoted by the actor's position on the issue. The position expresses the policy preference of the actor, while the salience expresses the relevance of the issue compared to other (perhaps unspecified) issues. These two elements — position and salience — are combined into a utility function for each actor that specifies the value the actor attaches to each feasible alternative outcome on the issue in question. The policy position, then, denotes the point on the continuum that has the highest utility for the actor. For any actor, the utilities of the other alternatives are assumed to be a function of their distance from the actor's most preferred position, taking the salience of the issue into account.

The next basic assumption has to do with the transformation of the preferences of the actors into a collective outcome — a final decision. This step requires a third element in which actors differ fundamentally, namely, their capability to influence the collective outcome. In both models this is the third empirical element that needs to be specified within a field of application. The models differ slightly in their assumptions about how this transformation occurs. The Bueno de Mesquita expected utility models take the median voter position as the predicted outcome, whereas the Stokman and Van Oosten exchange models take the mean of the votes as the predicted outcome.

The similarity of basic assumptions in the models makes it possible to compare them in terms of their fundamental difference, namely, the assumed dynamics in the decision-making process. Both models do not take the initial median vote or mean vote as the predicted outcome, but as the starting point from which actors try to improve their utility through the decision-making processes. The Bueno de Mesquita expected utility model gives actors the opportunity to challenge the positions of other actors if they expect a positive outcome from such a possible confrontation. In this process actors may be forced to take less attractive stances if they have no better alternatives. These challenges may, therefore, result in forced or negotiated shifts of policy positions for some actors and consequently may imply shifts in the predicted collective outcome. This process is repeated until no further important effects on the outcome of a decision can be observed.

The Stokman and Van Oosten exchange model assumes that the dynamics in decision making result from the possibility of actors exchanging voting positions over a set of decisions. For instance, consider two actors with opposing policy positions on two issues. Let us furthermore assume that the first actor has less interest in the first issue than in the second and that the reverse is the case for the second actor. Then both actors can expect to gain utility if the first actor supports the policy position of the second actor on the first issue in exchange for support from the second actor for his own policy position on the second issue. In this model, actors do not challenge one another; they cooperate by logrolling to get a better expected solution for all. Whereas the actors behave strategically in the expected utility model, they are sincere and cooperative in the exchange model.

The two dynamics of the models reflect two alternative views of collective decision making. The first view, represented in the expected utility model, conceives collective decision making in terms of conflict resolution — a noncooperative game — fundamentally different from exchange relations in economics. The second view, represented in the exchange models, does not see fundamental differences between economic exchanges and political decision making. It conceives of collective decision making as a cooperative game in which all actors can gain under certain conditions and in which promises to shift positions are taken as binding commitments. We are convinced that in reality both processes take place simultaneously. Regretfully, we are not yet able to formulate the conditions under which the one is more likely than the other. We can only state the conditions under which cooperation is possible, but cannot say when cooperative behavior is an equilibrium of a noncooperative game, as suggested by Bueno de Mesquita's approach, and when it is a consequence of a cooperative game, as implied by Stokman and Van Oosten.

Bruce Bueno de Mesquita

4 Political Forecasting:
An Expected Utility Method

The European Community's rules seemingly make policy formation (and policy prediction) on important and controversial
questions all but impossible. The European Parliament requires only a qualified majority to reject a "common position"
of the EC's council and commission, while the council requires unanimity to overrule the parliament and approve the
common position. This institutional structure suggests that
the individual sovereign interests of the member states reflected in the parliament can readily thwart policy, while the
supranational elements of the EC can overcome the parliament only under extraordinarily demanding conditions. The
process seems to be biased in favor of protecting individual
sovereign interests and against reaching agreement on important matters. Yet, decisions are frequently taken on issues
that arouse intense disagreements between the member
states. It seems likely, therefore, that considerable give and
take occurs outside the EC's formal institutions, resulting in
political accommodations that can make it through the EC
process.

The successes of the community inevitably lead to fundamental questions about politics and sovereignty. Do national representatives acquiesce in agreements that are contrary to the interests of their state and if so why? Can we
predict the dynamics that lead to agreements and the substantive contents of the informal bargaining process that results in EC policy? If we can, how dependent is that process
on the actual institutional arrangements within the European
Community? These are the central concerns that motivate
the elaboration of the model of policy formation set out here.

I delineate a model grounded in the micro- economic assumptions of expected utility maximization and illustrate the

application of components of the model with a single case: the European Community decision on the timing of the introduction of emission standards on mid-sized automobiles. In chapter 6, Organski and I explore several other automotive issues, as well as radiation control and air transport issues, using the model explained here.

In building the theory, including its predictive and process-oriented features, I focus primarily on the application of two theorems. Black's (1958) median voter theorem, which is explained below, is adapted to predict policy outcomes. A theorem about the monotonicity between certain expectations and the escalation of political disputes (Bueno de Mesquita and Lalman 1986; Banks 1990) is adapted to illuminate the unfolding decision-making process and to make predictions about the political ramifications of alternative proposals. The conjunction of these theorems and concepts from bargaining theory help foster the development of a dynamic model that includes detailed expectations about the agreements or compromises that various players are willing to make over time and the implications of those compromises for the ultimate resolution of the issues in question.

The Model

A general model for predicting policy choices and the attendant pulls and tugs that accompany political decisions is developed here. The model itself is designed with the objective that it will contain testable propositions about behavior. In that sense, it is intended as an example of applied formal modeling, an approach that can shed practical light on real-world problems as well as a tool for analyzing abstract propositions. Two constraints are assumed to facilitate prediction and explanation: that issues are unidimensional, so that preferences can be represented on a line segment, and that preferences (and associated utilities) for potential outcomes diminish steadily the farther in Euclidean distance a possible settlement is from one's preferred outcome.

The two constraints — unidimensionality and single-peaked utility functions — are necessary for the application of the median voter theorem. Black's theorem demonstrates that the outcome desired by the median or middle voter is the winning position under the constraints just assumed, provided a simple majority is required for victory. For a one-dimensional issue under these constraints, the median voter is the Condorcet winner; the alternative that in head-to-head competition defeats each other alternative.

To be sure, the median voter theorem has some important limitations (see, e.g., Kramer 1972; Davis, DeGroot, and Hinich 1974; McKelvey 1976; Schofield 1976). If an issue contains two or more independent dimensions over which preferences are defined, then even single-peaked utility functions and majority rule cannot guarantee the existence of an alternative for which the coalition of support dominates all others. Nevertheless, enough issues appear to remain or collapse into a single dimension so that unidimensionality and single peakedness need not be viewed as such severe or such simplifying conditions as to render subsequent analysis trivial. Chapter 9 evaluates the model proposed here in light of real decisions within the EC and finds strong evidence to support the claim that the approach can be a valuable and accurate tool for policy analysis.

The median voter theorem might appear to be an especially poor starting point for evaluating EC decision making. After all, the EC provides for qualified majority rule only under rather confined circumstances. Some choices institutionally involve a qualified majority, but others require unanimity. Of all the issues assessed in this volume only two did not formally require unanimity. We must wonder whether a model based on simple majority rule helps make accurate assessments.[1]

Furthermore, it is well known that the median voter theorem does not hold when issues are multidimensional or when participants in the decision-making process engage in logrolling or trades across issues. Indeed this latter point forms the foundation of the exchange models proposed by Frans Stokman and Reinier Van Oosten in chapter 5. Of course, whether these reservations are critical is an empirical, not a theoretical, question. Still, how are we to reconcile the assumption of majority rule against the explicit rules of the EC? The answer lies in the ability of decision makers to anticipate at least some procedural consequences that follow from their actions.

Issues expected to fail within the European Community setting probably do not get raised by any member state in the first place. The paucity of examples of such proposals is a hint of how well informal screening mechanisms work to select issues to be pushed forward and to identify issues that should be dropped. Ushering a proposal to defeat is a costly process that is best avoided. One way to avoid the costs of failure is to form rational expectations about what will happen if a proposal is pursued and to abandon those proposals for which the costs of action are expected to be larger than the benefits from action.

Expectations about a proposal's performance can be formed by engaging in an informal bargaining process, using informal discussions as a crucial screening device prior to bringing a subject into the EC's institutional framework. Indeed, such informal screening is likely to be especially important when the institutional rules require unanimity. Why should this be so?

The member states of the European Community presumably value the

1. It should be noted that the model as applied here assumes simple majority rule, but that the model is easily adapted to other rules involving special or super majorities.

EC as an institution. Otherwise, it would cease to exist. If they fail to reach compromise settlements on issues requiring unanimity, then the failure may threaten the very survival of the Community. By contrast, when decision makers fail to agree on questions that require only a qualified majority no one participant's dissent can threaten the viability of the Community's institutions. Consequently, the institutional framework makes it relatively "cheap" to be in the opposition when only a qualified majority is needed, but makes it quite costly to be opposed when unanimity is involved. In the latter case, the decision to oppose must be weighed against the damage that might be done to the entire Community framework of trust and cooperation, rather than being weighed only against the local costs and benefits of the specific decision.

When decisions do not require unanimity, I speculate that domestic political considerations in each member state become critical factors in determining the bargain that a member state's representative is or is not willing to pursue in the Community. The model proposed here can, of course, just as readily be used to evaluate the internal political process that produces the nation's policy toward the EC as it can to evaluate how that policy, once determined, evolves during the EC's own bargaining process.

A central hypothesis of this investigation is that EC policy choices can be predicted based on models of the informal bargaining process that almost surely precedes formal discussions within the Community structure. The model suggested here provides an analytic representation of bargaining in an informal setting, while taking into account specific features of the EC's rules that may influence such bargaining. An approach that helps predict the most likely outcome in such informal policy debates surely is of value, but it alone is inadequate for understanding the political dynamics that produce a settlement and that influences the relations among the actors. Many decision makers are reluctant to achieve victory on an issue at the expense of alienating prospective supporters and future allies, especially if the alienation is expected to escalate into a very costly situation.

The risks of escalation of a dispute is addressed by Bueno de Mesquita and Lalman's (1986) conjecture and Banks's (1990) theorem, which demonstrates that the probability of confrontation or political strife over an issue is an increasing function of the expected utility — or cost-benefit analysis — from such a confrontation. As Banks notes with regard to an earlier version of the model discussed here, "This justifies the assumption in the expected utility models of Bueno de Mesquita and Lalman (1986) and Lalman (1988) that a decision maker with a higher expected utility from war will be more likely to go to war; indeed Lemma 1 shows this to be the *only* assumption consistent with rational behavior in an incomplete information environment" (p. 605). Here I apply Banks's theorem to normal interactions among European states. Banks's monotonicity theorem highlights an important feature of all politics. It tells us that the more one expects to gain from challenging a rival perspective, the more likely one is to undertake the challenge.[2] This simple statement turns out to have interesting and sometimes surprising implications for political intercourse.

Through the use of the monotonicity result and the median voter theorem I suggest a simple model of perceptions and expectations. That model helps us comprehend bargaining and shapes an understanding of the conditions that can lead a negotiation to become excessively conflictual or to break down. I capitalize on the perceptual features of the proposed model by using comparative static techniques to describe the process by which negotiations unfold, moving from one set of circumstances (and outcomes) to another and another.

In the sections that follow I delineate the method for predicting policy choices, for influencing the stance of other actors, and for reshaping policy decisions. The model is a game in which actors simultaneously make proposals and exert influence on one another. They then evaluate options and build coalitions by shifting positions on the issue in question. The above steps are repeated sequentially until the issue is resolved. In the game, each player knows three factors: the *potential power* and *policy position* of each actor on each issue examined, and the *salience* each actor associates with those issues. The decision makers, or players, do not know how much each other actor values alternative outcomes or what perceptions others have about their risks and opportunities. Each decision maker chooses based on his or her perceptions and expectations, with these perceptions and expectations sometimes proving to be in error.

Predicting Policy Choices

When issues are unidimensional and preferences are single-peaked there must be a Condorcet winner, an alternative that cannot be beaten by any other alternative in a pairwise election process. Many, perhaps most, political choices, however, do not involve elections in which each voter casts a single vote. Nevertheless, the median voter theorem and the spatial theory of voting (Downs 1957) provide a theoretical foundation from which we can gain assistance in predicting the resolution of multilateral disputes.[3]

2. More precisely, Banks has shown that in any Bayesian asymmetric information game, an actor's likelihood of engaging in tough, escalatory behavior is a monotonically increasing function of the actor's expected utility from such behavior.
3. For applications to settings that do not involve conventional voting see Bueno de Mesquita 1984 on the selection of Khomeini's successor in Iran; Bueno de Mesquita 1990 for an analysis of the prospects of a multilateral peace conference over the Arab-Israeli dispute; Bueno de Mesquita, Newman, and Rabushka 1985 on the Sino-British

Let $N = \{1, 2, 3, \ldots, n\}$ be the set of actors trying to influence a multilateral decision. An actor might be a government representative, an official from a faction within a political party or a bureaucracy, a leader of some interest group, an influential private citizen, and so forth. Shortly I shall identify the precise characteristics that define a group, player or actor in this model. For the purposes of this book, an actor is the representative of a member state in the European Community.

Let $M = \{a, b, c, \ldots, m\}$ be the set of issues in a multilateral negotiation and let R_a be the line segment, bounded for convenience between 0 and 100, that describes the unidimensional policy continuum for any individual issue a selected from among the larger set of issues M. Let each actor i, $i \epsilon N$ (in other words, i is a member of the set of actors trying to influence the decision), have its own *preferred* resolution of issue a, with that preferred resolution denoted as x_{ia}^*, such that on the issue continuum R_a, $0 \leq x_{ia}^* \leq 100$. In other words, actor i has a preferred solution to the issue in question and that preferred solution can be located on a continuum of possible resolutions ranging from one extreme to the other.[4]

For any feasible, proposed outcome on issue a, say k's proposal, x_k (with feasibility defined in terms of the proposal falling within the range of outcomes for which there is at least some support), i's utility for x_k, $u^i x_k$, is a decreasing function of the distance between the proposal and i's preferred resolution, so that $u^i x_k = f \mid x_k - x_i^* \mid$. This means that proposals farther away from actor i's preferred outcome are of less value to i than are proposals closer to i's preferred outcome.[5]

Each actor i is assumed to be an expected utility maximizer, by which is meant that i calculates the expected value of alternative strategies and pursues the one that he or she believes is in his or her best interest. Of course, that belief may be incorrect. The theory of decision making proposed here does not assume that people choose to do what is best for them — even after the fact it may not be possible to know what would have been best — but rather that they choose what they think is best at the time they have to make a choice. In choosing a course of action they

negotiations over the future of Hong Kong; Morrow 1986; Morgan 1984, 1989, and 1990.

4. The outcome actor i has revealed to be preferred on issue a is denoted as x_{ia}^*. It may or may not be i's true ideal point. We generally do not know for sure what another actor's true ideal point is as there are strategic incentives for an actor to misrepresent his or her ideal point. Because the model developed in this chapter assesses policy decisions on one issue at a time, I drop the issue-denoting subscript (a, or b, and so on) from the notation so that henceforth x_i^* is the preferred position of actor i on the issue being evaluated at the moment.

5. This condition implies single-peaked preferences. Later I suggest an estimation procedure for specifying the function.

may be mistaken about the intentions of others or about the actual structure of the situation they are in. No decision maker has a crystal ball that guarantees making the right choice. Indeed, later in this chapter I shall suggest means by which decision makers can utilize the tools described here to exploit misperceptions so as to gain some advantage.

Of the infinitely many possible proposals to resolve some issue a, how are we to predict which will be chosen? To answer this question, let us first learn a little more about each actor i. In this analysis, each decision maker is endowed with three characteristics. Each player attaches some *utility* to each possible outcome on issue a, as already noted. Each participant in the bargaining process is also endowed with the *power* to exert some influence on decisions. Let c_{ia} be the capabilities (or power) actor i could bring to bear on issue a, such that the sum of the capabilities of the participants in a multilateral decision-making setting is 1.[6] The term c_i is actor i's share of the total potential influence that could be brought to bear in the negotiations over some issue a. Each participant has its own agenda of priorities or *salience* that it attaches to the issues that must be confronted. Thus, i may attach considerable importance to issue a and considerably less importance to issue b. Denote the salience of issue a for actor i as s_{ia}, with $0 \leq s_{ia} \leq 1$. Each actor is described by the values of $u^i x_k$ for all i, $k \in N$, c_i, and s_i on each issue. Any aggregation of individuals with identical values on all three of these variables can constitute an actor for the purposes of this model. Differences on the available pool of resources or on preferred outcomes or on salience mean that the aggregation of individuals make up more than one group and must so be treated.

So far, three pieces of information have been identified that define an actor or decision maker and that are the crucial (and only) variables required to solve the forecasting and perceptual model. Before turning to the model, however, I offer table 4.1 as an illustration of the minimal information needed to solve the forecasting and perceptual components that are explained below. In the table, each actor has an array of three values: c_i; x_i^*; and s_i. The issue, which arose in 1984–85 in the European Community during the period of the Europe of Ten, involved the timing by which emission standards were to be imposed on medium-sized automobiles in Europe. In this instance, c_i is the institutionally assigned voting weight for each EC member. The term x_i^* represents each nation's preferred date, measured in years, by which emission standards should be applied to medium-sized automobiles as revealed at the outset of discussions on the issue. The term s_i is the salience, or importance, each nation attached to the timing of emission standards on medium-sized cars. The

6. Again I will drop the a subscript from the notation throughout, but the reader is alerted to the fact that the model does not assume that an actor's capabilities or potential power is the same on all issues.

Table 4.1
Introduction Date for Emission Standards: Mid-Sized Automobiles

	Capabilities		Position (x_i)	Salience (s_i)
	Votes	c_i		
Netherlands	5	.08	4 years	80
Belgium	5	.08	7 years	40
Luxembourg	2	.03	4 years	20
Germany	10	.16	4 years	80
France	10	.16	10 years	60
Italy	10	.16	10 years	60
United Kingdom	10	.16	10 years	90
Ireland	3	.05	7 years	10
Denmark	3	.05	4 years	100
Greece	5	.08	7 years	70

data and decisions for this and other issues are explained in greater detail in chapter 3. I carry this particular automotive issue forward throughout this chapter as an illustration of key features of the model.

The median voter theorem provides the foundation for beginning our effort to turn the data in table 4.1 into concrete predictions about policy choices. In doing so, the reader should bear in mind that the insights derived from the median voter theorem can be applied to almost any political setting. Even in authoritarian regimes, the exercise of power may be understood as a form of voting. When alternative courses of action are pitted against each other, the array of forces on either side often determines victory. Of course, this array depends on more than the relative power of the competing interests. It depends also on the willingness to spend influence on the issue in question [s_i] — a budget constraint — and the intensity with which each actor prefers one proposed settlement, say j's proposal, ($u^i x_j$), to another proposal, say k's $u^i x_k$). Thus, each group has a total number of potential votes equal to its capabilities, a factor that may be influenced by external considerations or by the institutional arrangements (as in this case) that provide structure to the decision-making process. Each group's votes are discounted by the group's salience for the issue and by how much it prefers the particular options under consideration. This discounting is done because some decision makers may choose to withhold their power, saving it for other issues about which they care more at the moment (in other words, issues with higher salience), or because, although they care deeply about the issue, they do not care very much about the difference between the proposed settlements before them. The votes cast by actor i in a comparison of alternatives x_j and x_k are said to equal v_{ia}^{jk} where

$$(v_{ia}^{jk} \mid x_j, x_k) = (c_i)(s_i)(u^i x_j - u^i x_k). \tag{1}$$

Equation (1) states that the vote or power mobilized by actor i in a comparison of two alternatives (x_j and x_k) is equal to the potential capabilities of i discounted by how important the issue is to i (in other words, s_i) and by how much i prefers one proposal to the other ($u^i x_j - u^i x_k$). The less important i thinks the issue is, the less willing i is to spend its capabilities on the issue. What is more, the less i cares about one outcome as compared to another, the less willing i is to spend its influence in trying to promote a particular alternative at the moment.

The voting scheme reflects some institutional content in that the particular power of each actor is determined by the structure of the situation. The European Community has attempted to codify the relative power of its members through its weighted voting system. That codification is the source of c_i here. Yet, this institutional restriction is relaxed somewhat in the model because the assigned power is discounted by the willingness of each member nation to "spend" its resources on the issue in question. Thus, the model evaluates both institutional and extra-institutional considerations, including the bargaining that is likely to be concluded before a proposal works its way through the formal decision process. It is, if you like, a model of what takes place "inside the smoke-filled room" before the formal, visible process occurs. It assumes that the formal process echoes the agreements reached beforehand. The particular specification of how stake holders cast votes is, of course, ad hoc. Many alternative functions would capture the same theoretical properties. All of the specifications that are consistent with the logic of the model, however, would produce essentially similar results. The explanatory stories, if you like, would be the same, although some of the details would vary as the specific functional specifications varied. It is conditions such as the specific voting rule that makes it feasible to apply the model proposed here to concrete, real-world political situations.

The prospect that a proposal will succeed is assumed to depend on how much support can be mustered in favor of the proposal as compared to the feasible alternatives. In the model this is calculated as the sum of votes across all actors in a comparison between x_j and x_k. This sum equals v^{jk} with

$$v^{jk} = \sum_{i=1}^{n} v_i^{jk}. \tag{2}$$

If v^{jk} is greater than zero that implies that x_j defeats x_k because the tacit coalition in favor of j's proposal is more motivated and powerful than the coalition supporting k's proposal. If v^{jk} is less than zero, x_j is expected to be defeated by x_k and if v^{jk} equals zero the competing interests are collectively indifferent between the two alternatives.

In any negotiation, there are likely to be many more than two proposed settlements. By pitting all alternatives against one another two at a time, the outcome preferred by the median voter (weighted by power, salience, and intensity of preference) is found. Barring perceptions or beliefs that lead decision makers to switch their position, the median voter position is the predicted outcome (Black 1958).

In practice, perceptions or beliefs often lead decision makers to grant concessions or to give in to a rival's point of view, sometimes even needlessly. Such concessions or capitulations can change the location of the median voter. After explaining a method for estimating perceptions I shall return to this point and elaborate on how the dominant outcome is identified. That dominant outcome is the predicted resolution of an issue within the confines of the model proposed here.[7] For now we need only note that the initial median voter outcome can be the dominant outcome provided key actors do not switch positions in a way that alters the location of the median voter. Of course, it is crucial to provide an accounting of when such switches in position are expected to take place.

Continuing with our illustrative example, ignoring for the moment differences in risk-taking orientations among decision makers, we now calculate the median voter prediction using the data in table 4.1. In this simplified example, in which each actor is assumed to be neutral toward risks, I assign to that actor a utility of 1.0 for any proposed outcome that is the same as its preferred outcome. So, for instance, the Netherlands is assumed to have attached a utility of 1.0 to a four-year time delay, while the United Kingdom is assumed to have assigned a utility of 1.0 to a ten-year delay in the introduction of emission standards comparable to those in the United States or Japan. Any outcome that differs from a nation's preferred resolution by six years in this example is assigned the utility 0, reflecting the fact that this is the greatest possible disparity between feasible solutions to this issue. Finally, any proposed solution that differs from a nation's preferred settlement by three years is given the utility

7. It can be possible to defeat the dominant outcome by capitalizing on the procedures outlined here for estimating other people's perceptions. Later I explain how to use comparative static techniques for shifting an outcome strategically to favor some result that otherwise would be defeated. To defeat the dominant outcome it is necessary for one or more actors to have information that normally is not available to decision makers unless they have access to and use a model like this.

value of 0.5, reflecting the fact that it is halfway between the extremes. For instance, Belgium is assumed to have attached a utility of 0.5 to the proposals of both Germany and Italy, while Luxembourg is assumed to have assigned a utility of 0.5 to the seven-year proposal of Ireland.[8] These hypothetical utility values reflect the assumption that preferences for proposed outcomes decline as the proposal moves farther and farther away from the actor's preferred solution.

Using the above building blocks, I calculate v_{ia}^{jk} for the seven-year proposal versus the four-year proposal (in that order) as follows:

$$c_i \times s_i \times (u^i x_j - u^i x_k) = v_{ia}^{jk}$$

Netherlands	$0.08 \times 0.80 \times (0.5 - 1.0)$	$= -0.032$
Belgium	$0.08 \times 0.40 \times (1.0 - 0.5)$	$= +0.016$
Luxembourg	$0.03 \times 0.20 \times (0.5 - 1.0)$	$= -0.003$
Germany	$0.16 \times 0.80 \times (0.5 - 1.0)$	$= -0.064$
France	$0.16 \times 0.60 \times (0.5 - 0.0)$	$= +0.048$
Italy	$0.16 \times 0.60 \times (0.5 - 0.0)$	$= +0.048$
United Kingdom	$0.16 \times 0.90 \times (0.5 - 0.0)$	$= +0.072$
Ireland	$0.05 \times 0.10 \times (1.0 - 0.5)$	$= +0.003$
Denmark	$0.05 \times 1.00 \times (0.5 - 1.0)$	$= -0.025$
Greece	$0.08 \times 0.70 \times (1.0 - 0.5)$	$= +0.028$

From these calculations we can see that Belgium, France, Italy, the United Kingdom, Ireland, and Greece apparently would support a seven-year delay over a four-year delay. Summing each row gives the overall vote between these two alternatives. The support given to a seven-year delay easily defeats those who back a four-year program, with only .124 weighted votes in favor of four years and with .215 weighted votes in support of a seven-year delay. Of course, we would also have to compare the proposed seven-year delay to the ten-year program before determining the Condorcet winner.

Even with this simplified example, which ignores variations in risk-taking propensities and associated perceptions, we can see value added by the modeling approach. A naive view of the initial vote might mistakenly have given the edge to the backers of a four-year proposal. With the official EC weighting of votes, the backers of the four-year proposal controlled twenty votes (32 percent of the available total), while supporters of the seven-year proposal controlled only thirteen (21 percent of the available total). Such a view might also have been consistent with German threats to implement the policy on a unilateral basis. With the more so-

8. I reiterate that in the actual computation, the utility values are estimated differently and this can make a substantial difference.

phisticated calculation that includes differences in risk-taking propensities, as elaborated below, the seven-year proposal easily defeats the four-year delay and barely wins against the backers of a ten-year wait. Without taking into account the utility differences implied by the risk-taking component and without discounting for salience, the typical evaluation would have been that the ten-year program would win easily as thirty potential votes back that outcome, against twenty and thirteen respectively for the four-year and seven-year program.

The basic, median voter prediction is not the final prediction of the forecasting model. The beliefs and perceptions of the relevant actors frequently suggest compromises and concessions that one or another actor is willing to pursue and that other actors are willing to accept. These beliefs and perceptions may influence the array of interests sufficiently to necessitate re-estimating the median voter, perhaps several times, until perceptions and positions stabilize around the dominant outcome. In order to undertake such before-the-fact analytic updating it is necessary first to develop the means to estimate the relevant beliefs and perceptions.

Altering the Expected Outcome: Manipulating Perceptions

The forecasting element of the model reveals what decision makers should expect if everyone acts sincerely in accordance with their underlying preferences. What, however, can a decision maker do if the predicted outcome is not to his or her liking? Is there anything that can be done to improve the expected outcome?

It is possible and indeed likely that actors will cooperate in private, sophisticated deals to rearrange the prospective resolution of a controversial issue. Such deal making is, in fact, the essence of negotiations. The perceptual model guides inquiries so as to facilitate our understanding of which deals are feasible and which are not. In that way it points out the means to construct the dominant outcome or other strategically sophisticated approaches to resolving an issue.

If an interest group is dissatisfied with the expected outcome, there are essentially four courses of action by which this group — the focal group — might improve its prospects. The group leadership can:

1. alter its own level of effort (in other words, change s_i);
2. shift its revealed position, selecting x_i such that $u^i x_i^* \neq u^i x_i$;
3. influence those who are willing to make concessions to the focal group so that those other groups alter their level of effort (in other words, s_k); or
4. influence those who are willing to make concessions to the focal group so that those other groups alter their revealed position x_k so that $u^k x_k^* \neq u^k x_k$.

Here I focus only on point 4, maneuvers that involve persuading other groups to switch positions, with the direction and magnitude of any changes in position being dictated by the logic behind the model.

Decision makers interested in ascertaining what leverage they can exert could benefit from estimating the beliefs held by each other actor. To do so requires a focus on the three characteristics — $u^i x_j$ for all $i,j \in N$, s_i, c_i — used to estimate each player's expected utility from challenging or not challenging the policy proposal backed by each potential rival and for approximating the utility each actor i believes its rival expects to derive from challenging or not challenging the policy goals of actor i. In the model envisioned here, decision makers are assumed to calculate the expected consequences of challenging and of not challenging alternative proposals. The expected utility for i from not challenging rival j's position is denoted as $E^i u^i \Delta x_j \mid \overline{d}$, with $\overline{d}$ denoting the failure to challenge or make a proposal. This expected utility is estimated by projecting what the relevant decision maker believes is likely to happen in the absence of the exertion of pressure on a rival to persuade the opponent to alter its behavior. One of three contingencies may arise.

First, actor i may anticipate that with some probability (Q^i) rival j will not alter its current policies over the time period of concern to i, and so interest group i will derive whatever utility it receives from the preservation of the status quo between itself and j ($u^i \Delta x_j \mid \overline{d}$). Alternatively, i may anticipate that j's position on the issues will change, in which case there is some chance (T^i) that, from i's perspective, the policies of j are anticipated to get better (with $u^i \Delta x_j^+ \mid \overline{d}$ being the associated utility) or to get worse $(u^i \Delta x_j^- \mid \overline{d})$, so that $u^i \Delta x_j^+ \mid \overline{d} > u^i \Delta x_j \mid \overline{d} > u^i \Delta x_j^- \mid \overline{d}$. From i's point of view, j's policy on an issue gets better if j switches to a position closer to that supported by i and j's policy gets worse if j moves still farther away from i's preferred position. This follows directly from the assumption of single-peakedness. The expected utility of i if it leaves j's proposal unchallenged is described as:

$$E^i u^i \Delta x_j \mid \overline{d} = Q^i u^i \Delta x_j \mid \overline{d} + (1 - Q^i)[T^i u^i \Delta x_j^+ \mid \overline{d} + (1 - T^i) u^i \Delta x_j^- \mid \overline{d}]. \quad (3)$$

Equation (3) says that the value i expects to receive if it does nothing is the value it attaches to the status quo, discounted by i's subjective estimate of the likelihood that the status quo will prevail plus the value to i of j moving toward or away from i's preferred position in the absence of any effort by i, again discounted by actor i's subjective estimate of the likelihood of such moves by j.

By proposing a change in j's position, i can challenge j's position on issue a. In doing so, actor i presumably takes into account the probability that j does not care enough about the issue to resist the proposed settlement by i $(1 - s_j)$. Actor i also considers the possibility that j will resist

i's proposal (s_j), in which case there is some likelihood that i will succeed in its efforts to enforce its wishes on $j(P^i)$ and some probability that it will fail $(1 - P^i)$. Should i succeed, then i will derive the utility associated with convincing j to switch from its current policy stance to that supported by i. This is denoted by $u^i\Delta x_j^+ \mid d$, which equals $u^i(x_i - x_j)$. Should i fail, then it confronts the prospect of having to abandon its objectives in favor of those pursued by j, denoted by $u^i\Delta x_j^- \mid d = u^i(x_j - x_i)$. The expected utility for challenging j's proposed resolution of the multilateral dispute $(E^i u^i \Delta x_j \mid d)$ is

$$E^i u^i \Delta x_j \mid d = s_j\{P^i[u^i\Delta x_j^+ \mid d] + (1 - P^i)[u^i\Delta x_j^- \mid d]\}$$
$$+ [1 - s_j][u^i\Delta x_j^+ \mid d], \qquad (4)$$

so that the overall expected utility of i with respect to j's outlook on issue a is

$$E^i u^i \Delta x_j = E^i u^i \Delta x_j \mid d - E^i u^i \Delta x_j \mid \bar{d}. \qquad (5)$$

If equation (5) is greater than zero, then i believes that challenging j's position is superior to not challenging it, and so i is assumed to make a proposal of its own. If equation (5) is less than zero, then not challenging is preferred and i is said to be deterred. If (5) equals zero, then i is indifferent between challenging and not challenging j's proposed settlement. Each actor evaluates equation (5) vis-à-vis each other actor. In doing so, actors take the expected actions of third parties into account. The estimates of P^i include calculations of how i expects all other parties to respond to a dispute over policy settlements between i and j. In particular, P^i places each other actor in i's coalition, j's coalition, or in a neutral position as indicated by each third party's preference for i's policy proposal or j's. Actor j makes a comparable calculation (as does each $k\epsilon N$). Because equation (5) includes such subjective elements as utilities and subjective probabilities, it is possible to estimate a complete matrix of expected utilities that capture all possible confrontations, compromises, and capitulations among all the participants in the relevant political arena.

Each of the various components of equation (5) must be measured if the model proposed here is to have practical value. I have explained the measurement procedures in considerable detail elsewhere (Bueno de Mesquita 1985; Bueno de Mesquita, Newman, and Rabushka 1985; Bueno de Mesquita and Lalman 1986; Bueno de Mesquita 1990), so here I provide only brief, summary descriptions of the methods used for estimating each of the key variables.

The estimation of the probability of success for i's preferred outcome in a competition with j's preferred outcome is accomplished using the following specification:

$$P^i = \left(\sum_{k|u^k x_i > u^k x_j} v_k^{ij} \right) \Big/ \left(\sum_{k=1}^{n} |v_k^{ij}| \right)$$

for all $k \epsilon N$.

The probability calculation has a straightforward interpretation. The numerator represents the "power" or capabilities expected to be brought to bear by actor i and its supporters against j. The denominator is the sum of all of the capabilities expected to be utilized in the prospective policy dispute between i and j. As such, the overall equation treats the probability of gaining one's objectives in terms of gambling odds. The higher the proportion of resources in the would-be dispute on i's side, the higher i's chances of gaining what it wants. The probability calculation is subjective in that i's estimate of its chances for success may be quite different from j's estimate of the same value. The subjective component is introduced through the use of estimates of the individual risk-taking profiles of each decision maker. In particular, the utilities for the specific proposals (e.g., $x_i, x_j \epsilon R_a$) that enter into the calculation of v_k are evaluated, so that

$$u^i x_j = 1 - | x_i - x_j |^{ri} \qquad (6)$$

with ri — the indicator of risk-taking propensities — estimated as described below or in Bueno de Mesquita (1985).

The risk-taking component is fairly complex and involves two auxiliary assumptions. First, the positions decision makers take publicly on any issue are assumed to always represent some trade-off between what they really want (i.e., the unknown ideal point) and what they believe is pragmatic or safe. Second, what each decision maker really wants in his or her heart of hearts is always more radical than what is practical. Consequently, the risk indicator estimates the size of the trade-off made by each decision maker by evaluating the position taken by each decision maker, *ad seriatim,* controlling for the distribution of capabilities, salience, and expressed or anticipated positions of each other actor. The closer in expected utility terms an actor's public position is to the least vulnerable position (i.e., the median voter of the relevant configuration of preferred outcomes), the more risk averse the decision maker is presumed to be. This presumption follows from the notion that the actor has chosen a position that minimizes threats to its security at the expense of pursuing what it really wants. The farther the decision maker's expected utility score is from being at its possible maximum, while still remaining within the feasible set of alternative proposals, the more risk acceptant the decision maker is presumed to be. Algebraically, the risk calculation is

$$R_i = \frac{2 \sum\limits_{j=1}^{n} E^i u^i \Delta x_j - \sum\limits_{j=1}^{n} E^i u^i \Delta x_j(\text{max}) - \sum\limits_{j=1}^{n} E^i u^i \Delta x_j(\text{min})}{\sum\limits_{j=1}^{n} E^i u^i \Delta x_j(\text{max}) - \sum\limits_{j=1}^{n} E^i u^i \Delta x_j(\text{min})}$$

and

$$r_i = (1 - R_i/3)/(1 + R_i/3),$$

so that r_i ranges between .5 and 2.

The fundamental feature behind the risk indicator is the notion that actors choose positions on issues by trading implicitly between security and policy goals. Every decision maker is assumed to want to maximize utility in terms of the policy outcome and in terms of security against costly challenges by rivals. Alas, it is usually the case that security can be gained only at the expense of policy objectives and that policy or issue goals can be attained only at the expense of some sacrifice of security. The measure of risk taking provides one perspective on how much each decision maker appears to have exchanged security for policy goals or visa versa. In doing so, the risk-taking measure also provides a basis for estimating the value attached to the status quo.

The first term in the numerator of the main expression for estimating risks is equal to the security and policy value of actor i's actual or "real" position, while the next two terms place the "real" value within the boundaries of what could have been attained in terms of security or policy. That is, the "real" sum of expected utilities is the estimation of the actor's status quo value. It is conceived of here as being an endogenous choice variable of the decision maker. In this comparative static view of risks and of the status quo, the maximum and minimum possible sums of expected utilities are determined by exogenous conditions for each actor, with those exogenous conditions being the distribution of the power, position, and salience of each other actor.

The specification of the risk measure and, indeed, of the attendant utilities and probabilities is one of many possible ways of estimating these variables. The model is not dependent on these measurement specifications, although, of course, the empirical results are. Some such specification is necessary to ensure that we are providing an applied model — not one designed strictly for its theoretical properties, but rather one that consciously sacrifices some theoretical purity in exchange for practical applicability. Having said that, it should also be noted that in tests of the efficacy of this measure of risk-taking propensities across large numbers of European disputes, the measure has proven quite reliable in capturing actual differences in the risks taken by decision makers (Bueno de Mesquita 1985; Morrow 1987; Conybeare 1992; Lalman and Newman 1991). The same appears to be true of the other measures proposed here.

Utilities for the marginal gains $[(u^i \Delta x_j^+ \mid d$ and $u^i \Delta x_j^+ \mid \overline{d}]$ or losses $[(u^i \Delta x_j^- \mid d$ and $u^i \Delta x_j^- \mid \overline{d}]$ from shifts to alternative proposals are evaluated, using the basic building block just described, in the manner delineated in Bueno de Mesquita and Lalman (1986) and in accordance with equation (6). The utilities $u^i \Delta x_j^+ \mid \overline{d}$ and $u^i \Delta x_j^- \mid \overline{d}$ are approximated by comparing the value actor i attaches to the current median voter prediction to the value i attaches to the median anticipated if i accepts j's preferred outcome.

Equation (5) is estimated from four perspectives, with relevant superscripts on equation (5) indicating from whose perspective the calculation is being viewed:

1. i's expected utility vis-à-vis each rival j's proposal;
2. i's perception of each j's expected utility vis-à-vis i's proposal;
3. j's expected utility vis-à-vis each i's proposal; and
4. j's perception of each i's expected utility vis-à-vis j's proposal.

The expected utility values summarized in (1) and (2) and in (3) and (4), respectively, describe each actor's perception of its relationship vis-à-vis each other actor. It is these beliefs about the expectations of rivals that forms the basis for each stake holder playing out the bargaining game implied by the model.

With Banks's monotonicity of escalation theorem in mind, these expected utility relationships can be described in continuous form. According to Banks's theorem, the probability with which an actor anticipates confronting a given rival increases with its expected utility for challenging the rival's proposal, so that the higher some actor i's expected utility is with regard to persuading some other actor j to accept i's position, the higher the likelihood that i will confront j.[9] Using this theorem, we state the following applied expectations:

Pr(confrontation) = $[P^i$(confrontational)$][P^j$(confrontational)$]$
Pr(i gains concessions) = $[P^i$(confrontational)$][P^j$(not confrontational)$]$
Pr(j gains concessions) = $[P^i$(not confrontational)$][P^j$(confrontational)$]$
Pr(status quo) = $[P^i$(not confrontational)$][P^j$(not confrontational)$]$

with P^i(confrontational) = an increasing function of expression (5) calculated in accordance with i's expectations, while P^j(confrontational) is an increasing function of j's estimation of its expected utilities.[10] The specific functional relationship assumed here is

9. Recall that the theorem holds for all Bayesian, asymmetric information games.
10. Bueno de Mesquita and Lalman (1986) show that P^i(confrontation) = $f(r$ cosine $\theta)$ and P^j(confrontation) = $g(r$ sine $\theta)$, with r being the hypotenuse of a triangle with i's expected utility value as the base and j's expected utility value as the vertical arm. The

$$P^i(\text{confrontational}) = (3 + E^i u^i \Delta x_j)/6 \qquad (7)$$

and

$$P^j(\text{confrontational}) = (3 + E^j(u^j \Delta x_i)/6. \qquad (8)$$

Of course, the specific functions are ad hoc, but they are consistent with the monotonicity principle argued for by Banks (1990) and Bueno de Mesquita and Lalman (1986). By identifying the values of equations (7) and (8) for each actor we can evaluate all of the interactions that can arise and thereby assess the likely conditions under which an issue might be settled. It is important to recall that each pairwise relation has already taken into account all third-party interactions through the calculation of the discounted effort of each third party for each member of the pair under review.

The likelihood with which confrontation or concessions occur can be easily displayed in a polar coordinate space. For ease of presentation, I divide such a space into six sectors, with the boundary between each reflecting a fundamental turning point in the probability functions. Figure 4.1 displays such a polar coordinate space, along with relevant labels for each of the six sectors, reflecting the general likelihood of alternative outcomes in accordance with Banks's monotonicity theorem. Figures equivalent to this are used to summarize perceived and actual relationships among competing interests.

When the expected utility values (as perceived by either or both actors) favor a challenge by both i and j then a confrontation is likely in which neither actor is inclined to offer concessions or to bargain. Such conflictual situations involve high political costs and great uncertainty regarding the ultimate outcome. When, however, one actor expects to gain more by challenging a rival's position than by doing nothing and the other actor anticipates greater losses than gains in a confrontation, then the costs of resolving the issue are greatly reduced and the prospects of an amicable settlement are enhanced. If one side expects to gain more than the other side is prepared to give up then there is an opportunity to negotiate over the difference in expectations. In the event one protagonist anticipates losing more than the other protagonist believes it stands to gain, then we expect that the side anticipating a loss will willingly give in to the relatively modest demand of its rival. Finally, if both sides believe there is more to be lost than there is to be gained by challenging the other party's position, then the status quo between them is expected to prevail. In this case any demands or proposals that are made are likely to be mere bluffs and bluster without credible substance behind them.

---

symbol θ is the angle from the horizontal in a polar coordinate space defined by i's expected utility along the horizontal axis and j's expected utility along the vertical axis.

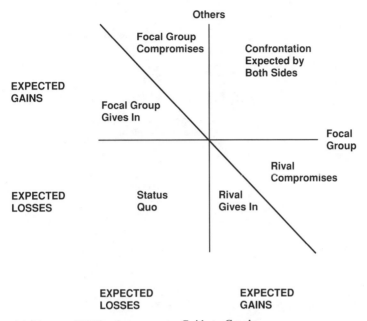

4.1: Expected Utility Assessments: Guide to Graphs

By examining the distribution of information in graphs like figure 4.1, it is possible to approximate the private information available to each participant in a dispute or negotiation. From that information it is possible to estimate how each party will behave and what consequences are likely to ensue. Of course, these are only approximations and not necessarily a faithful revelation of that private information. How faithful the approximation is remains an empirical question that is best addressed by evaluating how accurately the model predicts behavior.

What information does the perceptual model reveal in the context of the illustrative issue on which we have focused? Recall that every decision maker is assumed to know the array of potential power, positions, and salience of each other decision maker. That information is common knowledge. The private information possessed by each decision maker involves the shape of its own utility function and the belief it holds about the expected utilities of each other actor. Thus, everyone is assumed to know the basic information that goes into the expected utility model. Everyone knows the shape of their own utility function but can only form a belief about the shape of the utility functions of other decision makers.

Although there are considerable variations in perceptions from actor to actor, I illustrate the implementation of the perceptual model with figures that typify the key beliefs of EC members backing each of the three proposed introduction dates for emission controls on medium-sized cars.

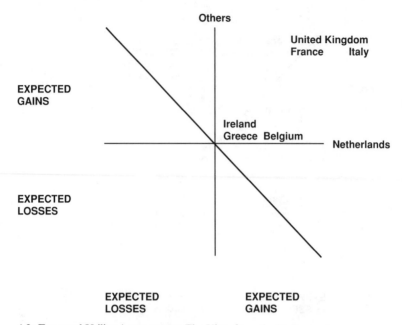

4.2: Expected Utility Assessments: The View from the Netherlands

Figures 4.2, 4.3, and 4.4 show the expectations of the Netherlands, Belgium, and France, respectively.

Evidently, the Netherlands — supporting a four-year delay — anticipated a highly confrontational environment in which its proposal would be vigorously opposed by everyone who did not share its point of view. Belgium had a quite different view of things. As a proponent of a seven-year delay, Belgium enjoyed the support of quite a broad coalition. Nevertheless, Belgian beliefs appear to have been very pessimistic. As can be seen from figure 4.3, the Belgians seem to have believed that they would be compelled to give in either to the coalition backing the ten-year delay or to the group favoring the four-year delay. The only nation the Belgians were not prepared to capitulate to was Luxembourg according to this assessment. To whom the Belgians might actually yield, however, depended on who would actually demand or propose a concession from them and on the choices Belgium had once such demands were made.

We have already seen that the Dutch (and their followers) expected a strife-ridden confrontation. Nevertheless, the Dutch thought that they had the upper hand in several relationships. Their perception of expected gains (as estimated here) should have led them to conclude that they stood to gain more than their rivals in a confrontation. The Dutch, for instance, seemingly held such an expectation about their relationship with the Belgians.

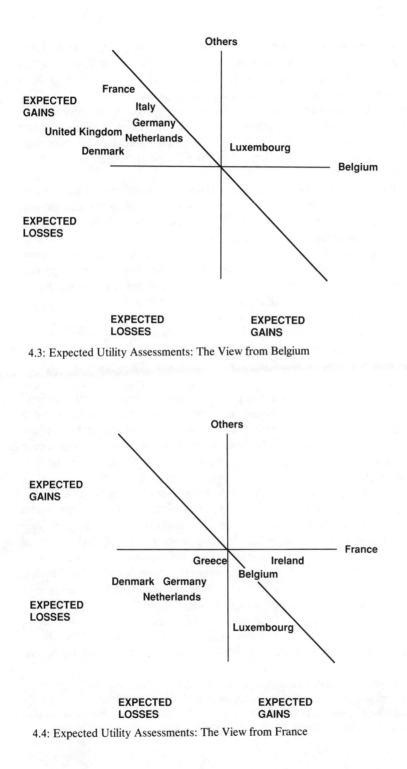

4.3: Expected Utility Assessments: The View from Belgium

4.4: Expected Utility Assessments: The View from France

The French apparently were not concerned about a highly costly political exchange. Rather, as suggested by figure 4.4, the French believed that the representatives of Belgium and Luxembourg would give in to them and that they could reach a compromise agreement with the Irish. The French view also supported a belief in a status quo oriented stalemate vis-à-vis the Netherlands, Germany, Denmark, and Greece. Thus, France and the members of its tacit coalition seem to have perceived opportunities to extract low-cost concessions, while the Dutch and their tacit coalition partners did not.[11]

The beliefs of each actor imply actions. Those actions, in the form of the extraction or granting of concessions over support for this or that specific position, lead to a re-evaluation of the situation by each decision maker. As representatives to the EC respond to revised proposals — with their responses supported by their beliefs and expectations — the prospects for a favorable or unfavorable settlement change for many participants. Beliefs and expectations provide the foundation for a kinematic (if not dynamic) assessment of the evolution of issue positions and to recalculations of the location of the median voter.

When actors are persuaded or coerced into accepting a proposal different from their initial (or current) position on an issue the decision process enters a new phase. Coalitions change and the support or risks associated with alternative proposals vary. New proposals are brought forward as revised beliefs and expectations open new possibilities or foreclose old ones. Each such sequence of revised stances on an issue is called an iteration. The model computes as many iterations as it takes for the policy issue to resolve itself by reaching a stable outcome — an outcome from which there is not a meaningful possibility of change given the estimated expectations of the actors.

The model portrays a process of decision making during each iteration. To gain an intuitive sense of what happens within the logic of the model during each iteration, think of the decision makers as being engaged in a game of cards. At the outset, each player is dealt a hand. The quality of the hand dealt to each player depends on the commonly known characteristics of each player. Stronger players (or those with strong backing from others) generally draw better cards than weaker players. Because of variations in salience, some players pay closer attention to their cards and to the whole playing out of the game than do others and so form different perceptions of the situation. Based on the cards they hold and the known characteristics of other players, decision makers form perceptions about

11. It should be noted that not everyone holding the same objective necessarily perceives the situation in the same way or has the same expectations. Indeed, there are important differences in the perceptions estimated by the perceptual model in this illustrative case. These differences play a crucial role in the ultimate settlement of the issue.

how good the hand is of each rival relative to the hand dealt them. With that information, each player decides on proposals or bids to make to the other decision makers. It is as if they are playing a game of bridge with a potentially large number of other players and they are bidding without knowing who their partners are.

If a player believes his or her hand is very weak compared to a specific rival, then no proposal is made to that actor. If i expects to lose to j, for instance, then i does not make a proposal to j. If, however, i thinks it holds a good hand relative to j, then i makes a proposal in the form of a suggested change in position by j on the issue at hand.[12] If i thinks j stands to lose quite a lot, then i will propose that j accept i's current position.[13] If i thinks it has a good enough hand to shift j's position, but not so good that j will give in to what i wants, then i proposes a compromise somewhere between i's position and j's.[14]

After all the players have submitted their secret proposals to one another, each player now reviews the new cards — the proposals — that it holds. Of course, some proposals are better for the recipient than others. Indeed, some proposals turn out to be frivolous in that the proposer cannot enforce the proposal, something that the proposer might only learn at the end of the round of proposal making. Other proposals received by a decision maker are potentially enforceable but fall by the wayside because a superior, enforceable proposal was made by a different player. Each player would like to choose the best offer made to it, and each proposer enforces its bids to the extent that it can. Those better able to enforce their wishes than others can make their proposals stick. Given equally enforceable proposals, players move the least that they can. Each actor selects from among the bids it made and the bids it receives. The bid that is chosen is the proposal that is the optimal choice for the player given the constraints under which it operates. These constraints include its own perceptions and the reality of which proposals turn out to be enforceable and which turn out to be beaten back by rivals or rejected outright as unenforceable by the recipient.

12. Actor i makes a proposal if, in figure 4.1, the conjunction of i's expected utility and i's estimate of j's expected utility falls between zero degrees from the horizontal axis and 45 degrees or falls between 270 degrees and 360 degrees from the horizontal axis. That is the domain within which i believes it has a comparative advantage over j and i expects more gains than losses from challenging j's position.
13. A proposed capitulation by j to i's wishes is made if i locates the conjunction of the respective expected utilities in the wedge that falls between 270 degrees and 315 degrees below the horizontal axis in figure 4.1 or in the wedge between zero degrees and 45 degrees. In the latter instance, i expects resistance from j, but i believes it can enforce its demand. In the former case, i expects no resistance from j.
14. A compromise is proposed if i believes the conjunction of the relevant expected utilities falls between 315 degrees and 360 degrees from the horizontal axis in figure 4.1.

At the end of a round of proposal making, players learn new information about their opponents. If, for instance, a player finds that some proposals it thought of as enforceable are successfully rejected, then it learns the proposal was unenforceable (i.e., the player has less support than it thought). By monitoring responses to its proposals, a player learns how much leverage it has with other decision makers. If a proposal is accepted, then a player learns that it made the best offer among all the proposals made to the recipient of its accepted bid.

When the players finish sorting out their choices among proposals, each shifts to the position contained in the proposal it accepted, thereby helping to create new coalitions, strengthening some old coalitions and weakening others. Of course, when a decision maker agrees to a compromise with another actor, it hopes that the other player will also live up to its end of the compromise bargain. But this is a game in which promises are not binding. Proposals are enforceable if a decision maker has the wherewithal to make sure that another actor does what it says it will do. Each player is free to renege on a proposed deal so long as it can enforce some other agreement or so long as someone else can enforce an agreement on it. Thus, i and j may agree to a compromise settlement in which j moves from, say, a seven-year position to a five-year position with the expectation that i will move from its four-year position to the five-year position. But i may have had an alternative proposal before it that was superior in terms of the expected impact on the ultimate outcome of the issue. Thus i may only move, say, to support a 4.5-year delay in the introduction of emission controls even though it proposed the five-year settlement to j. In this case i makes the more limited move because it is better for i's welfare and because i believes that the new or improved coalition of supporters that it attracts at this new position is sufficient to offset any effort by j to punish i for failing to fully live up to its part of the bargain.

What consequences follow from the actions implied by the first iteration through the model? How do those actions influence the location of the median voter? How do we determine when the median voter outcome at a particular iteration is to be taken as the actual resolution of the issue at hand? To answer these questions we must understand better the concept I call the *dominant outcome*.

The Dominant Outcome: Analyzing Comparative Statics

The initial median voter prediction ignores variations across actors in their beliefs and perceptions. Yet such variations may profoundly alter the outcome of a policy negotiation. Figure 4.2, for instance, reveals that the Dutch seemed to expect that their support for a four-year delay in emissions standards would strain relations with Belgium. Yet, figure 4.3 shows that, from the Belgian perspective, such a proposal would have been taken quite seriously, albeit the magnitude of the Dutch demand in expected utility terms made it less attractive for Belgium to give in to them than for Belgium to capitulate to a demand from the French or the Italians.[15]

Such differences in perceptions may operate in several ways to encourage errors of commission or of omission. Suppose, for instance, that group i mistakenly believes group j is willing to give in to i's goals. In pursuing its belief that j will capitulate, i mistakenly proposes that j shifts its support to favor the goal of i. From j's perspective, i is seen to be bluffing so that j, perhaps, believes it can extract concessions from i. In such a circumstance, i makes a demand expecting j to give in, but instead finds that j resists and makes a counterdemand of its own, perhaps leading to a strife-filled confrontation. That is a very different circumstance from one in which i holds the belief that j will capitulate, and j shares that perception. In cases where the combined perspective of i and j is expected to lead j to capitulate to i (or is expected to lead j to make concessions to i), we expect i to pursue its opportunity *and* for the opportunity to bear fruit. In such cases it is appropriate to assume analytically that the situation becomes restructured by a switch in position by actor j, provided no better, enforceable opportunity is before i or j.

Figure 4.4, for instance, reveals that France seems to have believed that Belgium would give in to the ten-year proposal. Figure 4.3 suggests that the Belgians were ready to do just that. Yet the model suggests that a compromise arrangement would be made in which Belgium, Italy, and France all agree to endorse a delay of about 8.4 years. How does this arise?

Figure 4.4 shows that the French thought an agreement could be reached with Ireland, but that it would take some concessions on their part. In particular, the model shows that the predicted outcome on this issue would have been a seven-year delay if the French remained intransigent, but that France could persuade the Irish to go along with a longer delay. According to the model, the French probably pressed for an agreement to support a delay of 8.36 years. The Belgians preferred a seven-year delay rather than a longer one, but they were not in a position to enforce their wishes. The same was true for Ireland. Given Belgium's apparent belief that they would be better off giving in to France than trying to fight them on this issue, the model predicts that Belgium would accept the French compromise proposal, placing Belgian influence behind a delay of 8.36 years before emission standards would be enforced on mid-sized automobiles.

15. The value of equation 5 for the Belgians vis-à-vis the Dutch on this issue is -0.495, while the value with respect to the French is -0.406, implying a smaller loss for the Belgians in giving in to the ten-year proposal than in capitulating to the four-year position.

Giving in to the French-Irish compromise position was better for Belgium than acquiescing to France's original proposal (ten years). Because France itself was abandoning that position, it appears that the French also calculated that the value to them of gaining Belgian and Irish support for an 8.36-year delay was better than obtaining only Belgian support for a ten-year delay. Indeed, the French compromise proposal is found by the model to be supported to a greater or lesser extent by Italy, Ireland, and Greece, as well as Belgium and France.

Belgium faced several alternative proposals. The Belgian delegation to the EC could have backed Dutch interests, or interests part way between what the Dutch wanted and what Belgium wanted. Or Belgium could have endorsed proposals for a longer delay than the seven-year period they preferred. The model selects the proposal that Belgium is expected to have preferred. The selection process is straightforward as it simply assumes that the Belgian delegation would have done whatever was best from the Belgian perspective, given the challenges they faced and the credibility of alternative threats to their position. That is, any compromise proposal offered to Belgium by an actor with a credible basis for making a demand would have been accepted if it were closer to the initial Belgian position than any other proposal, if the proposer could make its bid stick because it utilized enough clout to do so, and if it enhanced the probability that the outcome would be better for Belgium (from their perspective). If more than one proposal were equidistant from Belgium's starting position (e.g., proposals to support a five-year delay or a nine-year delay), then the Belgian representatives would have chosen the one that yielded the greatest expected utility gain or, if a loss were involved, the smallest expected utility loss.

More generally, if j is confronted with a circumstance in which it is prepared to capitulate or compromise with the wishes of two rivals with equally enforceable interests, each of whom has antithetical goals, then I assume that j gives in to the adversary whose goal is closer to j's. To do otherwise would be irrational given the assumption that utility declines with Euclidean distance from the actor's preferred outcome. If two actors demand concessions of equal distance from j's preferred position, but in opposite directions, then j is assumed to choose in favor of the move that j believes will cost it less in expected utility terms. Likewise, i enforces the proposals it makes that maximize its expected utility.

If j believes it must offer a concession to actor i but is not prepared to give in to i's demand, and if i believes that j will offer a concession, then a negotiated compromise can be achieved without escalating the dispute. In such a case, the concession is assumed to equal the distance on R_a between x_i and x_j multiplied by the ratio of the absolute value of j's expected utility to i's expected utility. This treats the compromise as the weighted average of the perceived enforceability of the demand and is quite similar to the Nash bargaining solution.

The above steps can be used to simulate the sequence of discussions, negotiations, or confrontations that are likely to take place between each possible pairing of groups involved in the resolution of some issue. The simulated bargaining process is very much like the intuition suggested by the analogy with a card game. No group is expected to make a concession that is contrary to its perceived interests and no group is assumed to forego the opportunity to seek a concession that it believes is attainable and is in its interest. Should an opportunity arise to gain a concession that ultimately yields deleterious consequences for the group pursuing it, then I assume that the actor, being rational, will forego the concession and avoid the longer-term negative results. The notion here is that decision makers are forward looking rather than myopic.

Through a sequence of iterations the above method allows the simulation of the evolution of positions on an issue. Along with that evolution there are constantly changing perceptions brought about by changes in the structure of the situation. As noted earlier, players learn by observing the actions of their rivals and so improve their information about the "cards" held by their opponents. Thus, each scenario (or configuration of positions, capabilities, and salience) may imply a new scenario. Generally, after two or three rounds the iteration-specific median voter prediction converges on a stable predicted outcome. When no group continues to believe that it can influence an actor who also believes it is susceptible to being influenced, then the result has converged on what I call the dominant outcome.[16] This is the outcome predicted for the issue in question.

Let us return to the illustrative example. Several backers of the seven-year outcome and of the ten-year outcome appear to have been prepared to reach a compromise agreement of about 8.36 years. The model automatically simulates such moves until a dominant outcome is reached. The new median voter prediction increases from seven years to 8.35 years. As noted, the model indicates that this proposal should have received broad support that was far from unanimous.

According to the analytic procedure suggested here, the British are expected to have broken with France and Italy by rejecting their compromise proposal and continuing to insist on a ten-year delay. The backers of a four-year delay probably also split somewhat, with Denmark, Germany, and the Netherlands willing to agree to a delay of nearly five years, while Luxembourg apparently stood firm at four years.

By assuming that the actors discount small gains on the outcome by

16. The model has built-in time-discounting rules so that small changes in positions become less and less attractive the longer, in relative time, that negotiations are expected to go on.

the costs associated with continuing to haggle over the issue, the model predicts that this specific issue would have been resolved relatively quickly. The dominant outcome would be, as indicated above, a lag of 8.35 years. However, if the participants were prepared to bear the costs of slightly prolonged negotiations, then the model's predicted dominant outcome rises to 9.05 years and stabilizes at that point. Thus, the prediction on this issue from the expected utility model is for the EC to have agreed to a delay of 8.35 or 9.05 years. The actual resolution was for a delay of 8.833 years.

Strategic Intervention to Alter the Dominant Outcome

The study of policy is incomplete without an analysis of strategic intervention to deflect or shape events. For policymakers in government, industry, or international bureaucracies, the most important questions are what will happen and how one might change undesired results. What will happen depends, as we have seen, on the perceptions of the actors in a negotiation setting. How events might possibly be changed depends upon the acquisition of additional information beyond that perceived by the actors, as specified by the controlling strategy approach, which is explained below.

In applying the expected utility models it often is of interest to ascertain how strategic maneuvers can shift expected outcomes toward or away from particular results. To the extent that decision makers behave as if they make the calculations described in the expected utility framework, the proposed model can be a useful tool, but first it must be sensitized to the strategic efforts to manipulate outcomes that are at the heart of bargaining processes.

One available strategic modification for an interested party is to alter its level of effort (salience). Sometimes, by spending more resources and carrying a bigger stick, a group is able to offset its political opposition. By doing so, the group enhances its relative "votes," shifting the expected outcome in the direction it desires. Depending on the particular structure of interests and influence, it is also possible for increased effort to facilitate the formation of a counter-coalition, thereby diminishing the prospects of moving the political settlement in the direction desired by whoever's utility one is trying to maximize. Figure 4.5 provides an illustrative demonstration of just such effects. In the example on which figure 4.5 is based, there are only three actors, A, B, and C, with the capabilities of A, B, and C fixed. So, too, are the initial policy preferences of the actors. Finally, A's and B's salience is fixed, but C's is allowed to vary between zero and 100. As is evident from the figure, increasing effort by C can have surprising effects. While an increase in C's salience generally improves C's bargain-

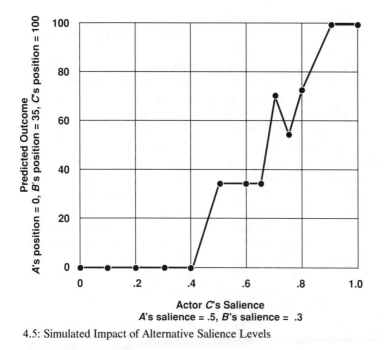

4.5: Simulated Impact of Alternative Salience Levels

ing leverage, there is a range in this example in which C's increased effort decreases the quality of the outcome from C's point of view.

The model presented here allows one to simulate the effects of shifts in level of effort so as to identify the optimal resource expenditure.[17] Furthermore, the model reveals cases in which no change in level of effort by the interested group will appreciably affect the predicted outcome. In such cases, other strategies — alone or in combination with this one — may be necessary if there is any hope of altering the anticipated dominant outcome. In any case, changed levels of salience introduce new information into everyone's decision calculus. As such, shifts in effort reshape the bargaining process by altering perceptions. Of course, increasing salience is costly as it involves dedicating more resources to one issue at the expense of some other issue or issues. Consequently, such shifts cannot occur casually; rather, they probably reflect calculations that the political costs of a relatively low profile have become larger than the costs involved in making a greater effort, especially when evaluated relative to the anticipated gains. Shifts in salience represent costly signals that must, naturally,

17. Current research by Frans and Jasper Stokman (1992) suggests ways to determine optimal salience allocations endogenously, representing a potentially very important improvement in the methodology for testing the effects of alternative salience levels.

be consistent with advancing the interests of the player in question. As figure 4.5 reminds us, such increases sometimes have no effect and other times have a counterproductive impact.

Shifts in policy stances are commonplace during negotiations. Indeed, in some sense this is the essence of bargaining. As interested parties move to more moderate or more extreme positions, they alter the level of support or opposition given to their position and they signal others about their flexibility on the issue being negotiated. Sometimes, by moderating a position, a group is able to attract support from significant actors who previously had been in opposition. Other times, however, moderation fosters outcomes supported by extremists. This can be accomplished by breaking away marginal elements from an opposed coalition, pivoting just enough power in a polarized situation to force a sharp swing toward the opposite extreme and, thereby, maximizing the interested party's expected utility.

It is also true that moves away from moderation and toward more extreme positions can shift outcomes toward the center or away from the center depending upon the particular structure of interests in the political setting. Since that setting is defined by the structure of preferences, capabilities, and salience within the model proposed here, the precise effects of a shift in position can be ascertained through simulation, by moving group positions on the issue continuum utilized by the model and then solving the model under these altered assumptions. Perhaps such simulations of alternative scenarios can even help forestall the implementation of some sophisticated strategies that backfire in actual practice.

When a single group is unable through its own actions to alter appreciably the expected outcome of a decision in the direction it desires, then it may consider the possibility of coordinating its efforts with other groups. Obviously, this is more difficult and hence more costly than moves that can be implemented unilaterally. When coalition building is dictated, the model can be especially helpful in providing useful guidance. The perceptual analysis, for instance, reveals which groups believe they should compromise or grant concessions to which particular other groups. It does so through the evaluation of beliefs about the probability that a given rival is inclined to be confrontational or not. The enactment of such beliefs is at the heart of the development of the dominant outcome. However, the dominant outcome takes advantage only of knowledge presumed to be possessed by the decision makers in question.

If a decision maker could gain insight into what a rival is thinking, such information might reveal opportunities for strategic intervention that were not readily perceived by the decision maker in question. The perceptual component of the expected utility model appears to be unique in making this possible. Because the perceptual analysis fully maps each actor's beliefs about each other actor (and even each other actor's beliefs about third parties), it is possible for the policymaker utilizing this model to assess the availability of concessions that the policymaker is unlikely to have recognized on his or her own. Naturally, even a group that is willing to grant concessions will not volunteer them unless asked. Therefore, an essential ingredient for sophisticated strategic intervention is to know, or at least approximate, the opponent's mind and to act upon that knowledge.

Using the perceptual analysis, any interested group (or an interested analyst) can identify the candidates prepared to succumb to someone else's objectives if pressed. A group leader should, of course, be most inclined to pressure those who believe they must grant concessions to the group's demands. The larger the probability that a rival will not be confrontational, the lower the costs expected to be associated with extracting gains from the foe, thereby making such an actor an especially attractive candidate for influence attempts. By focusing efforts on groups believed to have a high probability of granting concessions, the interested party can most efficiently organize the coalition — with altered levels of effort or revealed policy preferences — that will shift the outcome to be most in line with the organizing group's preferences. Again, simulation facilitates evaluating the impact of alternative coalitions so that the one actually constructed yields the best possible outcome at the lowest political cost.[18]

The comparative static techniques just described allow the analyst to evaluate the impact of alternative strategies. This can be done from the perspective of any interest group or of all groups. What is more, the process can proceed in stages, first identifying the best strategic reaction to the initial, base case, circumstance, then analyzing strategic responses to the initial strategy to alter the base case, and so forth. In this way, a "movie" of the unfolding process of negotiations, of moves and counter-moves, can be constructed.[19]

If a *controlling strategy* — a strategy that allows the full exploitation of hidden beliefs — exists it is likely to be discovered through this iterative process. Like the dominant outcome in which each actor relies on its own perceptions, this controlling strategy assumes that each actor pursues its own best interest. Unlike the dominant outcome analysis, the assessment of a controlling strategy takes advantage of the calculation of other players' beliefs, revealing information to a policymaker and then simulating its use by the policymaker. The controlling strategy takes information that previously was the private knowledge of an opponent and exposes it to a

18.   Again recall that the potential power, position, and salience of each group is common knowledge, but how it translates into perceptions and expectations is not. The model is a helpful tool for "revealing" or approximating the expectations and perceptions of decision makers. This information is generally otherwise within the domain of their private information.

19.   For a detailed example (drawn from Italian politics) of such an application of the model, see Beck and Bueno de Mesquita 1985.

decision maker who is privy to the assessments of the perceptual analysis of the expected utility model.

The utilization of the perceptual component of the model does not guarantee the existence of a controlling strategy. It is important to recognize that the processes outlined here neither provide a crystal ball nor a magic solution to insurmountable opposition. But these techniques have proven highly reliable in practice. Controlling strategies often are possible and can help shift the dominant outcome toward this or that objective, even if the precise goal cannot be attained.

Estimating the Model

Political outcomes — whether they involve intra- or inter-governmental relations or negotiations between public and private organizations or even within a single organization — can be and have been predicted using the model delineated above. To do so, however, requires converting theoretical concepts into practical application. Although this can be an extremely difficult task, there is, fortunately, a body of knowledge that can be called upon to estimate the critical variables. By combining the perspective of this rational-actor model with the knowledge and expertise of area or issue experts, it is possible to estimate the variables of interest and to solve the perceptual and voting components of the model discussed here.

As table 4.1 indicates, solving the forecasting and perceptual models requires identifying the groups or actors interested in trying to influence a policy outcome on the issues in question. For each actor, data must then be estimated on three variables: capabilities, preferred outcome, and salience. Sometimes, in institutionally structured settings, it is also important to take into account structural constraints that operate to help shape outcomes. In the EC, for instance, under some procedures certain countries are given more votes than others, and so this feature is important to take into account when those procedures are relevant. With just this minimal information in hand, and without any other information regarding, for instance, the history of the situation, the history of relations between particular actors within the situation, other sunk costs, or without even interviewing the actors involved to assess their own judgment about their beliefs and expectations, it is possible, as I have illustrated, to predict what the likely outcome will be. This is true whether the issues being investigated are as well defined and structured as those that typically come before the EC or whether the issues and their institutional setting are less clearly set out.

Where are the necessary data estimates to come from? Probably the best source is individuals with area or issue expertise. Such individuals have great insight into who the players are likely to be on an issue. What is more, although area experts often doubt that they possess the essential information to quantify capabilities or salience, through careful interactive techniques it is generally possible to elicit such information. The essential features behind the development of such estimates is to begin by identifying the most powerful actor and assigning that actor a score of 100 on capabilities. All other actors can then be rated as a proportion of the most capable group, as well as proportionate to each other. Issues must be defined precisely enough so that actor preferences can be located on a continuum. This also is not particularly problematic with suitable training.

The full details of such estimation techniques are too lengthy to enumerate here. It should be noted, however, that it is possible to achieve a very high level of accuracy and cross-expert agreement on the essential information, even when the experts in question disagree markedly with one another on the likely outcome or evolution of discussion on an issue. The greatest power and insight from such an approach can be attained by combining the analytic consistency of models such as those explained here with the nuanced and rich insights of area or issue experts.

When issue experts combine their skills with the analytic strengths of these models, then accurate and subtle predictions are most likely to be attained. To be sure, an abstract model such as the one proposed here is of no value without the information from experts needed to turn its abstractions into practical estimates. Expert knowledge, of course, is quite valuable even without a model to suggest what information is critical and how that information should be organized. But in numerous controlled experiments it has been found that the predictions extracted from the model in conjunction with the information from area experts is substantially more reliable than the predictions made by the experts themselves.

The perceptual, forecasting, and proactive model delineated above is a tool for assessing policy choices. The perceptual component allows the analyst to estimate perceptions and beliefs and provides a framework for anticipating the maneuvers that are likely to take place in a bargaining setting. The perceptual elements also provide clues as to when there is no longer room for maneuver so that an issue is finally resolved.

Through the use of comparative static techniques, the perceptual elements are combined with the median voter theorem to predict outcomes during a sequence of stages in a decision-making process. When the analyses indicate that relevant actors no longer perceive opportunities to alter an outcome, then the dominant outcome is the prediction at that stage of the bargaining sequence.

The model outlined here is an exercise in applied modeling. Some sacrifices to deductive rigor have been made to construct a tractable, useful model. Most notably, specific conditions have been assumed to give shape to utility functions and to facilitate the approximation of private information. Learning is assumed to take place during the model's iterations. Such learning has been treated as an explicitly specified function of changes in available information as revealed by the policy shifts of players, but the degree of learning and changed beliefs has not been computed strictly in terms of Bayesian updating. This is regrettable in many ways, but it is a necessary sacrifice to the great complexity of a game, like this one, that can have a very large number of players. The method used does permit the representation of learning in an applied setting and so trades away some theoretical purity for the sake of practicality. As such, the specific method is open to doubt and to subsequent revision. Ultimately, the value of any social science tool — whether it be axiomatic modeling, historical analysis, or crystal ball gazing — is the extent to which it helps explain and predict behavior.

How well does the expected utility approach proposed here perform in the context of important EC decisions? An attempt to answer that question, in the context of the framework suggested here and in terms of the models proposed by Stokman and Van Oosten in chapter 5, is made in chapter 9. The issue-by-issue predictions of the expected utility model are presented in chapter 6, along with illustrations of ways it can be used to influence policy choices and to structure the political environment of negotiations.

Frans N. Stokman and Reinier Van Oosten

5 The Exchange of Voting Positions: An Object-Oriented Model of Policy Networks

In chapter 4, Bueno de Mesquita presented his expected utility theory of forecasting political decisions. In his theory, each actor is assumed to be an expected utility maximizer — that is, each actor evaluates different strategies and pursues the one that he or she believes gives the highest expected utility. His theory allows actors to evaluate strategies solely on one issue at a time. Actors are not given the opportunity to maximize expected utility by connecting their voting positions on one issue to their respective positions on other issues. In this chapter it will be demonstrated that, under certain conditions, two actors can gain expected utility simultaneously by exchanging voting positions on two decisions or issues. Subsequently, a model is presented to predict the exchange rates of such potential trades, to compute the expected utility gains for the actors, and to simulate the realization of exchanges and their effects on the outcomes of decisions in a system of N actors and M decisions.

Our exchange or logrolling model is based on many of the same fundamental assumptions as the Bueno de Mesquita model. In particular, we assume single-peaked utility functions and the unidimensionality of each issue. We focus, however, on the multidimensional linkage across issues rather than on compromises within each separate issue. As our exchange model opens new strategies for actors over several decisions, it can be seen as an extension of the Bueno de

We thank Siegwart Lindenberg, Gwen Moore, Chris Snijders, Jeroen Weesie, Allen Whitt, and Evelien Zeggelink for their extensive comments on earlier drafts. The computer implementation of the model was supported by IBM under a study contract between IBM and the Interuniversity Center for Sociological Theory and Methodology of the University of Groningen, ICS.

Mesquita model. Our model deviates considerably from earlier exchange models of collective decision-making processes that are conceptualized in terms of exchange of control.[1]

Previous Exchange Models

In the early 1970s, Coleman (1972, 1973) presented his well-known social exchange model. Coleman applies Walras's model of economic exchange on a perfectly competitive market to more general exchange processes in decision making by assuming that actor preferences are consistent with a Cobb-Douglas utility function (see Coleman 1990, pp. 674–75). His model is built on a simple conceptual framework consisting of actors and events. Actors vary in their control over and interest in events. Coleman shows how changes at the collective level stem from the exchange between actors of control over one event for control over other events. Exchanges are motivated by differences in the distribution of control over events among the actors compared to their interest in the events. Actors are hypothesized to exchange control over events in which they are less interested for control over events in which they are more interested.

The resources of each actor are defined as his or her amount of control over valued events, whereas the value of an event is defined in terms of the interests of resourceful actors in the event. If the distribution of control over actors and their interests in events are known, the values of the events, the resources of the actors, and the distribution of control at equilibrium can be computed.

Coleman's exchange model is very simple for divisible and private events without market restrictions. Control represents the proportion of that event in the actor's possession. A recent study by Coleman (1990) shows that the model can be fruitfully used for and adapted to a wide variety of social phenomena. One of the most important extensions of his exchange model is its application to indivisible goods in collective decision making. Even in cases of constitutionally fixed sets of rights and multistage procedures of decision making (as in the American Constitution), Coleman states that the system can be modeled in terms of transactions of control among actors:

> The fact that there is generally a stream of collective actions rather than an isolated action means that individuals might be given rights which extend over a class of those actions and allowed to allocate them as they see fit within that

1. The development and application of the model were facilitated by the availability of a modern computer technology, object-oriented modeling, where actors are represented by objects. Like actors in the physical world, they have an internal structure that enables them to reason and to communicate with other objects.

class. . . . [T]his would constitute a means by which the
constraint of indivisibility of actions would effectively van-
ish: One person would use his resources to gain control of
those collective actions that most interested him, another
would gain control of those collective actions that most interested him, and so on. (Coleman 1990, p. 373)

The extension of Coleman's model to indivisible goods, however, is
neither simple nor straightforward. First, it requires redefinitions of control and interest. Control can no longer be defined as the proportion of an
event in the actor's possession if events are indivisible. Instead, control
is now defined as the actor's ability to effect an event outcome consistent
with his or her preference. In a similar way, interest is linked to the actor's
preferences by defining it as the extent to which the well-being of an actor
varies with the outcome of that particular event (Podolny 1990, p. 361).
Second, Weesie (1987) and Coleman (1990, pp. 822–25) show that interest
does not operate in the same way when the interests of actors in an
indivisible event are complementary or opposed. This is the first point for
which it becomes clear that the extension of the model is not straightforward. In the extension, actors exchange a good (control), the ideal of
which lies for all actors in the same direction, characterized by a non-
decreasing preference function (the more control, the better). In collective
decision making, however, we are dealing with the possibility of opposed
preferences and consequently different effects for exchanges among actors depending on whether they have interests that are opposed. Moreover, we are often dealing with single-peaked preferences. For example,
when the event concerns a decision on the height of a new public building,
actors will have different preferences on the ideal height, and they will
oppose a building that is either too high or too low. Therefore, we develop
a new model in which opposed and single-peaked preferences are explicitly dealt with. The exchange of control over events remains the heart
of all of the adaptations of the original Coleman model to collective decision making. Again, this focal concept is not straightforward in social
systems where rights to control are constitutionally fixed and decision
making is a multistage procedure.[2]

2. That adjustment of a wrong model might have serious consequences can be seen in the
    study of Podolny (1990). He — like Marsden (1983) — is primarily interested in the
    question of which exchange relations among actors are actually established in a collec-
    tive decision-making situation. He investigates whether such exchanges primarily take
    place among actors with like interests or opposed interests. In his experiments, he
    rewards the simple collection of votes by the participants without differentiating be-
    tween pro and con votes and concludes that exchange relations are more likely to occur
    among actors with like interests. One may wonder, however, whether any significance
    should be given to the collection of like votes and, by implication, why the total number

The above observations lead us to the position that Coleman's exchange model is not appropriate for decision making on collective goods. In our opinion, an exchange model is required that takes seriously the following elements of collective decision making and, by implication, uses these as cornerstones in the model:

1. Control is fixed and often embedded in a multistage decision-making procedure. The control of actor i on the outcome of decision a in such procedures is denoted by his or her *voting power* (v_{ia}).

2. Actors differ in their preferences for outcomes over collective decision-making issues. At the highest level of abstraction, actors are assumed to have monotonically increasing utility functions related to universal goals — like physical well-being and social approval — but they have different instrumental preferences for the means that lead to the ultimate goals (Lindenberg 1990, p. 741). In this perspective, outcomes of collective decision making can be perceived as instrumental goals: whereas one outcome can produce social well-being or social approval for one set of people, another outcome can be better for others. In other words, each actor orders outcomes in terms of the contribution the outcome makes to the actor's universal goals. These outcomes are not necessarily dichotomous, but they may well consist of a certain amount of an outcome (e.g., the size of a budget, the height of a new building, or, in the example below, car emission rates). The most preferred position of actor i on decision a is called his or her *policy position* (x_{ia}^{*}).

3. Actors differ in their interests in decisions. The interest of actor i in decision a is denoted by the *salience* of decision a for the actor i (s_{ia}).

4. Actors ultimately are willing to vote for less preferred policy positions on less salient issues in exchange for a vote for their policy position by other actors on more salient decisions. The final stance of actor i on decision a is called his or her *voting position* (x_{ia}).[3]

---

of collected votes has any relevance. What matters in collective decision making is the number of votes that have been reversed so as to favor an actor's own preference on the basis of an exchange.

3. The reader should be aware that our notation differs from Coleman's. He used the symbol x to denote the interest of an actor and the symbol c to denote the control of an actor. The reason for our deviant notation is that the symbol c is used to denote dyadic control relations between actors in the Stokman–Van den Bos model, as is commonly done in social network research, whereas voting power is a relation between an actor and an event. In the Coleman models with opposed interests, the symbol y is

In other words, in collective decision making, outcomes of decisions are instrumental goals for actors, and actors try to maximize their utilities by searching for outcomes that are as close to their policy position as possible. If actors have different saliences and policy positions on decisions, they can produce more utility by exchanging voting positions. This makes sense only when actors have voting power on decisions in which they are willing to support a position other than their own policy preference. This implies that in collective decision making actors do not exchange control, but rather exchange voting positions.

The exchange — or logrolling — model is based on pairwise exchanges between two actors on two decisions. In a larger system of N actors and M decisions, each actor investigates his or her potential exchanges with all other actors on any pair of decisions. Subsequently, which potential exchanges are realized is modeled in such a large system by assuming that each actor tries to realize his or her best potential exchanges. In order to model this exchange process, four simplifying assumptions are made. The first assumption specifies the utility functions of actors on the outcomes. The second is related to the information actors possess during collective decision making. The third excludes strategic behavior, and the fourth is related to the exchange equilibrium the actors aim at. The assumptions are:

ASSUMPTION 1: SPECIFICATION OF UTILITY FUNCTIONS. *On each issue a, actors have single-peaked preference functions. The expected utility of actor i on some issue a is a function of the salience of the issue for the actor, s_{ia}, and the distance between the outcome of decision a and the policy position of actor i on decision a. Denoting the expected outcome of decision a as O_a, the expected utility for actor i on decision a is given by the following linear function:*[4]

$$EU^iO_a = -s_{ia}|O_a - x_{ia}|. \tag{1}$$

The total expected utility for actor i over all M issues is assumed to be the sum of his or her utilities over all issues:

$$EU^iO = \Sigma_a U^iO_a. \tag{2}$$

---

often used to denote the signed interest x. In our model, however, we need an extra symbol because the voting and policy positions of actors are unrelated to their interests in events. For that reason x^* and x are used to denote respectively the policy and voting position of an actor and the symbol s to denote his or her salience or interest.

4. Decisions can have very different ranges. For that reason, all decisions are normalized between 0 and 1 by dividing the policy and voting positions of actors through the range. The expected utility function is therefore defined on the normalized decision. Note that, except for the risk factor, this function is similar to the expected utility function of Bueno de Mesquita in chapter 4.

ASSUMPTION 2: FULL INFORMATION. *Policy and voting positions, voting powers, and the saliences of all actors are assumed to be common knowledge. On the basis of these elements and the decision rules, all actors are able to compute the expected outcomes of decisions when no exchanges of voting positions take place.*

ASSUMPTION 3: NO STRATEGIC BEHAVIOR. *Strategic behavior of actors is not allowed. This has two implications:*

1. *Exchanges of voting positions on two issues a and b between two actors i and j are restricted to actors with policy positions on opposite sides of the expected outcomes of both issues: $(x_{iu}^* - O_u)(x_{ju}^* - O_u) < 0$ for $u = a,b$.*
2. *After the exchange, actors take voting positions in the interval $[x_{iu}^*, x_{ju}^*]$ for $u = a,b$.*

ASSUMPTION 4: SYMMETRY EQUILIBRIUM AFTER EXCHANGE. *When an actor exchanges voting positions with another actor, she or he accepts no smaller gain of expected utility than the other actor.*

Assumption 1 specifies the same loss function as that in the Bueno de Mesquita model if we disregard the risk-taking component. The risk-taking component makes it possible to model all kinds of strategic behavior. Its elimination from our loss function is justified because we purposely aim to exclude strategic behavior in our present, first elaboration of the model in order to investigate the effects of mutually beneficial exchanges between actors on pairs of decisions. Therefore, assumption 3 restricts the exchanges to those between two actors on opposite sides of the expected outcomes. For such pairs of actors, exchange of voting positions on two decisions is the sole possibility for a joint increase of utility, whereas actors on the same side have possibilities to increase their utility on only one decision without having to give something away on another decision (e.g., by choosing more extreme voting positions that are advantageous for both actors). In combination with assumption 3, assumption 2 is not very restrictive because incomplete information is primarily relevant for effective strategic behavior that will not immediately be observed and compensated for by other actors.

The fourth assumption specifies the symmetric effects that the actors aim to achieve through the exchange. Although the assumption of equal expected utility gain for both actors seems intuitively appealing, two objections can be made.

The first objection is that the assumption seems to imply a comparison of utilities between actors which is problematic and not allowed. Each actor does not compare his expected utility gain with that of the other, but with his perception of the expected utility gain of the other actor. By assumption 2, however, this perception is equal to the actual expected utility gain by the second actor. Here, but also later, we see that our model maximizes expected utilities of actors and not utility itself. It implies, however, that any extension of the model to include strategic behavior requires the explicit reformulation of assumption 4 in terms of the perceptions of the actors and not in terms of their actual utilities.

The second objection is that this equilibrium is based on intuitive reasoning and is not derived from a theory of the underlying micro-process. If we solely had to deal with the micro-process, a better alternative would have been available, but that alternative gives too many complications at the next stage of our model, namely, the selection of the realized exchanges from the pool of potential exchanges in a system of N actors and M decisions. That alternative is the Raiffa–Kalai–Smorodinsky solution given in bargaining theory (Friedman 1990, pp. 218–23). Reformulated in the context of our own research problem, actors compare their utility of the expected outcome without exchange (the so-called status quo situation) with the ideal situation, that is, the expected outcome if the other actor is prepared to vote for his or her policy positions on both issues. From a number of desirable axioms, an equal percentage of utility gain — instead of equal utility gain — is derived as the equilibrium after exchange. This solution is proven to be Pareto optimal for both actors, and it does not involve intersubjective comparison of utilities. In future extensions of our model, we aim to investigate the possibility of incorporating this exchange rate in our model, but we do not see the possibility to do so now.

In actual practice, the four assumptions are, of course, unrealistic. How serious this is can be observed when we apply the model to actual decision making and use our model to predict outcomes of decisions. If the model results in wrong predictions, we can relax the assumptions to build more complicated models according to the method of decreasing abstraction (Bueno de Mesquita 1981; Lindenberg 1990). The simplifying assumptions are therefore not essential for the chosen approach.

Collective decision making quite often consists not only of taking decisions on a set of prior issues, but also of the inventive creation of new choices. This is accomplished by splitting issues into a number of choices so as to provide for optimal compromises across the divergent interests of actors (Riker 1986). By properly specifying the salience actors attach to underlying dimensions instead of on the issues as a whole, our exchange model is able to predict the generation of these new choices.

Voting Power and Outcomes in Multistage Procedures

In general, the outcome of an issue depends on the policy positions of the actors, the decision rules, and the weights of the actors. In this section, we present a definition of voting power that takes into account both the weights of the actors and the decision rules. In the previous section we dealt with single-peaked, unidimensional decisions. The voting power measure is based on the assumption that such decisions in the formal voting procedure are converted to pro and con votes and that actors vote for the alternative that gives them the highest expected utility. The proposed voting power measure can be aggregated over different phases of a decision-making procedure. As such, the measure can fully represent the constitutional arrangements of the collective decision-making process, even when these are based on a multistage procedure.[5] Such a definition should be independent of more informal ways to influence outcomes of decisions or of exchanges of voting positions among actors. An appropriate definition of voting power was given by Stokman and Van den Bos (1992) who develop their concept of voting power precisely to represent the institutional settings as a separate element in their two-stage model of the political process.[6] They define the voting power of an actor as the proportion of collective decisions that is consistent with the policy position of the actor over all possible combinations of policy positions of the actors who participate in the decision process. According to this definition, the voting power of actors varies from .5 for actors without voting power to 1 for a dictator. For computational reasons, we rescale the voting powers to the interval from 0 to 1, resulting in a voting power of 0 for all actors without voting power. Actors with positive voting power are denoted as public actors.

As an example, let us consider the West German Bundestag after the 1987 general election. The simple majority criterion is 249 votes. As the German parties are rather homogeneous, we may consider them as

5. Such an aggregate measure is particularly useful for a global analysis of the decision-making process. In specific analyses of subprocesses with given policy positions of actors, prediction of the outcomes of decisions on the actual number of votes of actors and the specific decision rule might be preferable.

6. Their definition of voting power relies on the concept of decisional power of Hoede and his collaborators (Hoede and Bakker 1982; Hoede and Meek 1983; Hoede and Redfern 1985). Hoede and Bakker (1982) define the *decisional power* of an actor as the proportion of collective decisions that is consistent with his or her inclination over all possible combinations of inclinations of the actors. It depends on the decision rule (simple majority, qualified majority, or unanimity), the weights of the actors, and the control relations among the actors by which certain inclinations are converted to other preferences because of the existing control relations. The voting power of an actor in the Stokman–Van den Bos model deviates from Hoede and Bakker by modeling the conversion of certain inclinations via existing control relations to other preferences separately in the first stage of their model. Their definition of *voting power* is equivalent to that of decisional power in Hoede and Bakker when no influence relations among actors are taken into account. It is comparable to the Shapley-Shubik power index (Shapley and Shubik 1954).

the public actors in the Bundestag. The parties are the Christian Democratic Union/Christian Socialist Union (CDU/CSU) with 223 seats, the Social Democratic Pary (SDP) with 186, the Free Democratic Pary (FDP) with 46 seats, and the Green Party with 42 seats. The voting powers of the four actors are .75 for the CDU/CSU and .25 for each of the three other parties. The equal voting power for the three other parties is due to the fact that CDU/CSU can get a majority with each of them, whereas the only majority excluding the CDU/CSU requires the cooperation of all three parties.

The voting powers of the actors can be specified in a matrix, V. If we have N actors and M collective decisions, the order of the matrix is $(N \times M)$ and its entries v_{ia} specify the voting power of actor i with respect to decision a.

Stokman and Van den Bos also give an extension of the definition of voting power to multistage decision-making procedures. When research relates to more complicated decisions, as when different executive and legislative or supervisory boards are involved in the formal process, a single dimension may be insufficient for a proper representation of the institutional arrangements. To handle such situations, the voting power measure has been extended to enable the specification of several dimensions.[7]

Two examples may clarify the wide variety of institutional arrangements that can be represented in this way. First, let us extend the example of the German Bundestag. A legislative decision requires both the consent of the German government and that of the Bundestag (disregarding the senate for simplicity). After the 1987 election, a German government was formed consisting of a coalition of CDU/CSU and FDP. We assume that any legislative measure requires the consent of both coalition partners in the government. We can represent this multistage decision-making process by specifying two dimensions. On the first dimension (representing the German government) we give the CDU/CSU ministers and the FDP ministers an equal weight of one vote and specify as the decision criterion the need for two votes. That is, unanimity is required in the government. The second dimension represents the Bundestag and its specification is the same as above. The voting powers of the public actors now become: .25 for the CDU/CSU and for the FDP ministers, .186 for the CDU/CSU Bundestag fraction, and .0625 for the three other parties.

A second example illustrates how institutional arrangements in corporatist systems can be represented. Typical of corporatist systems is the requirement that all social partners simultaneously agree, and that the majority of parliament also agrees. This system can be depicted by spec-

7. This extension is due to Tom Snijders of the University of Groningen, who is also the author of a Pascal program to compute the voting power measure. In the program, up to five dimensions can be specified. The program is available on request.

ification of one dimension in which the corporatist, social partners have positive weights with unanimity as its decision rule. A second criterion indicates that the political parties are weighted by their number of seats in parliament, with simple majority as the decision rule. When relevant, a third criterion might be specified for the government if its consent is necessary for implementation of the decision, as when the government can exercise a veto.

In this definition of the voting power of actors, their respective weights and the decision rules in a multistage decision-making procedure are already incorporated. When using this measure, it seems inappropriate to take these elements into account again in predicting the outcome of a decision based on the voting positions and voting powers of the actors. In the Stokman–Van den Bos model, the outcomes of collective decisions are, therefore, predicted by taking the average of the voting positions of the public actors, weighted according to their voting power. The voting positions of actors need not be the same as their policy positions due to several processes in which public actors can adapt their voting positions. In Stokman–Van den Bos such adaptations are due to informal influence processes in the first stage of their model. Here we elaborate on adaptations or fluctuations in voting positions that result from exchanges or deals among public actors in the second stage. Following the notation given in the previous section, the predicted outcome of a decision a, O_a, is given by

$$O_a = (\Sigma_i x_{ia} v_{ia})/(\Sigma_i v_{ia}). \tag{3}$$

When we apply equation 3 to the original policy positions of the actors, we denote the predicted outcome as the *base model*. Under the base model specification, the formal decision rules are applied to the original policy positions of the public actors without taking into account differences of interests among the actors and any changes due to informal processes or exchanges of voting positions. The base model can be seen as a kind of realistic null model. We expect that our models will predict decisions better than the base model

When the decision rule requires unanimity among all public actors (as is the case with almost all EC council decisions considered in this book), all actors have equal voting power. Nevertheless, it is well known that in the EC council the policy positions of large member states informally have a larger weight than those of smaller member states. It is also evident that differences in interests among the member states are taken into account. Although it is our opinion that such differences should be modeled by focusing on the processes by which policy positions are transformed to voting positions, Van den Bos (1991) modeled these differences more or less directly by taking the number of votes assigned to each member state in majority decisions as voting weights and by including weights for the saliences of actors in the outcome function.[8] He called this model the *compromise model* and assumed that the president of the council would formulate a compromise in which the policy positions of the member states were weighted according to their votes and their saliences. The following alternative outcome function can be defined, representing the compromise model of Van den Bos:

$$O'_a = (\Sigma_i x_{ia} v'_{ia} s_{ia})/(\Sigma_i v'_{ia} s_{ia}). \tag{4}$$

These two definitions of the predicted outcome as a weighted average of voting positions can be applied directly to decisions involving purely numerical issue positions, such as the amount of money to spend or the height of a public building. However, it is not possible to apply these relations to binary choices to accept a bill or not. In the Stokman–Van den Bos model, actors can take voting positions on the whole range of pro or con choices (which we designate as falling between $+1$ and -1), indicating their inclination to vote for or against a proposal. In the exchange model below, voting positions between -1 and $+1$ on such decisions are also allowed as inclinations to vote in favor or against. In these situations, the use of the weighted average of the voting positions, as given in equations 3 and 4, also seems appropriate for predicting outcomes. A pro outcome is then predicted when this average is positive, a con one when it is negative. The difference from zero may be interpreted as the probability that our prediction is correct.

Conditions For Exchange of Voting Positions Among Public Actors

To clarify the exchange of positions or logrolling in decision making, we will consider the simple case of two decisions — a and b — on which actors i and j have voting power. As an illustration, the policy positions (preferences), voting power, and saliences of Germany and the United Kingdom are given in figure 5.1 for two issues introduced in chapter 3: the amount of tax incentives in deutsche marks that EC countries are permitted to give for large and medium-sized cars that already fulfill strong exhaust emission standards. Germany and the United Kingdom have different policy positions on both issues. Germany favors high tax incentives, namely, DM 3,000. The United Kingdom wants to permit no tax incentives. The policy positions can be related to the different positions in which the respective car industries are situated. At the time of the decision (1987), the required technology was already available for the German car industry. They considered this technology to be necessary for German autos to remain competitive in markets outside Europe, whereas this was

8.   In majority votes the member states have the following number of votes: France, Germany, Great Britain, and Italy, 10 each; Spain, 8; Belgium, Greece, Netherlands, and Portugal, 5 each; Denmark and Ireland, 3 each; and Luxembourg, 2.

Policy positions on tax incentives for large cars before
(x^*_{ia} and x^*_{ja}) and after (x^*_{ia} and x_{ja}) exchange

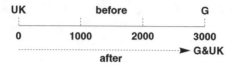

$S_G = 1$; $S_{UK} = .6$; $V_G = .0195$; $V_{UK} = .0195$

Policy positions on tax incentives for medium cars before
(x^*_{ib} and x^*_{jb}) and after (x_{ib} and x^*_{jb}) exchange

$S_G = .7$; $S_{UK} = 1$; $V_G = .0195$; $V_{UK} = .0195$

5.1: An Exchange of Voting Positions: Outcome Function of the Base Model

not the case for the British car industry. The German car industry supported the position taken by its government, a position also dictated by the grave condition of German forests and the resulting public pressure to take measures to protect the environment. As the German automobile industry did not fear Japanese competition in the large-car market segment at that time, tax incentives (in combination with an early introduction date for strong emission standards) for that sector of the market had very high priority for Germany. The British automobile industry, however, primarily produces for the medium-car market segment, making the prohibition of tax incentives in combination with a late introduction date and low emission standards for that segment of the market very important. This is reflected in the saliences of the two countries for the two issues, as given in figure 5.1. Germany has a larger interest in tax incentives for large cars than for medium cars, whereas the opposite is the case for the United Kingdom.

To investigate the necessary conditions under which an exchange of voting positions between two actors is attractive, let us assume, for the sake of convenience, that actor i asks actor j to shift its voting position on issue a, whereas actor j asks actor i to do that in return on question b. We will denote a as the *demand issue* for actor i and the *supply issue* for actor j. Consequently, decision b is the demand issue for actor j and the supply issue for actor i. We formulate the following necessary conditions under which an exchange of voting positions between two actors is attractive to them:

THEOREM 1. *For two actors i and j with policy positions on opposite sides of the expected outcomes of two issues a and b, an exchange of voting positions on decisions a and b increases their overall expected utility only if the three conditions below are simultaneously met (decision a being the demand issue for actor i and decision b for actor j):*

1. *ΔO_{ja}, $\Delta O_{ib} > 0$, where ΔO_{ku} denotes the change of outcome on decision u (u = a,b) brought about by a change of voting position of actor k (k = i,j) given no change in the voting positions of other actors so that for both actors, a change of voting position on the supply issue should result in a positive change in the expected outcome.*
2. *s_{ia}, $s_{jb} > 0$, so that both actors attach positive salience to the demand issue.*
3. *$s_{ja} = 0$ or*

$$\frac{s_{ib}}{s_{ia}} < \frac{s_{jb}}{s_{ja}} \qquad (If\ s_{ja} > 0),$$

so that either the salience on the supply issue for actor j is zero or else the ratio between actor i's saliences on his or her supply and demand issue is smaller than the ratio between actor j's saliences on his or her demand and supply issue.

Proof. Let us denote a shift by actor j on decision a as Δ_{ja}, where $x_{ja} = x_{ja}^* + \Delta x_{ja}$. Then a shift of Δx_{ja} in the direction of the policy position of actor i results in an increase in expected utility for actor i of $EU^{i+}\ \Delta O_{ja} = \Delta O_{ja}s_{ia}$. The resulting decrease of expected utility for actor j is $EU^{j-}\ \Delta O_{ja} = \Delta O_{ja}s_{ja}$. To compensate for actor j's loss, actor i shifts Δx_{ib} on decision b in the direction of the policy position favored by actor j. This increases the expected utility of actor j by $EU^{j+}\ \Delta O_{ib} = \Delta O_{ib}s_{jb}$, and decreases the expected utility for actor i by $EU^{i-}\ \Delta O_{ib} = \Delta O_{ib}s_{ib}$. Exchange is attractive only if actor i and j can improve their expected utility simultaneously. This is true if both $EU^{i+} > EU^{i-}$ and $EU^{j+} > EU^{j-}$. In other words, both $\Delta O_{ja}s_{ia} - \Delta O_{ib}s_{ib} > 0$ and $\Delta O_{ib}s_{jb} - \Delta O_{ja}s_{ja} > 0$. This implies, first of all, that $\Delta O_{ja}, \Delta O_{ib}, s_{jb}, s_{ia} > 0$, the first two conditions of the theorem. Moreover, in combination with the first two conditions, actor i gets an expected utility gain only if

$\Delta O_{ja}/\Delta O_{ib} > s_{ib}/s_{ia}.$

Similarly, actor j gets an expected utility gain in combination with the first two conditions only if $s_{ja} = 0$ or

$\Delta O_{ja}/\Delta O_{ib} < s_{jb}/s_{ia}$ for $s_{ja} > 0$.

Combined they give the third condition in the theorem.   QED

When two issues meet the three conditions for two actors, the conditions uniquely determine which issue is the demand issue for one actor and which is the demand issue for the other actor. If more actors and decisions are considered, however, a given issue can simultaneously be a demand issue in one potential exchange and a supply decision in another potential exchange for the same actor.

Condition 1 from theorem 1 can easily be specified for the outcome functions in equations 3 and 4. The outcome function in equation 3 holds that the voting power on the supply issue should be positive for both actors. The outcome function in equation 4 holds that the product of voting power and salience on the supply issue should be positive for both actors. These results are given in the following two corollaries.

COROLLARY 1.1. *If the outcome function given in equation 3 is used, condition 1 in theorem 1 can be specified as v_{ja}, $v_{ib} > 0$ if a is the demand issue for actor i, and as v_{ia}, $v_{jb} > 0$ if a is the demand issue for actor j.*

Proof. Assume that a is the demand decision of actor i and that actor j is the only actor shifting its position on a. According to equation 3 with O_a^* denoting the outcome on a after the exchange

$$O_a^* = \frac{\sum_{k \neq j} x_{ka}^* v_{ka} + (x_{ja}^* + \Delta x_{ja}) v_{ja}}{\sum_k v_{ka}}$$

$$= \frac{\sum_k x_{ka}^* v_{ka}}{\sum_k v_{ka}} + \frac{\Delta x_{ja} v_{ja}}{\sum_k v_{ka}}$$

$$= O_a + \frac{\Delta x_{ja} v_{ja}}{\sum_m v_{ma}} . \tag{5}$$

Since by assumption, $\Delta x_{ja} > 0$, $|\Delta O_{ja}| > 0 \Leftrightarrow v_{ja} > 0$. In an analogous way it can be proved that $v_{ib} > 0$.   QED

COROLLARY 1.2. *If the outcome function given in equation 4 is used, condition 3 in theorem 1 can be specified as $(v_{ja}'s_{ja})$, $(v_{ib}'s_{ib}) > 0$ if a is the demand issue for actor i, and as $(v_{ia}'s_{ia})$, $(v_{jb}'s_{jb}) > 0$ if a is the demand decision for actor j.*

The proof of corollary 1.2 is analogous to the proof of corollary 1.1.

In figure 5.1, Germany and the United Kingdom are at opposite ends of the policy spectrum on both issues, with the expected outcome at an intermediate position. Moreover, if the large car issue is taken as the demand issue for Germany and the medium-sized car issue as the demand issue for United Kingdom, we observe that the three conditions of theorem 1 are met:

- The two actors have positive voting power on the supply issue (in fact they have voting power on both).
- The two actors have positive saliences on their demand issues.
- The ratio between the supply issue and demand issue for Germany is smaller than the ratio between the demand and supply issue for the United Kingdom (for Germany the ratio is .7; for the United Kingdom 1.7).

The next problem is to specify the state of equilibrium after a position exchange. This requires the specification of the exchange rate between the voting positions and the determination of the total size of the exchange.

THEOREM 2. *If for two decisions a and b and two actors i and j the conditions of theorem 1 are met and if a is the demand issue for actor i, then the exchange rate between the shifts of outcomes on a and b is*

$$\Delta O_{ja} = \frac{(s_{ib} + s_{jb})}{(s_{ia} + s_{ja})} \Delta O_{ib}. \tag{6}$$

Proof. By assumption, a is the demand decision for actor i. A shift of Δx_{ja} in the direction of the policy position of actor i results in an increase in expected utility for actor i of $EU^{i+} \Delta O_{ja} = \Delta O_{ja} s_{ia}$. The resulting decrease in expected utility for actor j is $EU^{j-} \Delta O_{ja} = \Delta O_{ja} s_{ja}$. To compensate for actor j's loss, actor i shifts Δx_{ib} on issue b in the direction of the policy position favored by actor j. This increases the expected utility of actor j by $EU^{j+} \Delta O_{ib} = \Delta O_{ib} s_{jb}$ and decreases the expected utility for actor i by $EU^{i-} \Delta O_{ib} = \Delta O_{ib} s_{ib}$.

For the two actors the net improvement in expected utility will be equal (assumption 4) if

$$EU^{i+} \Delta O_{ja} - EU^{i-} \Delta O_{ib} = EU^{j+} \Delta O_{ib} - EU^{j-} \Delta O_{ja}$$

or

$$\Delta O_{ja} s_{ia} - \Delta O_{ib} s_{ib} = \Delta O_{ib} s_{jb} - \Delta O_{ja} s_{ja}$$

$$\Delta O_{ja}(s_{ia} + s_{ja}) = \Delta O_{ib}(s_{jb} + s_{ib})$$

$$\Delta O_{ja} = \frac{(s_{ib} + s_{jb})}{(s_{ia} + s_{ja})} \Delta O_{ib}. \quad \text{QED}$$

Theorem 2 expresses the exchange rate in terms of the outcomes on the issues. The necessary shifts of voting positions by the two actors depend on the decision rules and the weights of the actors. Corollary 2.1 gives the exchange rates between the shifts in voting positions of the actors if the outcome function of equation 3 is valid, whereas corollary 2.2 does the same if the outcome function of equation 4 is applied.

COROLLARY 2.1. *If the outcome function of equation 3 is used and if issue a is the demand decision for actor i, then the exchange rate for the shifts in voting positions of actors i and j is*

$$\Delta x_{ja} = \frac{(s_{ib} + s_{jb})v_{ib}\Sigma_k v_{ka}}{(s_{ia} + s_{ja})v_{ja}\Sigma_k v_{kb}}\Delta x_{ib}. \tag{7}$$

Proof. The relation between the shifts in outcomes of the decisions and the shifts in voting positions is now given by

$$\Delta O_{ja} = \frac{\Delta x_{ja}v_{ja}}{\Sigma_k v_{ka}}$$

and

$$\Delta O_{ib} = \frac{\Delta x_{ib}v_{ib}}{\Sigma_k v_{kb}}.$$

Substitution gives equation 7.   QED

COROLLARY 2.2. *If the outcome function of equation 4 is used and if a is the demand decision for actor i, the exchange rate for the shifts in voting positions of actors i and j is*

$$\Delta x_{ja} = \frac{(s_{ib} + s_{jb})v'_{ib}s_{ib}\Sigma_k v'_{ka}s_{ka}}{(s_{ia} + s_{ja})v'_{ja}s_{ja}\Sigma_k v'_{kb}s_{kb}}\Delta x_{ib}. \tag{8}$$

Proof. From equation 4, it follows that

$$\Delta O_{ja} = \frac{\Delta x_{ja}v'_{ja}s_{ja}}{\Sigma_k v'_{ka}s_{ka}}$$

and

$$\Delta O_{ib} = \frac{\Delta x_{ib}v'_{ib}s_{ib}}{\Sigma_k v'_{kb}s_{kb}}$$

Substitution gives equation 8.   QED

The corollaries show an important aspect of the exchange process, namely, that the exchange rates between actors is dependent on the decision rule and the weights of the actors as reflected in the outcome function. In other words, different decision rules and weights for the actors can lead to different exchanges! Under the outcome function of the base model (equation 3), the exchange rate between the shifts in voting positions of the United Kingdom on the large car issue and Germany on the medium-sized car issue in the example of figure 5.1 is $(1 + .7)/(1 + .6) = 1.063$ because the voting power of the two actors and the sum of the voting powers of all actors is assumed to be the same for the two decisions.[9]

9.   The latter is not always the case, as Hoede et al. demonstrated. The voting power of

When the outcome function of the compromise model (equation 4) is used (or is perceived to be used), the summation terms in equation 4 are not equal for issues a and b. Taking the relevant salience data from table 3.3 and the voting weights as given in note 8, the United Kingdom and Germany would apply another exchange rate,[10] namely, $((1 + .7) \cdot 7 \cdot 31.4)/((1 + .6) \cdot 6 \cdot 38.4) = 1.014$.

What remains to be solved is determining the new voting positions after the exchange takes place. Since we assume that the utility for alternative voting positions decreases on either side of an actor's stated policy position, actors are not interested in shifting the outcome across and beyond their policy position. Such an outcome might require a shift in the voting position of the other actor far beyond one's own policy position. However, this strategic behavior is excluded by assumption 3 where the shifts are confined to the interval between the two policy positions. The total amount of exchange is therefore determined by whichever of the two following conditions is met first:

$$\Delta x_{ja} \leq |x_{ia}^* - x_{ja}^*|$$

and   (9)

$$\Delta x_{ib} \leq |x_{ib}^* - x_{jb}^*|.$$

For the example found in figure 5.1, the resulting voting positions of the United Kingdom and Germany on the two issues are given in the last two parts of the figure under the outcome function of the base model (equation 3). Both actors realize an expected utility gain of .043 through this exchange. As decisions on these issues were taken before the entrance of Spain and Portugal into the EC, and Belgium and Greece are excluded from the computations because of missing policy positions, each of the remaining countries contribute .125 to the outcome. Normalizing the decision on the interval between 0 and 1, the net expected utility gain for Germany is $(1 \cdot 1 \cdot .125) - (.7 \cdot .941 \cdot .125) = .043$, and that for the United Kingdom $(1 \cdot .941 \cdot .125) - (.6 \cdot 1 \cdot .125) = .043$.

---

a system is maximal when all actors have equal weights and decisions are made by simple majority. Hoede et al. also derive several interesting results regarding total voting power in representational systems. For example, the present system in the General Assembly of the United Nations (one vote for each member state) gives maximal voting power only if all member states are ruled by dictators. At the time of the indirect elections for the European Parliament, they derived that the maximal voting power for the European Parliament would be obtained when the ratios between the numbers of national representatives are equal to the square root of the sizes of the national electorates.

10. Because of missing values for Belgium and Greece they are excluded from the computations.

A Dynamic Exchange Model

The most important characteristic of social processes in general, and collective decision-making processes in particular, is the fact that the outcomes of "macro" processes are not the result of a central (planning) authority in the policy domain. Rather, outcomes are the intended or unintended consequences of the simultaneous choices of decision makers. Actors try to realize their goals by choosing between the behavioral alternatives that are available to them under certain restrictions. This is the core principle in the structural individualistic approach (Boudon and Bourricaud 1982; Coleman 1986; Lindenberg 1985; Wippler 1978). The rationality of the decision makers that is implied in this principle, however, is seriously hampered by the fact that the actors are presumed to act simultaneously. This implies that their rationally chosen alternatives might appear to be suboptimal because they did not anticipate the actions of other actors. This limitation is reinforced because the actors, in contrast to central (planning) authorities, have limited information about the system and the intended actions of other decision makers. This makes it inevitable for actors in certain situations to define instrumental goals that are only roughly related to the ultimate instrumental goals in the system and to make ex ante assumptions that turn out to be unrealistic ex post (e.g., that other actors behave in a certain way). Actors, however, evaluate the ultimate success of these derived strategies and assumptions and have the possibility to adapt them in case of frequent failure. In other words, actors have the ability of adaptive learning from experience. This latter feature can be used to facilitate the design of an applied model by starting with a very simple model and then, in a stepwise process, adding assumptions when the simple model fails. This method of model construction is known as the method of decreasing abstraction (Lindenberg 1992).

For our exchange problem we need to generalize our given solutions for two actors and two decisions to a system of N actors and M decisions. In classical model building, this step would consist of formulating equations on the resulting equilibrium at the macro level, which is quite complicated and often not solvable. Since we are interested in designing a model that can be applied in practice as well as in principle, we eschew that approach. The recently available computer methodology of object-oriented modeling makes it possible to arrive at a direct representation of such a physical world of parallel operating actors (Goldberg and Robson 1983). In object-oriented models, these actors are represented by objects. Like actors in the physical world, they have an internal structure that enables them to reason and to communicate with other objects. As in the physical world, the reasoning of and communications between objects in object-oriented models may take place simultaneously, may result in a diversity of actions by different objects depending on the restrictions under which they operate, and may be adapted on the basis of past experiences (Lehrmann Madsen and Moller-Pedersen 1988). As such, object-oriented modeling incorporates the ideas of parallel distributed processing, whereas the representation of actors as adaptive learning objects gives these objects characteristics similar to self-organizing systems, such as are known from neural networks (see, e.g., Rumelhart and McClelland 1987).[11] The characteristics of social systems that are emphasized in the structural individualistic approach (parallel, operating under different restrictions, self-learning, and actors reacting to each other on the basis of which social phenomena develop) have their direct equivalences in object-oriented models. In other words, the principles of the structural individualistic approach and those of object-oriented modeling are so strikingly similar that object-oriented programming is seen as the appropriate means for an adequate representation of collective decision-making processes in general and exchange processes in particular. Object-oriented modeling permits the development of an applied model, one that can serve as a practical tool as well as an analytic construct.

The generalization of the exchange problem to a system of N actors and M decisions in the object-oriented model is solved by letting the actors negotiate with each other on the basis of the limited information that is available to them. This process is facilitated by the fact that the results of the exchange process can be represented as a network between actors. Object-oriented modeling facilitates the re-use of classes of objects. The necessary classes of objects for a network (graph, points, and edges) were previously developed,[12] so that these classes can be used directly to represent the result of the exchange process. Moreover, in a system of M issues not all prospective decisions may be suitable for exchanges of voting positions within a policy domain. For example, exchanges of voting positions on two issues might be restricted to decisions that are taken at a certain time interval, one after the other, or to decisions over which the contents are somehow related. The complexity of the system of N actors and M decisions can therefore sometimes be reduced by defining a network among decisions that delimits the pairs of issues that are suitable for

11.   The same guiding principles are used in a Ph.D. project on "Structure and dynamics of friendship networks in heterogeneous groups" by Evelien Zeggelink (1993), supervised by Frans N. Stokman, Cees Hoede, and Tom Snijders (ICS, Groningen).
12.   The network classes and the main elements of the computer application for the exchange process were developed by Reinier Van Oosten in Smalltalk-80. Smalltalk is the programming language that made the object-oriented paradigm popular. It is object-oriented to the extreme: everything in the system is an object. Smalltalk is not just a language, but also a very powerful programming environment for the language. Its powerful editing facilities, its powerful debugger, and its incremental compilation make Smalltalk a perfect fit for explorative and experimental research on social networks.

logrolling or exchanges. Again, the basic network classes can be used directly for these purposes.

We assume that actors are primarily interested in exchanges on pairs of issues on which they believe they stand to gain a lot. Because of assumption 4, the gains for the two actors are the same, which implies that an ordering of the exchanges in the system as a whole is at the same time an ordering of the exchanges for each individual actor. This would not be the case if the exchange rate had been determined on the basis of an equal percentage of utility gain for the two actors, the solution of the Raiffa–Kalai–Smorodinsky bargaining approach. It is for this reason that their solution creates problems in this stage of the modeling process and why at present the equal gain assumption is maintained.

The net gain on an exchange is highest if the gain on the demand decision is large and the loss on the supply decision is small. The first thing actors do in the model is to make a *demand list:* the actor orders the issues in terms of the maximal gain she or he can get. The more extreme the policy position of an actor on an issue and the higher its salience, the more an actor can gain by persuading other actors to shift their voting positions.

The exchange algorithm can now be summarized as follows:

1. Create a new network of potential exchange relations with the actors as its points.
2. Between any two issues on which actors are allowed to exchange voting positions, determine for each pair of actors whether they have policy positions on opposite sides of the expected outcomes of the issues and whether the three conditions of theorem 1 are fulfilled. For any pair of issues on which the pair of actors can exchange voting positions, create an edge (line) between the two actors in the network of possible exchange relations.
3. For each edge, determine the demand and supply decisions for actors i and j. Suppose (as we did above), the demand decision is issue a for i and b for j (that is, actor i is willing to move in the direction of actor j on issue b, and actor j is willing to do so on a).
4. For each edge, determine the maximal potential improvement of expected utility for the actors (which is the same for the two actors by theorem 2).
5. Order the edges in the network of potential exchange relations by the size of the maximal potential improvement in expected utility.
6. Define a new network of realized exchange relations with the actors as its points.
7. The edge with the highest maximal potential improvement of ex-

pected utility is the first realized exchange. It is moved to the network of realized exchange relations and deleted from the network of potential exchange relations. When several edges have the same value, one is selected at random.

8. Delete all other edges in the network of potential exchange relations for which decision b was the supply issue for actor i. Do the same for actor j regarding its supply decision a.

9. Continue steps 7 and 8 until no edges are left in the network of potential exchange relations.

10. Determine the voting positions of all actors on all decisions after exchange and compute the policy outcomes on the issues.

11. If random decisions have been made in step 7, repeat steps 5 to 9 several times to determine the means and standard deviations of the voting positions of the actors and the outcomes on the issues.

If no random choices between potential exchanges are made in step 7, the exchange algorithm results in a unique set of exchanges and a unique prediction of the resolution of the issues. The expected utility gain for each actor over all exchanges can be determined by cumulating his or her expected utility gain for each realized exchange. The total expected utility gain for the whole set of actors is then obtained by summing these expected gains over all actors. It should be realized, however, that these quantities do not represent the realized utility gains. If two actors realize an exchange, its effects on the resolution of the two issues result in utility gains and losses for all actors. Moreover, other exchanges among other actors may well nullify or enlarge the contemplated changes in outcomes and the expected utility gains for the exchange partners. Therefore, the realized utility gain for each actor and for the set of actors as a whole is another criterion to be taken into account in our judgment on the results of the exchange process. For example, as one of the analyses in chapter 7 shows, the final outcome may well result in an overall loss of utility and may, therefore, not be Pareto optimal for the set of all actors.

If random choices are made in step 7, the set of realized exchanges is not unique. Of course, different sets of exchanges may well result in the same predicted issue outcomes so that a unique prediction of the outcomes may result even in this case. In other situations, however, the predicted outcomes differ over different sets of realized exchanges. Then, the means of the predicted outcomes over one hundred simulations are taken as our predictions. Special attention will be given, however, to solutions that result in maximal expected utility gains and maximal realized utility gains for the set of all actors. The analyses in chapter 7 show that these two criteria vary quite independently from one another. We prefer the mean solution to one of these two because it is hard to defend a notion that suggests that actors optimize either the expected or the realized utility for the system as a whole instead of their own utility. In situations of uncertainty, the mean reduces the uncertainty more than any other statistic.

The exchange algorithm is extremely simple. First of all, actors do not anticipate the effects of other exchanges. In a more complicated model, we might give actors the ability to investigate whether certain seemingly less profitable exchanges should be given priority because these exchanges will block exchanges by the other actor in one or another way. Second, all exchanges and their expected utilities are related to the original expected outcomes of the decisions. An alternative would be to give each actor the opportunity to do his or her best exchange and to recalculate the expected utilities of the remaining potential exchanges in terms of the adapted expected outcomes before a second exchange is allowed.

The exchange model of voting positions developed in this chapter deviates fundamentally from existing exchange models. It takes the core aspects of collective decision as points of departure: the exchange of voting positions rather than the exchange of control; actors with single-peaked preference functions rather than linear increasing preference functions; multistage decision procedures rather than single-stage decisions. This model yields a number of relevant results:

1. a well-founded measure for the voting power of actors in multistage decision-making procedures;
2. the conditions under which exchange of voting positions is attractive for actors;
3. the prediction of exchange rates that actors will use; and
4. a direct representation of the negotiating process by the application of object-oriented modeling techniques.

In the models presented in this book, the exchange rates between voting positions are determined at the level of the pairs of actors; no prices at the system level emerge. This might be seen as an important disadvantage when compared with other exchange models of collective decision making. However, the absence of physical currency and prices at the system (market) level is seen as a fundamental aspect of exchanges in political systems by other authors as well (Parsons and Smelser 1956; Coleman 1970; Marsden 1983). According to Marsden, the absence of a physical currency and the inalienability of official decision-making authority (voting power)

> mean that trust in the operation of political exchange must
> be guaranteed in a manner distinct from that used in economic exchange. Bargains struck may involve one actor
> using resources in the interest of another at one time in

> exchange for a promised reciprocation by the other actor. These bargains are different from economic exchanges because the actor receiving political value does not surrender constitutional control over an equivalent amount of value at the time it is received. Instead, a promise is made concerning the disposition of equivalent value at a future time. But no mechanism such as money is available to insure that the promised future action will indeed be forthcoming. (Marsden 1983, p. 691)

From this perspective, the determination of the exchange rates at the level of the pairs of actors rather than at the system level can be seen as appropriate and advantageous to our model, facilitating its application in a variety of contexts. For example, the model can be applied to informal influence processes within policy networks. The exchange described above was confined to actors with voting power. In the phase before the final decision, however, opinion formation takes place in interactions among public and private actors. This results in indirect voting power for influential private actors, a process that was explicitly modeled by Laumann and Knoke (1987), as well as Stokman and Van den Bos (1992). Exchanges of positions among private actors with complementary interests may lead to a joint approach toward public actors. With the help of an extension of the model presented here, it is possible to explain this important — though often neglected — aspect of collective decision-making processes. This can be made more realistic by using information on informal networks. In fact, one can restrict the model to actors who are connected by the informal network or by other network ties. This possibility has been explicitly used by Marsden (1983).

In addition, the model can be applied to transaction costs (Williamson 1991). Transaction costs in collective decision-making processes can be assumed to depend on several factors. First, characteristics of the pair of decisions might be influential for transaction costs. If two decisions are to be taken within a large time interval, exchange of voting positions involves extra risks for the actor for whom the second decision is the demand decision. These risks depend also on characteristics of the two actors and on the relation among them. As our exchange model is based on a combination of networks among decisions and among actors, all relevant types of transaction costs can be taken into account and related to the exchange rates.

III Application of the Models

In the next two chapters we shall apply the contending models to a common set of sixteen issues. The policy decision for each issue, the identity of the actors, and the three basic variables for each actor (i.e., their capability, salience, and policy position) were given in chapter 3. The two classes of models were described in chapters 4 and 5. The aim of the next two chapters is to present the information each model implies about the underlying political processes that lead to decisions. Chapter 6 provides detailed information gleaned from the expected utility model, while chapter 7 presents the implications drawn from the logrolling approach. This should help the reader develop a fuller understanding of how predictions are derived from the models.

We hope to show in this section that the information regarding the underlying political process is rich for both models. In this respect, these approaches differ substantially from models in which outcomes are predicted on the basis of macrolevel or structural phenomena (such as is true of both neorealist approaches and interdependence models) or purely as analytic solutions of some statistical model. Unlike the techniques investigated here, statistical, structural, or macrolevel models generally do not provide insights into the transformation of individual, goal-oriented actions into collective outcomes. Of course, except where available evidence warrants a claim of accuracy, we do not maintain that the specific processes and interactions described in our models have actually taken place. That would require an extensive empirical investigation into the dynamics of EC decision making that we were unable to perform. The models provide, however, important clues as to how the outcomes might have arisen. That is, the models provide a plausible explanation of the political dynamics required to motivate the actions taken by rational decision makers and to provide a microfoundation for the predicted and observed policy decisions. Here we can see the "as if" principle at work. To the extent that decisions are consistent with our predictions, it increases our confidence that decision makers behave according to the processes assumed in our models.

In chapter 8 an extensive analysis of an important set of issues related to the development of a European Bank is presented. The chapter shows the possibilities the expected utility model provides for analyzing long-term developments on a complex issue like the Economic Monetary Union. The small data requirements of the model (as well as the other models) make this a powerful tool for developing longitudinal, dynamic analyses. The banking issue is followed through several European summits on the basis of expert data that were gathered prior to each summit.

For the last summit, that of Maastricht, data were also collected regarding several distinct aspects of European banking policy. This created the opportunity to predict outcomes from the Maastricht summit based both on the expected utility approach and on the exchange models. The outcomes of the summits were predicted correctly, except in the case of Maastricht. Here both the expected utility model and the exchange model predicted a somewhat less supranational variant of the European Bank than was actually chosen. It will be shown, however, that the predicted solution probably would have been much less controversial than the actual outcome. The model predicts that the actual policy chosen would face stiff opposition from the United Kingdom and from Denmark. Later developments have shown how right this prediction was.

Bruce Bueno de Mesquita and A. F. K. Organski

6 Policy Outcomes and Policy Interventions: An Expected Utility Analysis

The study of policy is the analysis of strategic intervention to deflect or shape events. For policymakers in government, industry, or international bureaucracies, the most important questions are what will happen and how one might change undesired results. What will happen depends on the power, preferences, and perceptions of the actors in a negotiation setting and is presented in the expected utility model's dominant outcome. How events might possibly be changed depends upon the acquisition of additional information beyond that perceived by the actors, as specified by the development of a controlling strategy. In this chapter we summarize the political dynamics behind dominant outcome predictions across the sixteen issues that form the core of our investigation. We also illustrate how the perceptual component of the expected utility approach can help identify prospective controlling strategies. This is done through applying appropriate techniques on one issue.

Sixteen policy issues — nine automotive issues, two questions concerning radiation emissions, and five air transport questions — of some importance to the European Community have been evaluated as a means of testing the theories of policy forecasting set out in this book. These issues are analyzed using the expected utility method and a model that is motivated by the median voter theorem and a monotonicity theorem. The latter facilitates the identification of probabilistic actions by actors seeking confrontations, capitulations, or concessions from their rivals. The former theorem translates the anticipated actions into predictions about policy choices. The substantive significance of the sixteen issues was summarized in chapter 3; here we summarize the perceptual and dominant outcome results.

Automotive Emission Standards: Date of Introduction

Three of the nine automotive issues on which we have data concerned the date by which automotive emission standards were to be imposed on large, medium, and small automobiles, respectively. These issues are of interest both from a substantive perspective and from a methodological and theoretical perspective. Substantively it is interesting to assess which countries were most likely to coalesce with which others according to the expected utility formulation and to identify the compromise settlements that the model predicts would be put in place as EC policy. Theoretically the e issues help demonstrate the value of an explicit model as a means of sorting out the dynamics underlying seemingly very similar issues.

Before turning to the substantive issue, let us take a moment to reflect on the theoretical issue. Many are skeptical of the value gained by engaging in the process of modeling decisions. Often this skepticism is well founded by the observation that a model is only as good as the information used to place values on its variables. Since we have used expert information to estimate values, it is appropriate to wonder whether anyone with the relevant information would do just as well at predicting outcomes, whether they had a model or not. We do not wish to avoid this question, but rather want to confront it head-on, and to do so we propose a simple experiment.[1]

Table 6.1 contains data on the voting power, policy position, and salience of three automotive issues. For the moment we will not say which issue is which. The voting power and policy stance of the ten EC countries was the same on all three issues. There are three columns of salience data in the table because the relative importance of the three issues varied from EC member to EC member across the issues.

We ask the reader to examine the data in table 6.1 and to write down a predicted outcome on each issue. Please do so without reading ahead and without turning back to chapter 3. Here is a place to write the predictions:

Issue 1: _____   Issue 2: _____   Issue 3: _____

Whatever estimate has been made is, of course, already helped by our having focused attention on a very small set of crucial variables. The

1. We have also conducted systematic, controlled studies to evaluate the extent to which the expected utility model merely echoes back the judgments of the experts who provided the informational inputs to the model. In those tests we have found that the model and the experts disagree about half of the time. When the two disagree, the model's predictions have turned out to be more accurate about 80 percent of the time. The United States government places the model's accuracy at 90 percent or higher. For documentation see James Ray, *Global Politics,* 5th ed. (Boston: Houghton Mifflin, 1992), p. 161.

Table 6.1
Power, Position, and Salience on Three Issues

	Power	Position	Salience		
			Issue 1	Issue 2	Issue 3
United Kingdom	100	10	90	60	60
France	100	10	60	100	60
Italy	100	10	60	100	60
Greece	50	7	70	100	40
Belgium	50	7	40	40	40
Ireland	30	7	10	10	10
Germany	100	4	80	30	100
Denmark	30	4	100	100	100
Netherlands	50	4	80	100	100
Luxembourg	20	4	20	20	20

choice of these variables is dictated by the demands of the various models evaluated in this volume. In that regard anyone's judgment is enhanced by the requirement that the key factors entering into an evaluation be made explicit. Still, at least in our experience, most people guess that the first and third issue would be resolved at a value of seven and that the second would be settled at a value of ten. The data on issues 1 and 3 in table 6.1 look almost identical, with only small and seemingly mutually canceling shifts in salience to differentiate the two. Yet the expected utility model's logic leads to sharply different predictions — a 4.7-year delay in the introduction of emission control standards on large automobiles (issue 3) and an 8.4-year postponement for mid-sized cars (issue 1). The model predicts a 9.0-year delay on the introduction of auto emission standards on small cars (issue 2 in table 6.1). In reality, issue 1 was settled at 8.8 years, issue 2 at 8.8 years, and issue 3 at 4.8 years. All three predictions are quite close to the actual decisions even though there is little that obviously differentiates the data on the issues, especially the first and third. The average error in the expected utility predictions for these three issues is under 4 percent. Experts with the data from table 6.1 available to them still err by an average of about 29 percent. The reduction in erroneous predictions is apparently one important contribution of the modeling process.

The logic of the expected utility model helps the analyst differentiate among the issues by focusing on complex interactions among the varia-bles. That ability to differentiate is one aspect of the value added of the modeling approach. Other aspects include the detailed and nuanced calculations about shifting coalitions, compromise agreements, and the timing of decisions. With your own estimates and the model's predictions in mind, we turn now to an evaluation of each of the sixteen EC issues that form the heart of our investigation.

Table 3.6 depicts the initial positions of the ten EC countries on each of the three automotive emission standards introduction date issues; the relevant salience data are reported in table 3.5. At the outset, three of the four largest members were in agreement in promoting as long a delay as possible in the introduction of emission control standards. France, the United Kingdom, and Italy all apparently supported a lax approach, while Germany wanted emission control standards introduced at the earliest feasible time. Yet the seeming agreement between France, the United Kingdom, and Italy was in important respects less significant than one might conclude at first blush. The British cared more about postponing such controls on mid-sized cars than they did with regard to large or small automobiles. Italian and French interest in the subject rose as the size of the automobile diminished, reflecting their stakes in the automotive market. Germany's interest, not surprisingly, diminished steadily as the issue moved from large to mid-sized to small cars.

Because of differences in their commitment to influence decisions on these emission control issues, the apparent British-French-Italian coalition was subject to different pulls and tugs depending on the segment of the market under regulatory scrutiny. As far as large cars are concerned, the expected utility assessments indicate that the coalition would hold together while going down to defeat in the face of the greater commitment and interest of the Germans and their supporters. The expected utility model leads to a predicted delay in the introduction of emission controls on large automobiles of 4.7 years. The actual decision, as we noted earlier, supported a delay of 4.8 years. Table 6.2 displays the predicted shifts in position through the bargaining process on this (and the other two) introduction date issues.

How did the positions of the decision makers evolve with respect to the introduction of emission controls on large automobiles? As we saw, at the outset the members of the EC divided into three distinct coalitions: those favoring a ten-year delay, a seven-year postponement, and those preferring the introduction of standards in four years. After a period of bargaining, the expected utility model suggests that the participants were divided into more and new coalitions. Belgium joined Germany, the Netherlands, and Denmark in endorsing a four-year delay, while Luxembourg appears to have been willing to abandon that position in favor of a compromise at 6.8 years. Ireland was expected to move toward the United Kingdom, France, and Italy by giving its support to a compromise settlement of 8.8 years.

Table 6.2
Bargaining Sequences: Introductory Date for Auto Emissions

T_0		T_1	
Large Autos			
France	10.0	United Kingdom	9.6
Italy	10.0	Italy	9.6
United Kingdom	10.0	France	9.6
Belgium	7.0	Ireland	8.8
Greece	7.0	Luxembourg	6.8
Ireland	7.0	Germany	4.0
Germany	4.0	Netherlands	4.0
Netherlands	4.0	Denmark	4.0
Denmark	4.0	Greece ·	4.0
Luxembourg	4.0	Belgium	4.0
Mid-Sized Autos			
United Kingdom	10.0	United Kingdom	10.0
France	10.0	Italy	8.4
Italy	10.0	France	8.4
Greece	7.0	Greece	8.4
Belgium	7.0	Belgium	8.4
Ireland	7.0	Ireland	8.4
Germany	4.0	Netherlands	4.8
Denmark	4.0	Germany	4.7
Netherlands	4.0	Denmark	4.6
Luxembourg	4.0	Luxembourg	4.0
Small Autos			
France	10.0	Ireland	10.0
Italy	10.0	Italy	9.0
United Kingdom	10.0	France	9.0
Greece	7.0	United Kingdom	9.0
Belgium	7.0	Germany	7.9
Ireland	7.0	Luxembourg	7.8
Netherlands	4.0	Greece	7.0
Denmark	4.0	Belgium	7.0
Germany	4.0	Netherlands	4.0
Luxembourg	4.0	Denmark	4.0

Note: T_0 refers to the base case in the model. T_1 refers to the first iteration of the model.

To better understand the model's logic, we illustrate the bargaining process behind these policy shifts by pursuing the decision rules that yielded the predicted outcome. Table 6.3 summarizes the proposals regarding the introductory date for large auto emissions made and received by each EC member according to the expected utility logic. If no value is contained in a cell, then we expected that no proposal was made or was enforceable by the row actor. Because of the way the model is set up, if A can make a potentially enforceable proposal to B then B cannot make a credible proposal to A at that juncture (other than to accept or reject A's bid). Therefore, column entries reflect the proposals by the row nation that potentially were enforceable on the column nation.

No entry is placed in a cell if A had an enforceable proposal but did not recognize that fact or if A made a proposal that was not potentially enforceable. In the event of a tie between the magnitude of the smallest policy concession in terms of policy distance demanded of B, B accepts the proposal that has the smallest associated expected utility loss. Thus, for instance, Belgium, with an initial position of 7.0, receives a proposal to back the United Kingdom, France, and Italy at ten years and to back the Netherlands, Germany, Denmark, and Luxembourg at four years. The expected utility loss associated with giving in to the ten-year coalition is -0.506 for Belgium. The Belgians expected utility loss for giving in to Germany (-0.467), the Netherlands (-0.453) or Denmark is smaller (-0.448). The proposal to endorse a four-year delay is, consequently, supported by Belgium over the suggested ten-year delay.

From table 6.3 we can see how compromises arose among the member states of the European community. According to the logic of the expected utility approach, the United Kingdom, France, and Italy made proposals to Belgium, Greece, Luxembourg, and Ireland. The proposals to Belgium and Greece apparently did not eventuate in an agreement because, as noted, these two countries probably received less costly pressure from Denmark and its supporters. Ireland, however, is believed to have accepted a compromise proposal under which it supported a delay of 8.8 years in exchange for a minor concession from France, Italy, and the United Kingdom. These three members are hypothesized to have offered to reduce their stance on a delay from ten years to just over nine and a half years. Luxembourg may also have been swept along as part of that compromise proposal, with Luxembourg agreeing to endorse a 6.8-year delay rather than the four-year period they initially backed. The conjunction of these agreements results in the dominant outcome shifting from seven years to about 4.7 years.

Once this set of bargains was struck, the expected utility model indicates that further adjustments represent only minor shifts in positions. The next round of bargaining, if it were held, would have altered the outcome too little according to the model's logic to warrant the costs of

Table 6.3

Introductory Date for Emission Controls for Large Automobiles: Enforceable Proposals

	France	Italy	United Kingdom	Belgium	Greece	Ireland	Germany	Nether-lands	Den-mark	Luxem-bourg
France				10.0 / −.506	10.0 / −.506	<u>8.8</u> / <u>9.6</u>				<u>6.8</u> / 9.8
Italy				10.0 / −.506	10.0 / −.506	<u>8.8</u> / <u>9.6</u>				<u>6.8</u> / 9.8
United Kingdom				10.0 / −.506	10.0 / −.506	<u>8.8</u> / <u>9.6</u>				<u>6.8</u> / 9.8
Belgium										
Ireland										
Germany				4.0 / −.467	4.0 / −.467	4.0 / −.865				
Netherlands				4.0 / −.453	4.0 / −.453	4.0 / −.862				
Denmark				<u>4.0</u> / −.448	<u>4.0</u> / −.448	4.0 / −.860				
Luxembourg										

Note: The first entry in each column is the policy position associated with a potentially enforceable demand made by the row decision maker to the column decision maker. The second entry in each column is either the expected cost for the recipient of complying with the proposal to give in to the row actor or, in the event of a compromise, the proposed new position of the row actor in exchange for the proposed policy shift by the column actor. Underlined entries are those that the expected utility model's logic predicts were enforced. Notice that Luxembourg agrees to shift to support for a 6.8-year delay from its initial position of four years in exchange for a minor concession from Britain, France, and Italy. Note also that these three nations accept a larger compromise, to 9.6 years, than the 9.8-year position they apparently indicated to Luxembourg. Luxembourg, of course, is delighted to have a larger concession and Britain, France, and Italy were apparently willing in order to gain additional support from Ireland and thereby place some additional upward pressure on the dominant outcome.

continued negotiations. As we have mentioned, the actual outcome called for a delay of 4.8 years.

The story for mid-sized cars was quite different from that for large autos. The British apparently were steadfastly committed to putting off as long as possible the introduction of emission controls. The French and the Italians, although initially favoring the same ten-year delay, were prepared to compromise quite quickly, breaking their tacit coalition with the United Kingdom. On this issue we expect that the United Kingdom found itself isolated, while France and Italy signaled the softness of their position and helped persuade Belgium, Greece, and Ireland to support positions akin to their own modified stance in favor of approximately an 8.4-year delay. In the end, the issue was settled with an agreement favoring an 8.8-year delay, while the prediction from the expected utility model anticipated an 8.4- to 9.0-year delay.[2]

The introduction of emission controls on small cars was resolved in exactly the same way as the policy toward mid-sized autos. The agreed-upon delay in the introduction of the standards was 8.8 years. The expected utility assessment of this issue looks quite similar to the evaluation of the large auto issue in that the British-French-Italian alliance appears to have held together, while compromising its position down from support for a ten-year delay to the endorsement of a delay of about nine years. An important difference in the resolution of this regulatory matter as compared to the first two such issues was the apparent willingness of the Germans — whose efforts were not concentrated on the small car market — to abandon their initial position. As can be seen in table 6.2, the initial German position in favor of only a four-year postponement shifted to a compromise position in favor of a seven-and-a-half-year delay. The upshot of this concession coupled with the moderated position and tenacious cohesion of the French-British-Italian coalition is for a predicted dominant outcome of just under nine years. The actual decision postponed the introduction of emission standards on small cars for 8.8 years.

Most notable among the differences between the three auto emission introduction date issues in terms of the expected utility logic is the degree of perceived intransigence or conflict among the decision makers. A basic pattern emerges, which can be characterized as the smaller the car, the more conflictual the issue. On the large auto issue there appears to have

2. From time to time we report a range of predicted outcomes from the expected utility model. This is because its dynamic, iterative process can be viewed as stopping at either of the two final bargaining rounds identified by the model, depending on one's view of the time costs of continued bargaining. When we evaluate the accuracy of this model we utilize the value identified by the model as the settlement beyond which further concessions are no longer worth the associated bargaining costs. That value is selected by the model's internal logic and not by the analyst.

been a widespread recognition of a need to accommodate German interests. Just 10 percent of the perceptions about bilateral relations on this issue appear to have involved an expectation of conflict. Yet, on mid-sized and small automobiles, the perceived frequency of serious disagreement was much higher. Twenty-nine percent of bilateral relationships appear to have been conflictual on the introductory date issue for mid-sized cars and nearly 40 percent reflected conflict with regard to small automobiles. That is, more of the decision makers were reluctant to compromise with one another on the small car issue than on the medium or large automobile issues. Still, sufficient compromises proved possible for the decision makers to reach agreement and to settle the questions in a manner consistent with the predictions from the expected utility model.

Tax Incentives for Different Sizes of Automobiles

As with the introductory date, the issues concerned with tax incentives were divided according to the number of cylinders that an automobile possesses. Each issue was extremely polarized. About half of the nations favored a 3,000 deutsche mark tax incentive, while the other half wanted no incentive at all. Again, the United Kingdom, France, and Italy represent a large tacit coalition opposed to the German position in favor of a DM 3,000 incentive. Salience values decline for Germany and rise for France and Italy as the number of cylinders decreases. British interest is highest with regard to mid-sized automobiles.

The initial median voter prediction on all three of these issues is for there to be no tax incentive. However, the expected utility analysis indicates a high degree of willingness among the backers of no incentives (France, Italy, the United Kingdom, and Ireland) to forge a compromise agreement. The members of the no-incentive coalition generally do not feel as strongly about tax incentives as do their counterparts who favor a substantial incentive. The initial negotiated compromise favors a tax incentive for large automobiles of DM 1,626, with all of the no-incentives decision makers agreeing to this as an intermediate effort at forging a winning coalition. The compromise apparently is not sufficiently compelling to break the pro-DM 3,000 coalition, which — according to our expected utility assessments — would hold firm. But the analysis also suggests that substantial room still remains for negotiation and further compromise. At DM 2,372 Germany and its supporters appear willing to work out a compromise agreement on tax incentives for large automobiles. The predicted outcome is for a tax incentive of DM 2,372, while the actual compromise supported a tax incentive of DM 2,200.

The story behind the tax incentive program for mid-sized cars is quite different from that for large automobiles. Again the British, French, and Italian coalition shows considerable willingness to support some incentives despite their initially hostile position. At the end of one round of bargaining, that coalition is prepared to accept an agreement to provide a tax incentive of DM 2,024. The flexibility of this group apparently is largely unrecognized as the Germans propose an agreement at DM 1,545 and Luxembourg suggests settling for DM 1,459. The divisions within the pro-incentive coalition are, according to our expected utility assessments, evident to the anti-incentive coalition. The upshot is a prediction that the issue would be settled at somewhere between DM 1,459 and DM 1,535. The actual resolution established a DM 2,200 tax incentive for mid-sized autos.

Why is the predicted decision for mid-sized auto tax incentives so different from the prediction regarding large automobiles? This is an especially important question because the expected utility prediction in this case is only moderately accurate. Perhaps we can learn something from evaluating the sources that underlie the predictive error.

Support for tax incentives on medium-sized automobiles was no less polarized than was the tax incentive issue for larger autos. The degree of importance attached to the issue, however, is different and this is the crucial factor that gives shape to the final predicted settlement. Because of the differences in salience, the tax incentive question for mid-sized autos is expected to have provoked more hostility than apparently arose regarding large autos. Both issues start off with similar levels of perceived hostility, but that level remains unaltered throughout the bargaining process over large car tax incentives and rises sharply over mid-sized auto tax incentives according to the expected utility analysis.

For both sizes of cars, the initial bilateral relationships apparently were anticipated by the decision makers to be conflictual in about 30 percent of the cases. By the end of discussions on mid-sized autos, that percentage reaches about 55, while it has remained steady at under 30 percent for large automobiles. This suggests that the agreement predicted for mid-sized auto tax incentives had pushed the decision makers close to their limits for concessions and quite a bit farther than was the case for large cars.

Perhaps the actual salience levels were less different across these two issues than our estimates suggest. The error of prediction derived from the model encourages us to look more closely at those estimates as they are almost certainly the source of the error. In any event, the compromises extracted from the pro-incentives coalition according to the expected utility assessments were larger for mid-sized cars than for larger ones. The actual concessions apparently were not so large. The actual outcome supported a tax incentive for such cars of DM 2,200.

The story for small automobiles is almost exactly the same as for medium-sized cars. The European Community was highly polarized and the initial median voter position supports no tax incentives. Again there is a rather widespread expectation of sharp disagreement and conflict. In this case, the expected utility calculations support a compromise arrangement and a dominant outcome of DM 1,271, while the actual decision endorsed a tax incentive of DM 750. Although again there is a sizable difference between the predicted and actual choices, the difference is smaller than in the case of mid-sized automobiles. The logic of the expected utility model did lead us to anticipate that the tax incentive would be smallest on small cars even though the initial preferences were identical across all three cylinder numbers.

The most significant features of the small car decision according to our modeling procedure have to do with the relative flexibility and unity of the competing coalitions. Again the anti-incentive coalition of France, the United Kingdom, and Italy (as well as Ireland) remains intact, while the pro-incentive coalition factionalizes. The Dutch and the Danes are hypothesized to have remained at their initial position in support of a DM 3,000 tax incentive. Apparently no one thought it was worthwhile trying to make a deal with them. The Danes were unappealing partners because they were unwilling to expend any influence on the issue (as reflected in their salience score of zero). The Dutch, according to our evaluation, probably overestimated their own leverage and so made proposals that were rejected by the anti-incentive coalition whose members had better opportunities than those offered by the Netherlands. The Germans are predicted to have abandoned their high incentive position at the first opportunity and to have given their support to a compromise settlement favoring an incentive of about DM 1,500, with Luxembourg being even slightly more accommodating at about DM 1,450. So, while one coalition remained united, the other split apart.

Unlike the predicted evolution of the decision regarding middle-sized cars, the anti-incentive small car coalition more accurately anticipated the flexibility and factionalization of the pro-incentives coalition this time. Consequently, the anti-incentives coalition did not seem to show as much willingness to compromise on the tax incentives for small cars as they seemingly showed for mid-sized autos. Their proposed settlement falls at DM 1,271, and this is the settlement predicted to prevail.

The model suggests that so long as the anti-incentives coalition stuck together, they could impose their will on the rest of the EC members because the key pro-incentive member — Germany — was not prepared to put up much of a fight on this issue. In reality it appears that the anti-incentive coalition offered a minimal compromise — even smaller than the one predicted here — and got sufficient support to carry the day. The initial and compromise positions of each decision maker for each of the tax incentive issues can be found in table 6.4. The settlement itself was for a tax incentive of DM 750.

Table 6.4
Tax Incentives on Automobiles (in DM)

Large Autos

	T_0	T_1	T_2
Germany	3,000	3,000	3,000
Netherlands	3,000	3,000	3,000
Luxembourg	3,000	3,000	3,000
Denmark	3,000	3,000	3,000
United Kingdom	0	1,626	2,372
France	0	1,626	2,372
Italy	0	1,626	2,372
Ireland	0	1,626	2,372

Mid-Sized Autos

T_0		T_1
3,000	Netherlands	3,000
3,000	Denmark	3,000
3,000	United Kingdom	2,024
3,000	France	2,024
0	Italy	2,024
0	Ireland	2,024
0	Germany	1,545
0	Luxembourg	1,459

Small Autos

	T_0		T_1
Netherlands	3,000	Netherlands	3,000
Germany	3,000	Denmark	3,000
Luxembourg	3,000	Germany	1,499
Denmark	3,000	Luxembourg	1,455
France	0	France	1,271
Italy	0	Italy	1,271
United Kingdom	0	United Kingdom	1,271
Ireland	0	Ireland	1,271

Note: Country names are repeated only for rounds of bargaining in which coalitions break apart.

Emission Controls On Automobiles

The issues concerning emission limits generally were not polarized the way the other automotive issues were. Rather, there was a substantial dispersion of interests and many opportunities to reach compromise agreements. We will discuss the decision surrounding emission standards on large automobiles later in this chapter when we describe the development of a controlling strategy, so we will skip over this issue for the moment.

For mid-size vehicles, the issue of emission controls appears to have been less volatile than with respect to large automobiles. Yet its resolution was also expected to be less amicable. According to the expected utility evaluation, this issue should have arisen with an expectation of a fairly confrontational backdrop, with 43 percent of bilateral relationships perceived to be conflictual. The fear of confrontation, however, was more imagined than real, but still may have acted to constrain compromises in ways that could have been altered through the implementation of a controlling strategy had the decision makers had the added information provided by the logic of the expected utility model. In any event, from the joint perspective that takes both sides perceptions into account, the anticipation of substantial disagreement and dispute appears exaggerated, with only about one quarter of the bilateral interactions anticipated to be conflictual by the joint expected utility assessments.

One of the most striking aspects of the predicted relationships among the EC members over this issue is the expectation that Denmark's position would not succumb to any compromises. The anticipated Danish intransigence emerged in reality as well as in the logic from the expected utility model. Had the decision makers' perceptions been more in line with our joint perspective, it appears that the issue could have been settled with a compromise agreement endorsing a standard of .533, reflecting moderate tolerance of pollutants, a resolution, incidentally, that would have been closer to Denmark's wishes. The Dutch might have led the process of building a coalition behind this outcome. Instead, however, given that the expected utility model assumes that decision makers only make proposals when they believe they stand to gain from doing so, the predicted outcome is for a laxer standard of .717 on our scale of tolerance for pollutants in auto emissions. Danish objections not withstanding, the model predicts a compromise settlement that ignores Denmark's wishes. The actual outcome supports a tolerance level of .792, so that the expected utility prediction was within 86.5 percent of the true value.

The fundamental feature behind the decision on mid-sized auto emission standards is that the seemingly hard-line initial position of Germany proves quite pliable. As table 6.5 shows, the Germans could be expected to have shifted from their initial stance in support of .448 tolerance for

Table 6.5
Compromises on Emission Standards

T_0		T_1	
Large Autos			
United Kingdom	1.0000	France	.9171
France	.9333	United Kingdom	.8695
Belgium	.9333	Italy	.8255
Italy	.7819	Luxembourg	.5772
Germany	.5486	Germany	.5486
Netherlands	.5000	Netherlands	.5000
Luxembourg	.5000	Belgium	.5000
Denmark	.4931	Denmark	.4931
Mid-Sized Autos			
United Kingdom	1.0000	United Kingdom	.7174
France	1.0000	Germany	.7174
Italy	1.0000	Italy	.5331
Belgium	1.0000	Netherlands	.5331
Netherlands	.5331	France	.5331
Luxembourg	.5331	Belgium	.5331
Germany	.4481	Luxembourg	.5331
Denmark	.4481	Denmark	.4481
Small Autos			
France	1.0000	Germany	.8705
Italy	1.0000	Belgium	.8566
United Kingdom	1.0000	Luxembourg	.8566
Belgium	.7619	Ireland	.8566
Luxembourg	.7619	Italy	.8496
Ireland	.7619	France	.8496
Netherlands	.4941	United Kingdom	.8496
Greece	.4941	Denmark	.6273
Denmark	.4941	Greece	.4941
Germany	.4941	Netherlands	.4941

Note: The scale refers to tolerance for pollutants in emissions.
Lower values reflect support for fewer pollutants.

pollutants to a willingness to live with more emissions (.717 on the scale) — a revised position quite close to the eventual settlement.

The initial prediction with regard to emission control on small cars is .947 toleration of pollutants, with Germany again favoring strict standards and France, the United Kingdom, and Italy supporting the weakest emission control standard. The positions of the decision makers seem to have been extremely fluid and, also, there seems to have been a consensual position. As is evident in table 6.5, the significant auto manufacturing countries in the EC are expected to have abandoned their diverse initial positions and converged on an agreement in the upper .8 range. The outcome predicted with the expected utility model for small cars is expected to be fairly noncontroversial at between .871 and .855. In reality, the issue was resolved by endorsing a standard of .762, reflecting considerable tolerance for pollutants.

We have now completed our summary of the nine automotive issues included in this study. A few words are in order about the general characteristics of the politics behind these issues. It is clear that all of these issues pitted German interests against the concerns of the other major auto-producing EC countries — the United Kingdom, France, and Italy. The smaller EC members frequently played a pivotal role in helping to provide compromise proposals and in mediating between the competing larger member interests. Were there winners and losers? In general, Germany fared poorly. The eventual policy choice was quite far from Germany's initial position on most of these issues.

Germany did do well on the question of the date for introducing emission controls on large automobiles. The Germans cared deeply about this issue and got pretty much what they wanted. Likewise, Germany fared rather well on the tax incentive issues for the two larger categories of automobiles. On the remaining automotive issues, Germany agreed to substantial concessions.

It would be a mistake to infer that because Germany did not win, the other large EC automotive manufacturers did. They, too, generally agreed to substantial concessions as part of the process of tacit bargaining that led to policy choices by the EC, despite the ostensible need within the rules for unanimous support. Italy got exactly what it wanted on large auto emission standards, but not because Italy carried the day. Rather, the Italian position represented a feasible compromise between the hardline stance of Germany at one extreme and the lax stance of the United Kingdom and France at the other extreme. The date for introducing such standards on mid-sized and small cars appears to have been more satisfactory from the French and Italian perspectives than was true for the British, but here, too, the actual decision still necessitated a significant compromise. Finally, the British, French, and Italians seem to have done relatively well on small auto tax incentives, although possibly at the price of not doing so well on tax incentives for larger automobiles. All in all, the process appears to have been one of considerable give and take, yielding, on average, outcomes quite close to those predicted with the expected utility model. The average error of prediction for these nine issues is about 15 percent, so that the typical predicted outcome was within 85 percent of the actual choice and several predictions were within 5 percent.

Radioactive Emissions

Following the Chernobyl disaster, the European Community focused attention on the implementation of standards for controlling radioactive contaminants in foodstuffs. Two issues are at the heart of our analysis of this policy area. Each was highly controversial. Indeed, the community treated these two issues differently from the other fourteen we are investigating precisely because of their controversial nature. Thus, the two radiation issues were settled under the qualified majority rule, while the other questions evaluated in this volume were resolved under the unanimity rule.

As we saw with the automotive issues, the unanimity rule did not preclude compromise, but rather seems to have encouraged it. However sharp the differences were among the member states, none were sufficiently willing to jeopardize the survival of the community to thwart a compromise settlement even if the compromise did not serve the member's interests on the issue in question. The qualified majority rule, by contrast, made it easier for opposition to be sustained, and it was.

The first radiation issue that we assessed concerns tolerable levels of radioactive contaminants. The Benelux countries together with Ireland and Portugal supported a standard of .1078, while the Germans took a slightly harder-line stance at .1000. Denmark at .2500 and Italy and Greece at .8125 represent the gulf between those supporting a high standard and those supporting a much weaker standard. No one fell in between these widely differing positions. Finally, France and Spain anchor the opposite end of the scale at 1.0000.

The base case median voter forecast is .8125, the Greco-Italian position. The issue is politically charged, with many of those at .1000 or .1078 anticipating a confrontation with those at the opposite end of the continuum. Indeed, the expected utility model predicts that no compromise proposals would stick and that the outcome would be a standard of .8125. In actuality the EC commission reported a proposed settlement of .815, or virtually exactly the outcome predicted by the model.

The commissions recommendation, however, did not prevail among the community member states. Instead, the issue became very heated, with prolonged debate and little compromise by some states. This is what we would expect on an issue being resolved through the qualified majority rule, a procedure that reduces the costs for remaining in opposition, thereby encouraging greater attentiveness by member states to their own domestic constituencies rather than to the politics of the EC itself. The actual settlement, after extended debate, was for .356 toleration relative to the maximum proposed level of tolerance for radiation. As this is the first issue we have assessed that was resolved under the qualified majority rule, it is interesting to consider the particular institutional procedures that were applied.

In accordance with the qualified majority rule, extreme positions could be excluded from the final vote and, of course, debate could be quite sustained. That is, this was an issue likely to be settled in two stages: first the EC commission would reach a proposed resolution and they did. That was equivalent to our prediction of .813. Then the member states would have a further go at it and, after prolonged negotiations, would reach an agreement that could exclude the interests of some participants. Indeed, we now know that the positions backed by Greece, Germany, and Denmark remained extreme and were excluded from the final vote.

What happens in the expected utility model if the issue is permitted to be negotiated over a more prolonged period than normally permitted by the model's time-discounting rules? The actual decision we now know involved about five or six rounds of negotiations. The expected utility model takes an interesting turn if permitted to go beyond the initially predicted result (.813 at the end of the first stage) and to iterate through six rounds of bargaining. Although in the initial rounds of bargaining the model's predictions hover around .813, the prediction experiences a precipitous drop by the fifth round and settles into a pattern during the sixth round of bargaining. The predicted outcome at that juncture is .475, a prediction quite close to the second stage choice made by the community member states. Having said that and having noted how greater attentiveness to the institutional or structural framework within which decisions are made can improve predictions, we nevertheless treat .813 as our prediction. By that standard the expected utility model does quite poorly on this issue, the first matter in our data set decided by the qualified majority procedure.

The second and final issue in this section concerns a yes or no decision to extend the radioactive contaminants standards following the Chernobyl accident. The post-Chernobyl preferences are even more polarized than in the previous issue. The EC appears initially to favor an extension. That is the prediction from the expected utility model. Since this was a simple yes or no vote, intermediate compromises are not really meaningful, but perhaps we can interpret intermediate positions between a yes vote and a no vote as the likelihood of supporting extension. In that sense, the predicted likelihood of extension according to the logic of the model was 84 percent. In reality the heightened standard was extended, precisely as anticipated by the model.

For the first radiation issue, the expected utility model based on the first stage prediction was inaccurate by a very substantial 50.8 percent. Compared to the first stage decision of the EC, however, this prediction was within 1 percent of the commission recommendation. If the second stage prediction is utilized for the first radiation issue, then the inaccuracy is reduced to 13.2 percent when compared to the final choice of the community. The second radiation prediction had no error component.

Air Transport Liberalization

The first of the five air transport liberalization issues on which we focus concerns permissible deep discounting of fares. This was generally a rather salient issue, with positions differing broadly mostly as a function of how much international air travel terminated or originated in the relevant country. The United Kingdom and the Netherlands, for instance, both wanted a minimal discount fare as the London and Amsterdam airports would be competitively advantaged under those conditions. Greece and Spain were more inclined toward substantial discounts.

The expected utility assessments lead us to expect that most members were willing to accept a compromise agreement, but that the British and the Dutch viewed the proposed compromise as highly controversial. As noted in chapter 3, this was the case. Because of Dutch and British hostility to the plan and because the issue was being decided under the unanimity rule, debate was extended in the hopes of promoting an agreement. The issue was ultimately settled with the member states agreeing to permit a lowest possible deep discount fare of 45 percent. The prediction from the expected utility model is for that deep discount fare to have been set at 50 percent, an assessment quite close to reality.

A second liberalization issue revolved around the distribution or sharing of seating capacity. The Netherlands and the British took a decidedly different position on this issue than did the other EC members. Both of these countries favored complete liberalization so that 100-percent sharing of seating capacity among members would be permitted. Italy, France, Spain, and Greece took the opposite position, favoring the maintenance of existing regulations. The Dutch and the British both perceived the situation as highly charged, leading them to make few effective proposals. Yet the expected utility analysis indicates that each could have exerted more effective influence by taking a calmer approach to the issue. It appears that they missed an excellent opportunity to exert a more positive influence on the decision over this policy area.

Our assessments indicate something of a roller coaster ride on seating capacity fluctuation. At first blush it appears the issue would be settled at

19.8 percent, but after one round of bargaining the outcome shifts to the view that the status quo ante should be maintained. The danger of such an outcome to the interests of several EC members seems to have provoked further bargaining and the construction of a stronger coalition in favor of sharing approximately 20 percent of seating capacity. The dominant outcome predicted using the expected utility logic is 19.9 percent, with France, Germany, Belgium, Denmark, and Portugal all giving that compromise their support. The actual outcome was an agreement to share 13.3 percent of capacity, a compromise outcome fairly close to that predicted by the model. Indeed, in some ways the actual outcome was even closer to that predicted by the expected utility model. For the first two years, the agreement was a 10-percent capacity, with 20 percent being the designated amount in the third and final year of the compromise agreement. Of course, 20 percent was the model's prediction.

A third issue focused on air transport exemptions between hubs and regional airports. Again the British and the Dutch (this time together with Ireland) found themselves coalesced against the broadly held sentiment in favor of accepting all exemptions. The issue appears to have been very heated, with just over half of all member relationships being conflictual according to the expected utility logic. The model suggests that the issue would be resolved by forging a compromise agreement that excluded the Dutch, Irish, and British, who seem to have preferred to stick to their initial position rather than grant support for the extension of exemptions. The model predicts a resolution supporting a substantial number of exemptions (2.7 on a scale where 1 means no exemptions, 2 means some, 3 is equivalent to many exemptions, and 4 accepts all exemptions). The actual outcome was to accept all exemptions. If the discrete, ordinal scale is treated as a continuous set of choices, then the expected utility prediction should be viewed as 2.7, but if the ordinality of the scale is taken seriously, then the predicted outcome is the nearest ordinal step, or 3.

As noted in chapter 3, we have also investigated the percentage of hub-regional traffic that was to be subjected to the capacity-sharing arrangement. As with the other air transport issues, the United Kingdom and the Netherlands (and Ireland) staked out a position at one extreme, opposing any capacity sharing, while France, Italy, and others wanted all hub-regional traffic to fall within the guidelines of the capacity-sharing arrangement. The other EC member states had interests on this issue that were spread broadly across the spectrum. Unlike some of the other issues, however, the United Kingdom and the Netherlands seem, according to the expected utility calculations, to have been willing to compromise somewhat in an effort to reach an amicable agreement. The prediction from the model is for an agreement for 70 percent of hub-regional traffic to fall within the capacity-sharing arrangement. In actuality the issue was settled at 80 percent, again an outcome rather close to the expected utility

Table 6.6
Deep Discount Fares

	T_0		T_1
Spain	60	Spain	59
Greece	60	Greece	59
Italy	55	Italy	56
Denmark	55	Belgium	55
France	50	France	50
Germany	50	Luxembourg	48
Portugal	50	Ireland	46
Belgium	50	United Kingdom	30
Luxembourg	50	Germany	30
Ireland	45	Portugal	30
United Kingdom	30	Netherlands	30
Netherlands	30	Denmark	30

prediction. The compromise positions on these four air transport issues are summarized in tables 6.6 to 6.9.

One final issue was assessed within the framework of air transport liberalization. Here the question called for a yes or no vote on whether the liberalization package would continue in force even if the member states could not agree on the next step in the process. The model predicts that the members would support termination, forcing the council's hand. The decision was as predicted. All those who wished for the liberalization package to continue in place even if further steps were not agreed upon felt put upon by the winning coalition according to the expected utility assessments. Indeed, had it not been a simple up or down vote, it is likely that the pro-continuation faction could have prevailed on almost every member to support a compromise, continuing some parts of the package but not others. However, this option was not available to the decision makers, and so the pro-termination coalition dominated.

The Process of Negotiations: Modeling Comparative Statics
The fifteen issues reviewed thus far have all been analyzed with an eye to accounting for the dynamics behind each policy decision and in the hope that the predicted outcomes and reality would match rather well. In chapter 9 we assess that accuracy. We have not, however, examined the possibility that decision makers might have helped negotiate alternative resolutions of these issues by the judicious use of the information suggested

Table 6.7
Capacity Fluctuation

	T_0		T_1		T_3
Netherlands	100	Netherlands	100	Netherlands	100
United Kingdom	100	United Kingdom	100	United Kingdom	100
Ireland	30	Ireland	25	Ireland	25
Germany	20	Luxembourg	25	Luxembourg	25
Portugal	20	Portugal	20	France	20
Belgium	20	Germany	20	Germany	20
Denmark	20	Italy	0	Portugal	20
Luxembourg	20	France	0	Belgium	20
Italy	0	Spain	0	Denmark	20
France	0	Greece	0	Italy	0
Spain	0	Belgium	0	Spain	0
Greece	0	Denmark	0	Greece	0

Table 6.8
Hub-Regional Exclusions

	T_0		T_1
Italy	4.0	Portugal	3.0
Greece	4.0	France	3.0
Denmark	4.0	Germany	3.0
Portugal	3.0	Denmark	2.8
Spain	2.0	Greece	2.8
Germany	2.0	Italy	2.0
France	2.0	Spain	2.7
Belgium	1.0	Luxembourg	1.6
Luxembourg	1.0	Belgium	1.5
Netherlands	0.0	Netherlands	0.0
United Kingdom	0.0	United Kingdom	0.0
Ireland	0.0	Ireland	0.0

Table 6.9
Hub-Regional Inclusion

	T_0
France	100
Italy	100
Greece	100
Spain	100
Portugal	70
Germany	60
Denmark	50
Luxembourg	50
Belgium	40
United Kingdom	0
Netherlands	0
Ireland	0

by the expected utility model. Our discussion of the final automotive issue will illustrate how the expected utility assessments might help policy makers in formulating negotiating strategies.

We shall provide two illustrations of how the expected utility models can be used to reshape events, producing results that are different from the dominant or median voter outcome that was developed in chapter 4. In one illustration, we show how Germany's interests could have been advanced had the German government had access to a model such as the one described here. In the second illustration we show an instance where access to the additional information reveals that France could not reshape the outcome even if it raised its own level of commitment and persuaded its ally, Italy, to do the same with regard to the issue of emission standards for large automobiles.

To assess alternative strategies and to ascertain which is most likely to maximize the welfare of this or that decision maker we utilize a simulation approach. Utilizing the information implied by the expected utility calculations, we identify feasible shifts in decision maker proposals, positions, or salience. By simulating those shifts we are able to evaluate — before the fact — what impact alternative strategies are expected to have.

The perceptual analysis provides the essential ingredient for simulating alternative strategies. Any interested group (or an interested analyst) can identify the candidates prepared to succumb to someone else's objectives if pressed. A group leader should, of course, be most inclined to pressure those who believe they must grant concessions to the group's demands. The larger the probability that a rival will not be confrontational, the lower the costs expected to be associated with extracting gains from the foe, thereby making such an actor an especially attractive candidate for influence attempts. By focusing efforts on groups believed to have a high probability of granting concessions, the interested party can most efficiently organize the coalition — with altered levels of effort or revealed policy preferences — that will shift the outcome to be most in line with the organizing group's preferences. This simulation process proceeds in stages, first identifying the best strategic reaction to the initial, base case, circumstance; then analyzing strategic responses to the initial strategy to alter the base case, and so forth. In this way, a "movie" of the unfolding process of negotiations, of moves and countermoves, can be constructed.[3]

If a *controlling strategy* — a strategy that allows the full exploitation of seemingly hidden beliefs — exists it is likely to be discovered through this iterative process.[4] Like the dominant outcome in which each actor relies on its own perceptions, this controlling strategy assumes that each actor pursues its own best interest. Unlike the dominant outcome analysis, the assessment of a controlling strategy takes advantage of the calculation of other players' beliefs, revealing that approximated information to a policymaker and then simulating the use of that information by the policymaker who otherwise would not have known it. Thus, the controlling strategy takes information that previously was treated as the private knowledge of an opponent and exposes it to a decision maker who is privy to the assessments of the perceptual analysis of the expected utility model. The controlling strategy, then, exploits the reduced search costs associated with our model's method for acquiring relevant information, making it attractive for decision makers to satisfice at a higher level than was previously the case.

Simulating a Controlling Strategy: German Opportunities Forgone

In the case of large automobile emissions, the issue produces an interesting political problem for Germany and an interesting anomaly for the expected

3. For a detailed example (drawn from Italian politics) of such an application of the model, see Beck and Bueno de Mesquita 1985.
4. Of course, it is possible that real-world decision makers already estimate what we are calling hidden beliefs. Certainly rational actors will exploit available information to improve their strategic choices as long as the costs of such exploitation are not expected to exceed the benefits. A computer-based search procedure such as is designed into the expected utility model makes those search costs much lower for us as analysts than they probably are for decision makers at this time. In that sense, we may be revealing hidden or private information that can be expected in the future to become common knowledge.

utility model. The actual outcome on this issue was to tolerate .782 percent of the most liberal standard regarding particulate emissions from large automobiles. Germany's preferred outcome was to permit only .5486 percent of that level of pollutants, a much lower level. The actual decision was exactly the outcome desired by the Italians whose automobiles were not nearly as well equipped to reduce pollutants as were German cars. Although Italy got its way, it was not the Italians who were necessarily central in shaping the decision. Rather, their position apparently represented a reasonable compromise among competing interests.

The expected utility model does relatively poorly on this issue. Although the model's initial median voter prediction of .779 is very close to the true outcome, the treatment of the hypothetical rounds of bargaining produces a dominant outcome prediction of .577, about 40 percent off the mark. Thus, the size of the error contained in the dominant outcome identified by the expected utility model on this issue is about two and a half times larger than the average predictive error of the expected utility model across the sixteen issues evaluated here.[5] Indeed, this is one reason for selecting emission control standards on large automobiles as an issue for special focus. We are interested in calling special attention to this issue in the hope of learning more about any specific structural or institutional limitations that were imposed on the decision makers in working toward an agreement on large automobile emission standards.

According to the expected utility model, had the issue been settled right away, the Italian position would have carried the day, just as it did in reality. However, the model predicts that several compromises were likely to be forged. Most notable among the prospective concessions is the indication that Belgium — not an auto-producing country — was willing to abandon its initial position in favor of very lax standards (.933 percent of the least restrictive proposal) and back the stiffer Dutch position. Other compromises were also likely. Italy, for instance, was predicted to endorse a slightly higher level of permissible pollutants than suggested by its initial position. The expectation is that Italy would do so in exchange for a reduction in the British position. The predicted compromises are reported in table 6.5.

Table 6.5 makes evident that the positions of the EC countries were likely to begin to converge toward the center, with the major uncertainty being over exactly where that convergence would lead in terms of an actual emission standard. From the German point of view, such convergence away from very lax standards was all to the good as it fostered the prospect of placing large German automobiles at a comparative advantage in the European marketplace. To realize the benefits from such a pro-

5. The predictions and the error rate for the expected utility model and for the other models examined in this volume can be found in chapter 9.

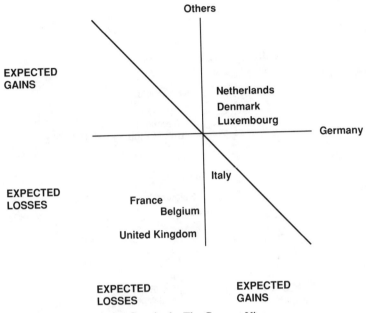

Others

EXPECTED
GAINS

Netherlands
Denmark
Luxembourg
Germany

Italy

EXPECTED
LOSSES

France
Belgium

United Kingdom

EXPECTED
LOSSES

EXPECTED
GAINS

6.1: Large Auto Emission Standards: The German View

spective advantage, however, the Germans were eager for the eventual agreement to impose considerably stiffer standards than ultimately arose. What might the Germans have done to enhance their prospects?

The answer lies in an assessment of our estimates of German perceptions and our estimates of the perceptions of the other EC members involved in the decision. Figure 6.1 depicts Germany's perceptions as approximated using the expected utility model, while figure 6.2 shows the estimated perceptions of each other country vis-à-vis Germany on this same issue. It is quite clear from the two figures that German expectations differed markedly from the perceptions of the other EC members.

In the German view, we see that only Italy was expected to accept the German position. This is consistent also with the Italian perspective. That is, the Italians believed the German's had a credible case to which they were willing to acquiesce if no other EC member made them a better offer. Alas for the Germans, the indications using the logic of the expected utility model are that Italy could strike a better bargain, gaining increased British support if only the Italians would shift their position modestly. Unforeseen by the Germans — but anticipated by the expected utility assessments — is a willingness by the French and the Belgians to accommodate German interests.

Belgium received little or no pressure from any country other than the Dutch. The Dutch position was even more stringent than the Germans

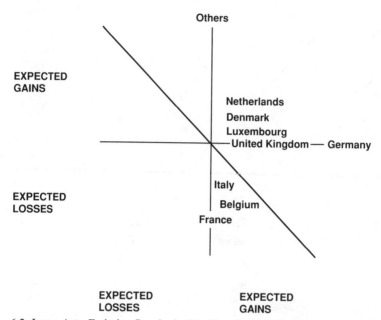

6.2: Large Auto Emission Standards: The Non-German View

wanted and much more stringent than the initial position endorsed by Belgium. Consequently, it would have been in Belgium's interest to respond to a German proposal if such an offering were forthcoming. The German representatives apparently did not believe they could convince Belgium to back their position and so probably did not try. Figure 6.2 indicates that Belgium would have been responsive so we can simulate as part of a controlling strategy a proposal by Germany to gain Belgian support.

According to the expected utility assessments the French representatives received no significant credible proposals from other members of the European Community on the issue of large automobile emission standards. Consequently, as evident in table 6.5, we predicted a rather stationary French position. Yet, figure 6.2 shows the French as being willing to accept the German position, a notion that is consistent with the broad-based coalition between France and Germany that others have observed on a variety of EC issues. According to the analysis reflected in figure 6.1, the Germans did not anticipate France's responsiveness, and so, probably, France was not approached on this particular issue. As part of a German controlling strategy, figure 6.2 indicates that France would have accepted the German position, and so we simulate the impact that such an alliance would have had.

Table 6.10 displays the initial national positions or preferences on large

Table 6.10
National Positions on Large Auto Emission Standards

| | Initial Bargained | | Simulated | | | |
| | | | German-French-Belgian Coalition[a] | | German-Belgian Coalition[b] | |
	T_0	T_1	T_1	T_2	T_1	T_2
Netherlands	.5000	.5000	.5000	.5386	.5000	.5337
Belgium	.9333	.5000	.5486	.5164	.5486	.5218
Luxembourg	.5000	.5772	.5772	.5486	.5772	.5486
Germany	.5486	.5486	.5486	.5486	.5486	.5486
France	.9333	.9171	.5486	.5185	.9171	.7965
Italy	.7819	.8255	.8255	.7103	.8255	.7878
United Kingdom	1.0000	.8695	.8695	.7105	.8695	.8695
Denmark	.4931	.4931	.4931	.5185	.4931	.5087
Forecast	.7794	.5772	.5486	.5486	.5486	.5486

Note: The scale refers to tolerance for pollutants in emission. Higher numbers indicate greater tolerance.
[a]A simulated controlling strategy in which Germany builds a coalition with France and Belgium. The feasibility of this coalition is indicated by the French and Belgian "perceptions."
[b]A simulated controlling strategy in which Germany builds a coalition with Belgium only. The feasibility of this coalition is indicated by the Belgian "perceptions" and is an easier coalition to construct than the French-Belgian alliance.

auto emission standards, along with the predicted change in positions based on the dominant strategy. It also displays the simulated effects that are likely to have arisen if Germany had built the coalition with France, Italy, and Belgium that we believe was feasible. The predicted outcome accompanies each round of hypothetical bargaining displayed in the table. As is evident, the simulated strategy would have produced a better outcome for Germany than that actually attained, at least according to the logic of the expected utility model.

A second, simpler controlling strategy was apparently available to Germany. Table 6.10 also summarizes the effect of a German-Belgian coalition without the support of the French. It is apparent from this analysis that French cooperation was not essential for Germany to move the results toward its objectives. The model's dominant outcome already suggests that Belgium was prepared to move to the Dutch position. There is little reason to doubt that Belgium would have preferred the German objective. Germany's initial position was closer to Belgium's than was that of the Netherlands. What is more, had Germany taken the unanticipated action of forging a coalition with Belgium, beliefs would have changed substantially among the other decision makers, leading gradually to more and more support for the German position. All the smaller EC partners would have gathered around Germany, eventually leading the French, British, and Italians — all of whom have large automobile industries — to support tougher emission standards.

Simulating a Controlling Strategy: Sparing France Wasted Effort

The focus on controlling strategies provides insights into errors of omission and commission. In Germany's case, it appears that there was a failure to exploit a chance to forge a much better policy outcome than was obtained. Sometimes, actors in a multilateral negotiation attempt to take actions that are counterproductive because of mistaken beliefs or inadequate evaluations of circumstances. Although we have no concrete evidence of such mistakes having been made by any EC members during the debates over the automotive issues, we illustrate two ways in which such errors might easily have occurred.

Sometimes an actor believes that a rival is willing to grant concessions when the adversary is not. In such cases it is even possible for the adversary to react in a highly confrontational way, making it politically costly for its opponent to have asked for anything. The failure to anticipate correctly the response of an opponent is a direct consequence of not being able to estimate the foe's beliefs adequately, perhaps because the costs of processing the available information more thoroughly are just too high. Such errors would be avoided if decision makers routinely examined their circumstances from the perspective afforded by the construction of controlling strategies and capitalized on the efficiency of models of the sort discussed here.

A second error that can be made is to pursue a controlling strategy without sufficient information about the long-term consequences of strategic choices. For instance, one might be able to forge a coalition in support of a desired position only to discover that the reconfiguration of positions enhanced the cohesion of rival groups. That is, we believe, what would have happened to France had they tried to build a controlling strategy without the comprehensive mapping of perceptions that can be provided by an expected utility perspective.

France and Italy, for instance, were positioned to build a compromise coalition in support of emission controls on large automobiles of around .8695 percent tolerance, a coalition that would have supported the modified British position. The Italians believed that such an arrangement with the French would be beneficial to them and so did the French. As we have already seen, in the absence of Germany's implementation of a controlling strategy, the Netherlands and Belgium could have been expected to co-alesce in support of a tougher standard, at .5000 on our tolerance scale. Luxembourg was prepared to align itself more closely with France and Italy than it did at the outset. Indeed, Luxembourg was apparently ready to shift from its initial position (.5000) to .7013 as a gesture of limited support for the Franco-Italian compromise. They apparently were not asked to make this limited gesture.

Had Luxembourg made the gesture it might actually have weakened France's interests, setting the stage for a sharp swing toward Germany's position. Even if France and Italy both raised their level of effort on the issue to its highest possible amount—100—still that would not have been enough to forestall the sharp swing toward Germany's goal.[6] By maintain-ing their initial level of effort and by not seeking a gesture of support from Luxembourg, France was able to construct a coalition that created support for a compromise outcome between the French goal and the German goal. Recall that the dominant outcome was .5772. In this case, the expected utility assessments suggest that the controlling strategy available to France was very risky, yielding an improved outcome only if negotiations were artificially protracted and rendering an inferior outcome otherwise. To try sophisticated strategic maneuvers apparently would have been to dissipate resources in a risky, if not fruitless search. The French, wisely, avoided such a mistake.

Sixteen European Community issues were evaluated using the tools delineated here in an effort to link the abstract modeling process to real-world choices. Although the issues were given only scant, summary at-tention, still considerable detail regarding who was likely to make what proposal to whom has been discussed. Perhaps subsequent research will reveal the extent to which the perceptual component is consistent with what actually went on within the relevant negotiations. Information cur-rently available suggests considerable consistency between the individual bargaining strategies predicted by the model and actual choices in the EC.

6. The predicted outcome, given the Italo-French coalition combined with significant additional support from Luxembourg, would have shifted downward slightly to about .55. However, if the bargaining period could have been protracted, then the above coalition would have benefited France, with the fourth round of bargaining — if there were one — yielding an emission standard of .8631, suggesting great tolerance of pollutants. This, of course, is much closer to the original French position than the actual decision or than any of the simulated decisions under the constraint of a more limited time for discussions.

In any case, the predicted dominant outcome and the actual outcome appear closely related.

The controlling strategy has been explained as a tool for policymakers who wish to intervene in the policy process in order to improve circumstances from their perspective. Such a tool can be a powerful device for anticipating actions and reactions to alternative approaches to any policy problem. It can help utilize resources in the most efficient way, avoiding ill-fated investments of time and energy and promoting the identification of efficient opportunities for the use of one's time, energy, and influence. The dominant outcome model combined with the model of controlling strategies provides a fairly comprehensive analytic focus on the policy process and the attendant pulls and tugs of multilateral negotiations or confrontations.

Frans N. Stokman and Jan M. M. Van den Bos

7 The Exchange of Voting Positions in the EC Council

In this chapter we apply the exchange or logrolling model that was presented in chapter 5. The model makes it possible to simulate logrolling between actors over different decisions and to investigate the effects of logrolling on expected policy outcomes. Logrolling in collective decision making should be profitable for actors on opposite sides of the expected outcomes as long as both actors have voting power on their supply issue and positive saliences on their demand issue and when either the salience on the supply issue of the second actor is zero or the ratio of the saliences of the supply and demand issue for the first actor is smaller than the ratio of the demand and supply issue for the second actor. The latter condition includes the intuitive idea that actors can exchange voting positions if one actor is more interested in the first issue than in the second and the other actor is more interested in the second than in the first. The condition is, however, considerably broader than this intuitive idea.

The model restricts the exchange process to actors who are on opposite sides of the expected outcome on both issues because the exchange of voting positions is the sole possibility for a joint utility gain for these actors. Without this restriction, all kinds of strategic behavior has to be considered, much of which has already been presented in the expected utility model of Bueno de Mesquita in chapters 4 and 6.

If we apply the logrolling model at the national level, decision making within coalition governments seems to be a more profitable field than decision making in national parliaments. Important decisions in coalition governments require the consent of all coalition partners. Without an extensive logrolling process, the achievement of this consent would be very difficult. Within this context, it should be realized that coalition formation implies the addition of another phase to the decision-making process. As long as the coalition operates as a united block, the decision within the coalition is decisive because of its majority in parliament. As a consequence, logrolling among coalition partners does not occur when determining the expected outcome in parliament, but does occur when determining the expected outcome within the coalition (Bueno de Mesquita 1975; Laver and Schofield 1990; Laver and Shepsle 1990). Furthermore, coalition formation opens the possibility for parties to logroll even if they are located on the same side of the expected outcome of a decision within the whole parliament. What is decisive is the location of both parties on opposite sides of the expected outcome within the coalition. By negotiating the most important future decisions at the time of coalition formation, the time congruence required for the exchange process to take place is also fulfilled. At the national level, the logrolling model is therefore better suited for decision making within cabinets than within parliaments.

In contrast to national politics, no longstanding formal coalitions are formed at the level of the European Community. EC decision making, therefore, places a strong emphasis on consensus. The sustained opposition of one country endangers the whole process of integration and the total functioning of the EC. Consequently, integration requires a decision-making process that emphasizes a fair distribution of gains and losses over the EC countries. This is even more urgent due to the unanimity or qualified majority that is required for decisions to be made. As a result, EC decision making can be characterized as a long process in which decisions are searched for that are beneficial to all. In this process, logrolling can contribute considerably to efforts to achieve the required majority or unanimity because of the utility gains that both exchange partners expect to get through this mechanism. Logrolling can therefore be seen as an important element on issues in which all member states find parts that are essential for their own interests. In all these respects, EC decision making exhibits many similarities with decision making within national coalition governments, albeit with an even stronger impetus on unanimity building as no alternative coalitions are available. EC decision making is therefore a good case to test the validity of the exchange model.

The controversial decisions introduced in chapter 3 will be used to test and evaluate the exchange model. We shall also investigate how well the set of decisions fulfills the basic condition for exchange of voting positions, namely, that actors with opposed policy positions differentiate their interests on the issues. The better this condition is fulfilled, the more likely it is that there will be exchanges of voting positions and the more such exchanges contribute to a common optimum. Given the results of the exchange model, we shall show the main exchanges and how well the model predicts outcomes, as well as identifying the actors who profit most from the predicted exchanges.

The exchange process will be simulated under the two alternative voting procedures introduced in chapter 5. In the first one — the base model — we assume that decision making within EC councils is based solely on the formal voting weights of the member states. This implies that in unanimity decisions all member states have the same voting weights, whereas their voting weights in qualified majority decisions are derived from the qualified majority criterion and the voting weights of the member states in the council. In the second one — the compromise model — we assume that an informal decision-making procedure is used in the EC council in which the policy positions of larger and more interested member states are weighted more than those of smaller and less interested member states. These different decision rules not only predict different outcomes, but also different exchange rates among exchange partners.

Emission Limits For Automobile Exhaust Gases

On the car emission limits for exhaust gases, three issues were at stake in the EC council: the definition of emission standards, the date of introduction of the new standards, and the implementation of fiscal incentives.

The original proposal of the European Commission of May 1984 contained uniform emission limits for all car sizes and one date of introduction—1995 at the latest. Although not specifically regulated in the proposal, the German contemplation of tax incentives for cars meeting the stricter emission standards quickly became controversial. From the very beginning, three groups of EC member states could be distinguished: Germany, the Netherlands, and Denmark supported strong, early measures and high tax incentives; Italy, France, and the United Kingdom took opposite positions, namely, relatively soft standards at a later introduction date and no tax incentives; the other EC member states were either unclear in their policy positions or took intermediate policy positions.

Initially the possibilities for a compromise and an exchange of voting positions were very limited because of the high salience of the three issues for all opposing member states. This, however, was drastically changed when the measures were separated according to car weights and capacities. Because of the special concerns in Germany about large and medium-sized cars, the special focus of the United Kingdom on medium-sized cars, and the concern of France and Italy for the small car category, the interests of the opposing member states differed strongly as a function of the car size categories. By splitting the three issues into nine decisions, logrolling among the member states became possible and may have contributed to finding a solution that was acceptable to all. In this respect, these issues are an excellent example of how conflicting interests can be

Table 7.1
Predicted Outcomes of the Exchange Model on the Car Introduction Date and
Tax Incentive Decisions

	Base	Compromise	Base Exchange	Compromise Exchange	Actual
Years until Implementation					
Large cars	6.7	6.97	5.64 (.22)	4.54 (.29)	4.83
Medium cars	6.7	7.40	5.98 (.15)	8.06 (.09)	8.83
Small cars	6.7	8.26	8.39 (.14)	8.96 (.11)	8.83
Tax Incentive (in DM)					
Large cars	1,500	1,471	2,326 (30)	2,643	2,200
Medium cars	1,500	969	906 (147)	390 (168)	2,200
Small cars	1,500	881	1,201 (187)	278 (130)	750

resolved by the creation of new issues along underlying dimensions on which the interests of actors are differentiated.

On 21 March 1985, the EC council decided on the classification of cars, the definition of emission standards, the date of introduction of the new standards, and the level of tax incentives. Decisions on emission standards themselves were taken on 27 June 1985. This indicates that the final determination of the emission standards was made without the possibility of linking these issues to policy decisions regarding the introduction date and tax incentives. In our exchange simulation on the three issues, we therefore split the group of nine decisions into two groups, a group of six decisions on the introduction date and tax incentives for large, medium, and small cars, and a group of three decisions on the emission standards for the three categories of cars. The data that were used as input for the exchange model were presented in tables 3.4 (actor capabilities), 3.5 (saliences) and 3.6 (policy positions). Moreover, we refer to the discussion on the base model and the compromise model in chapter 5.

Table 7.1 contains the results of the exchange simulations on the six introduction date and tax incentive decisions. The first column gives the predicted outcomes under the base model, the mean policy position of the member states weighted according to their formal voting power. As we are dealing with decisions that require unanimity, all member states were treated as if they were of equal weight. The second column contains the predicted outcomes under the compromise model. In this prediction the policy positions of the member states are weighted by the product of their saliences and their number of votes in qualified majority voting (as given in tables 3.5 and 3.4). The compromise model reflects the notion that the larger and more salient EC members receive greater weight in the decision-making process. If we compare the predictions of these two models with the actual outcomes, as given in the last column of table 7.1, we see that the compromise model results in better predictions than the base model. For most decisions, the compromise model successfully predicts some of the differentiation over the three categories of cars. However, on introduction dates and tax incentives, the actual outcomes show much more differentiation than the compromise model was able to predict. The compromise model particularly fails to predict the introduction period for large cars and the tax incentives for large and medium cars.

The third column of table 7.1 contains the results of the exchange model under the base assumptions. These results should be connected with the first two columns of table 7.2, where the expected and realized utility gains of the exchanges under the base model are given for the whole system and for the individual actors.

The computer generated two hundred possible exchanges under the base model. One hundred simulation runs generated no less than eighty-seven solutions due to different possible exchanges with equal expected utility gains. None of the solutions was generated more than three times. Nevertheless, the predicted outcomes do not have very large standard deviations (given in table 7.1 in parentheses), except maybe for the tax incentives for medium and small cars. The predictions of the base exchange model are better than the base model for large and small cars but worse for the medium cars. In contrast to the actual outcome, the model predicts that the introduction date for the medium cars is close to that for the large cars. In a similar way, the model predicts that the tax incentives for medium cars would be on the same order of size as that for the small cars, whereas in actual fact the decision was taken to allow high tax incentives for both medium and large cars. The highest expected utility gain is obtained in six different solutions. Two of these solutions generate exactly the same outcomes, although they are based on different underlying exchanges. Together, these two were generated five times. The outcomes are 5.95, 5.88, and 8.38 for the introduction dates for large, medium, and small cars, respectively, and 2,360, 718, and 1,548 for the tax incentives by auto size. The two solutions generate only a moderate realized utility gain for all actors, namely, 0.093. For the other solutions with the highest expected utility gain, the realized utility gain is rather moderate too. The predicted outcomes do not fundamentally differ from those given above. The highest realized utility gain, no less than 0.312, is obtained in only one solution with the outcomes of 5.65, 5.88, 8.08 for the introduction dates, and 2,360, 789, and 1,023 for the tax incentives. It was generated only once and has an expected utility gain of 0.988.

Under the base model, Denmark has six possible exchanges with the

Table 7.2
Expected and Realized Utility Gains: Exchanges for the Car Introduction Date and Tax Incentive Decisions

	Base Model		Compromise Model		Actual Outcome Compared to	
	Expected	Realized	Expected	Realized	Base	Compromise
Belgium	0.000	−0.191	0.004	−0.271	−0.329	−0.295
Denmark	0.223	0.015	0.017	0.132	−0.400	−0.025
France	0.182	0.264	0.110	0.185	0.282	−0.416
Germany	0.179	0.274	0.210	0.424	0.192	0.631
Greece	0.013	−0.335	0.000	−0.403	−0.559	−0.452
Ireland	0.015	−0.048	0.000	−0.068	−0.082	−0.074
Italy	0.108	0.165	0.085	0.068	0.325	−0.261
Luxembourg	0.012	−0.002	0.001	0.026	−0.037	0.117
Netherlands	0.071	−0.032	0.101	0.151	−0.112	0.632
United Kingdom	0.167	0.058	0.138	0.053	0.148	−0.439
Utility gain	0.97 (0.01)	0.17 (0.05)	0.67 (0.01)	0.30 (0.07)	−0.571	−0.582
Percentage gain		1.22		2.14		

highest expected utility gain, four with France and two with the United Kingdom. All these exchanges result in an expected utility gain of 0.078 for both exchange partners. From the point of view of Denmark, these potential exchanges result from the fact that Denmark was given the highest possible salience (100) on all three introduction date decisions and no salience (0) on all three tax incentive decisions (see table 3.5). France and the United Kingdom take policy positions that are opposite to Denmark on all decisions. France opposes tax incentives for medium cars and small cars with the highest possible salience (100). For France, however, the introduction date on medium and large cars is of less importance (salience of 60). These specifications imply that Denmark can exchange its voting positions on small and medium car tax incentives against the voting positions of France on medium and large introduction dates, resulting in four possible exchanges with the same expected utility gain. The United Kingdom was given the highest possible salience only on medium car tax incentives (salience of 100), whereas — like France — it had lower salience on two introduction date decisions, namely, on small and large cars (saliences of 60). This implies that Denmark can potentially exchange its voting position on medium car tax incentives with the British voting positions on the small or large car introduction date decisions, resulting in two potential exchanges. As all these six exchanges have the same expected utility gain, the exchange model chooses one of them at random.

Different solutions are generated over a number of simulation runs, as we saw. To give one example, in one of these solutions Denmark exchanges its voting position on small car tax incentive against the French voting position on large car introduction date and its voting position on medium car tax incentive against the U.K. voting position on large car introduction date. Both exchanges result in voting positions for Denmark of zero tax incentives for small and medium cars (its policy position was DM 3,000), and in voting positions of France and the United Kingdom for an introduction date of 5.31 years for large cars (their policy positions were ten years). After these exchanges, Denmark takes the same voting positions as France and the United Kingdom on the two tax incentive decisions, but France and the United Kingdom are not willing to support fully the policy position of Denmark (four years) on the large car introduction date decision. Otherwise, Denmark would have had a greater utility gain than France and the United Kingdom.

As can be seen in the first two columns of table 7.2, the expected utility gain from all exchanges under the base model was 0.97. The realized gain was only 0.17 or 1.2 percent of the original utility loss under the base model (13.83) (see assumption 1 of chapter 5). Notwithstanding this small percentage, the exchanges have substantial effects on the predicted outcomes, as we have seen. France, Denmark, Germany, the United Kingdom, and Italy expected substantial gains from the exchanges under the base model, but it was, finally, Germany, France, the United Kingdom, and Italy that realized substantive utility gains, whereas the expected gain for Denmark vanished almost completely due to exchanges among other member states. The result was agreement on later introduction dates for small cars. This decision was very salient for Denmark (100), with Denmark supporting an introduction date of four years. The realized utility gain for Germany is due to the fact that Germany was able shift the expected outcomes on large cars to its side. Similarly, France, Italy, and to a lesser degree the United Kingdom were able to do the same, particularly for small cars. For the countries with positions in the middle, the logrolled outcomes are worse because they deviate more from their ideal positions. This was particularly the case for Greece and Belgium with utility losses of, respectively, −0.335 and −0.191 compared to the base prediction.

These results can be compared with those reached under the compromise model. These are given in the fourth column of table 7.1 and in the third and fourth column of table 7.2.

Under the compromise assumption, the exchange model generates eleven different solutions. In comparison to the exchanges under the base model, the outcomes for the introduction dates are much better, being really very close to the actual outcomes. The results for the tax incentive decisions are also more extreme than those predicted under the base model. Under the compromise exchange model, only the tax incentive decision for medium cars went in the wrong direction. The model now predicts more variation among the outcomes than actually was realized. The highest expected utility for all actors (0.676) is linked with the solution with the following outcomes: 4.70, 8.12, 9.12 for the introduction dates, and 2,643, 495, and 420 for the tax incentives. This solution is generated eleven times under two different sets of exchanges. The realized utility gain for this solution is, however, very bad, being only 0.164. Compare this with the solution with the highest realized utility of 0.378. The expected outcomes of this solution are very extreme, namely, 4.36, 8.04, and 8.84 for the introduction dates, and 2,642, 116, and 388 for the tax incentives. This Pareto optimal solution was obtained twenty-seven times under two sets of exchanges. The expected utility gain for all actors was 0.670.

The exchanges under the compromise model are quite different from those under the base model. The most profitable exchanges under the base model between Denmark, on the one hand, and France and the United Kingdom, on the other, disappear under the compromise model. In the decision rule under the compromise model, policy positions of member states are weighted by their votes under the qualified majority rule and salience. As Denmark had no salience on the tax incentive decisions, its policy positions on these decisions are not taken into account and exchanges with Denmark would not effect the outcomes on these decisions. The best possible exchange is now between Germany and France. Germany is prepared to support the French policy position of no tax incentives on small cars against the French support of DM 2,661 tax incentives on large cars. This exchange will give an expected utility gain of 0.071 to both parties. The next best exchange is a similar agreement between Germany and the United Kingdom on medium and large car tax incentives, in which the United Kingdom will support the German position on large cars against a voting position of Germany of DM 40 on medium cars (expected utility gain 0.065). In the third exchange, Germany exchanges its voting position on the small car introduction date with Italy's voting position on large car tax incentives. After this exchange, Germany supports the Italian policy position of ten years for small cars against a voting position for Italy of DM 1,096 on large car tax incentives. This results in an expected utility gain of 0.038 for both exchange partners. In the fourth exchange, Germany is again one of the partners, this time with the United Kingdom. They exchange voting positions on medium and large car introduction dates for an expected utility gain of 0.036. After this deal, the United Kingdom supports the German policy position that favors a four-year delay for large cars against a voting position for Germany of 8.39 years on medium cars. After this exchange, random choices have to be made between exchanges due to equal utility gains.

From this overview of exchanges it will be clear that Germany is the big winner under the compromise model. This can indeed be observed in the third and fourth columns of table 7.2, which contain the expected and realized utility gains over the six introduction date and tax incentive decisions under the compromise model for each actor. Germany expected to gain most from the exchanges, followed by the United Kingdom and France. Germany and France also realized more utility gain than the other countries. Both gained even more than they expected, in contrast to the United Kingdom that realized less gain than anticipated.

Under the compromise model, the expected overall utility gains from all exchanges (0.67) is lower than under the base model, but in terms of the realized utility gains the compromise exchange model is better (0.30 against 0.17). Nevertheless, this utility gain is only a moderate 2.1 percent in comparison to the original utility loss under the compromise model (13.82). It is therefore remarkable how strong the effects of the exchanges under the compromise model are, as can be observed in table 7.1.

Let us compare, finally, the utility gains associated with the actual outcome. In a similar way to our computation of utility gains from simulated solutions, we compute utility gains from the actual outcomes in comparison to a chosen null model. The last two columns of table 7.2 contain these utility gains, the first one compared to the base model without exchanges, the second one compared to the compromise model with-

Table 7.3
Predicted Outcomes of the Exchange Model on the Car Emission Standards
Decisions

	Base	Compromise	Base Exchange	Compromise Exchange	Actual
Emission limits					
Large cars	.71	.72	.57	.57	.78
Medium cars	.75	.80	.79	.85	.79
Small cars	.73	.80	.80	.88	.76

Note: The scale refers to tolerance for pollutants in emissions. Higher numbers
indicate greater tolerance.

out exchanges. The actual outcome is far from optimal, as its overall utility
gain is negative compared to both the base model (−0.571) and the compromise model (−0.582). By implication, the actual outcome is worse than
the logrolled solutions. The base model and the compromise model have,
however, fundamentally different distributions of the utility gains across
the individual actors. As a consequence, the utility gains and losses of the
actual outcome are distributed quite differently over the actors in comparison to the two null models. If we take the base model as the basis for
comparison, only the four largest countries realized utility gains, whereas
all other countries had to take losses. In comparison to the compromise
model, the actual outcome is very favorable for Germany and the Netherlands, with a gain of .63 for each. Except for Luxembourg, all other
member states take losses against the compromise model. This holds particularly for France and the United Kingdom. As such, the actual outcome
may serve as a case in which most parties can claim that they gained in
the negotiations as long as the basis for the comparison remains implicit.

We now turn to the three decisions in which the emission standards
were fixed on 27 June 1985. The predictions under the various models and
the actual outcomes are given in table 7.3. Again the compromise model
displays better predictions than the base model. In both exchange models,
we see that less strict emission standards for medium and small cars are
supported in exchange for stronger standards for large cars. Both models
predict an outcome of 0.57 for the emission standards for large cars. Under
the base model this results in a very good prediction on the medium car
issue (0.79 against actual outcome of 0.79), but a moderately too high
prediction on the small cars (0.80 against an actual outcome of 0.76). As
was the case with the tax incentive decisions, the compromise model
predicts results that are too extreme, namely, 0.85 for the medium and
0.88 for the small cars.

Under both models, Germany is a partner in the first two best exchanges. This is because the policy positions of Italy, France, and the United Kingdom are the same and opposite to Germany, whereas the order of the saliences for Germany is different from the order of the saliences for these other member states. The base exchange model generates four solutions, but all have the same predicted outcomes. Similarly, the compromise exchange model generates two solutions with the same predicted outcomes. Under the base model, Germany supports the French policy position on small car emission standards in return for a voting position of France of 0.578 on large cars (expected utility gain for both partners is 0.048). The next best exchange is between Germany and the United Kingdom. The United Kingdom supports the German policy position of 0.549 on large cars in exchange for a voting position by Germany of 0.885 on the medium car emission standard. After these two exchanges a number of other exchanges are realized, but they are partly determined by random choices among potential exchanges because of equal expected utility gains. Under the compromise model, the best exchange is between Germany and the United Kingdom (expected utility gain of 0.041); the United Kingdom supports the German position on large cars against a voting position of Germany of 0.82 on medium cars. In the next exchange under the compromise model, Germany supports the French position on small cars against a voting position of France of 0.701 on large cars. The above exchanges result in large expected and realized utility gains for Germany under both models, as can be seen in table 7.4.

The base model and the compromise model result in about the same total utility losses: 7.95 for the base model and 8.10 for the compromise model. The exchange model gives a utility gain of 2.4 percent under the base model and one of 1.5 percent under the compromise model. The last columns of table 7.4 show that the actual outcome is less efficient than the outcome of the base model, but that it is very close to the prediction of the compromise model. Compared to the compromise model, the largest loss is for Germany, but it is modest.

Summarizing the results on all car emission decisions, we conclude that the compromise model gives the best predictions for the car emission standards, whereas the exchange model gives the best predictions for the six decisions on the introduction date and on tax incentives. It is somewhat unclear whether on these latter issues the exchange model fits better in combination with the base model or the compromise model. For the introduction dates, the combination with the compromise model results in almost perfect predictions, whereas the predictions for the tax incentive decisions are better in combination with the base model. As the role that Germany played in the actual decision-making process corresponds more with the former combination (see chapter 3), we are inclined to prefer the combination with the compromise model. According to this exchange

Table 7.4
Expected and Realized Utility Gains: Exchanges for the Car Emission Standards Decisions

	Base Model		Compromise Model		Actual Outcome Compared to	
	Expected	Realized	Expected	Realized	Base	Compromise
Belgium	0.000	−0.076	0.000	−0.133	0.118	0.078
Denmark	0.023	0.044	0.019	0.055	−0.295	−0.019
France	0.055	0.040	0.050	0.032	0.214	−0.024
Germany	0.080	0.146	0.081	0.158	−0.236	−0.074
Greece	0.000	−0.143	0.000	−0.139	−0.071	0.087
Ireland	0.000	−0.000	0.000	−0.014	0.007	0.009
Italy	0.026	0.067	0.028	0.061	0.200	−0.036
Luxembourg	0.000	0.037	0.000	0.011	−0.031	−0.004
Netherlands	0.021	0.044	0.030	0.055	−0.295	−0.019
United Kingdom	0.042	0.036	0.052	0.034	0.225	−0.010
Utility gain	.247	0.193	0.260	0.121	−0.164	−0.013
Percentage gain	2.43		1.50			

model, however, Germany was willing to trade its position on both small and medium car tax incentives — as well as on small car introduction dates — for endorsement of its position on large car tax incentives. Given the identical nature of the fiscal measures decisions, this may not be a realistic assumption. It also seems possible that France, the United Kingdom, and Italy formed a coalition in their opposition to Germany, thereby thwarting the German efforts to maximize the large car tax incentive. Moreover, the exclusion of Denmark from our analysis due to the absence of salience may have disturbed the predicted outcome. Had Denmark been given a slight amount of salience, then exchanges from the base model would also have been possible.

The discussion of the actual decision-making process in chapter 3 also gives a possible explanation for the emission standards results. As Germany had already gained much on the first six decisions, it wanted to have the issue settled quickly. Only then would it become possible to apply the fiscal measures and to have the court proceedings instigated by the commission dropped. As a result, Germany chose not to press for better results on the emission standards. This interpretation was corroborated by the expert that furnished our data.

Germany was a partner in all exchanges with substantial utility gains, and this might well explain why the exchange model did not work. In addition, the fact that the actual outcome is very close to that of the compromise model seems to validate the application of this model in cases with limited opportunity for exchange of policy positions when interested parties hold opposite positions and where a decision needs to be reached quickly.

Maximum Permissible Radioactive Contamination

The data on the radioactive contamination issue contain only two decisions: the height of the levels of the emergency system and the decision to renew the post-Chernobyl regime. The latter decision is a pro or con decision, whereas the former is a composite score between 0 and 1, based on a combination of different radiation norms. The saliences and policy positions of the member states on these two decisions were given in table 3.7. The group of member states who are in favor of high permissible levels (France, the United Kingdom, Spain, and — at a somewhat lower level — Italy and Greece) oppose renewal of the post-Chernobyl regime, whereas the other group of member states combine policy positions for low permissible levels with a policy position in favor of renewal of the regime. This implies that exchanges can result both in lower height levels with more opposition against renewal and in higher levels with renewal. Whether exchanges go mainly in one direction depends on whether the actors in opposite camps have systematically different saliences on both

Table 7.5
Predicted Outcomes of Exchange Model on the Radioactive Contamination
Decisions

	Base	Compro-mise	Base Exchange	Compromise Exchange	Actual
Height level emergency	.469	.568	.560	.653	.356
Renewal post-Chernobyl	.143	.013	.440	.239	1 in favor

Note: Higher values indicate greater levels of acceptable radioactive
contaminants.

issues or not. If one camp would primarily be interested in the height of
the levels and the other in the renewal decision, many exchanges in the
same direction are possible. Table 3.7 shows that this is not the case.
Greece and Denmark exemplify a pair that could agree to an exchange
leading to a lower permissible level and stronger opposition to renewal.
France, on the one hand, and Luxembourg and the Netherlands, on the
other, could agree to an exchange in the opposite direction. It is not
immediately clear from the saliences in table 3.7 whether the balance of
the exchanges will go in one direction or the other. Let us therefore look
at the results of the exchange model.

A comparison of the first two columns in Table 7.5 with the fifth column
(the actual outcome) shows that the base model gives a better prediction
of the actual outcome than the compromise model. The compromise
model, which — given equal saliences — weights the policy position of
large member states more, predicts higher permissible levels and a lower
support for renewal of the post-Chernobyl regime than the base model.
The actual outcome, however, shows lower permissible levels in combination with sufficient support for the renewal of the post-Chernobyl regime. This result might also indicate that the saliences of the actors were
misspecified by the expert, but two other factors complicate these decisions. The major one is the dichotomous nature of the renewal decision.
As a pro or con decision, all intermediate predictions are interpreted as
an inclination or likelihood for a positive or negative decision. Both the
base and the compromise model predict positive outcomes, albeit the
compromise model with a lower likelihood. The second problem concerns
the decision rule. These two issues belong to the category of policy decisions taken by qualified majority. Therefore, extreme positions, supported
by a high salience, can be ignored without halting the decision-making
process.

The exchange model under the base assumption results in two possible solutions with only slightly different predicted outcomes. In the first solution, France supports the renewal of the post-Chernobyl regime in exchange for Dutch support for higher permissible radiation levels (.772 instead of .108). The second solution differs from the first only in the replacement of the Netherlands by Luxembourg in this exchange. In both cases the exchange results in an expected utility gain of 0.039 for each exchange partner. The second exchange goes in the opposite direction. In the second exchange, Greece supports the position of Denmark on the quantity decision (.250) against less support by Denmark for the extension of the post-Chernobyl regime (.122 instead of 1.0). This deal is supposed to give a utility gain of 0.030 to each partner. Of the remaining three exchanges, two go in the direction of more support for renewal and higher levels against one in the opposite direction. As a result, the prediction of the base exchange model is both for more support for renewal and higher levels of radiation.

The exchange model under the compromise assumption results in a unique solution. The first exchange is between France and the Netherlands (expected utility gain of 0.023), resulting in support for the renewal decision by France and a voting position of the Netherlands of .544 on the height decision. In the next exchange the United Kingdom is willing to support extension against support of Germany for a maximum radiation level of .530. In this exchange, the extension of the post-Chernobyl regime is the demand issue for Germany. In a later exchange of Germany with Greece, the extension issue is the supply issue for Germany, resulting in a new voting position of .961 on the extension issue. The model forbids an actor to cheat in the sense that he or she may not twice give away a voting position on an issue. Here we see that the model does not forbid an actor first to convince another actor to support his or her own position while giving away his or her own position in a later exchange.

Another interesting case involves two exchanges by Spain. In a first exchange with Luxembourg, Spain changes its extension position from -1.0 to $-.175$. In a later logroll, Ireland supports the original position of Spain on the extension issue (-1.0) in exchange for support from Spain for a maximum level of .718. Again, in one exchange, the extension issue is the supply issue for Spain and in the other the demand issue, as was the case with Germany. The only difference is the order in which the two exchanges occur. Although one may question whether this behavior is allowed in actual practice, we decided to allow it in our model as an unforeseen side effect. The last exchange not yet discussed is that between Denmark and Italy, with an expected utility gain of .009. Denmark votes against renewal of the post-Chernobyl regime in exchange for Italy's support for a height level of .558. The overall result of all exchanges is both a higher maximal radiation level and more support for the renewal issue (see table 7.5).

With exchanges in opposite directions it is not surprising that the expected utility gains under both the base and compromise assumptions were higher than the realized ones (see table 7.6). Moreover, no large gains and losses for individual actors result from these exchanges. More interesting are, therefore, the last two columns in table 7.6, in which the utility gains and losses of the actual outcomes are compared with the predicted outcomes under the base and compromise models. Evaluated against the unweighted sum of gains and losses of the individual actors, the actual outcomes are more profitable than the predicted ones under both the base and the compromise model. This is due to the fact that the larger members accepted losses (with the exception of Germany) and the smaller countries gained.

A possible explanation for the willingness of large member states to accept such losses lies in the protracted character of decision making on this particular issue. A final decision was taken only following nineteen months of discussion and a number of intermediate decisions. It may seem surprising that Germany, Luxembourg, Denmark, and Greece voted against the final proposal on the permissible radiation levels whereas the data in table 7.6 would indicate stronger opposition from France, Italy, Spain, and the United Kingdom. Public opinion and corresponding electoral implications may, however, explain much of this behavior. Furthermore, it should be noted that it was not clear which member states would vote against until the final vote.

If we consider the above results for the two radioactive contamination decisions, we may conclude that the exchange model did not improve things by much. The exchanges increased the support for renewal of the post-Chernobyl issue but indicated wrongly a tendency for higher radiation levels. However, we may seriously question the applicability of the exchange model for these two decisions because of the dichotomous nature of the renewal decision and the qualified majority rule.

Air Transport Liberalization

The liberalization of civil aviation within the EC was a long-debated issue with strongly opposed preferences among the EC member states. As described in chapter 3, the United Kingdom, the Netherlands, and Ireland were in favor of extensive liberalization, whereas a restrictive policy was advocated particularly by Greece, Spain, and Italy. The other EC member states took intermediate positions. Decision making in the EC council on the first phase of the liberalization of civil aviation concentrated on five decisions in which we find the two groups at opposite ends of the issue domains (see table 3.9 for the policy positions of all member states on the

Table 7.6
Expected and Realized Utility Gains: Exchanges on the Radioactive Contamination Decisions

	Base Model		Compromise Model		Actual Outcome Compared to	
	Expected	Realized	Expected	Realized	Base[a]	Compromise[a]
Belgium	0.000	0.024	0.000	0.009	0.053	0.123
Denmark	0.030	−0.011	0.009	−0.027	0.114	0.242
France	0.039	0.063	0.024	0.066	−0.121	−0.238
Germany	0.006	0.048	0.019	0.019	0.107	0.246
Greece	0.030	−0.139	0.003	−0.104	0.006	−0.034
Ireland	0.012	0.004	0.001	−0.010	0.079	0.170
Italy	0.012	−0.051	0.009	−0.028	−0.061	−0.149
Luxembourg	0.031	0.068	0.004	0.038	0.082	0.199
Netherlands	0.026	0.068	0.024	0.038	0.082	0.199
Portugal	0.000	0.005	0.000	−0.001	0.028	0.061
Spain	0.006	−0.009	0.005	0.002	−0.055	−0.122
United Kingdom	0.019	0.001	0.015	0.014	−0.085	−0.182
Utility gain	.211	0.072	0.113	0.017	0.228	0.514
Percentage gain	1.00		0.23			

[a]In the computations for the utility gains and losses of the actual outcomes, the outcome of the renewal post-Chernobyl decision is set to the predicted outcome of the base and compromise model, respectively. The decision is a dichotomous one, and the predictions of the base and compromise models can be considered as the likelihood of a positive outcome. If the actual outcome would have been set to one, the utility gains for the actual outcomes would have been larger than those given in the table, but it would be hard to compare them with the other columns in the table.

five issues). The first decision concerns the deep discount rate, meaning the minimum percentage of the normal rate that may be offered as discount. The policy positions of the member states varied between 30 percent (the liberal position) and 60 percent (the restrictive position). The second issue concerns the capacity fluctuation margin, the maximum percentage difference in seating capacity distribution to be allowed between any two countries. The United Kingdom and the Netherlands wanted no restrictions at all and, therefore, supported a capacity fluctuation margin of 100 percent, whereas the restrictive countries and France did not wish to permit a fluctuation margin at all (a policy position of 0). Two other issues deal with the liberalization of air transport between hub airports in one member state and regional airports in another. The third question, then, concerns the number of exemptions from the liberalization measures for hub-regional traffic that a country is allowed to make. The most liberal position is no exemptions (0), the most restrictive is a maximum of four exemptions (4). The fourth decision concerns the percentage of hub-regional traffic that would fall under the capacity fluctuation margin. The liberal policy position is that hub-regional traffic should not be included in the capacity fluctuation margin (0 percent), whereas the restrictive policy position is that all hub-regional traffic should be included (100 percent). Finally, the fifth issue is related to the question of whether or not the package would continue after its termination if the EC member states were unable to agree on further steps toward liberalization. The liberal policy position is that the package would not remain in force (the policy position of 1), whereas the restrictive position is that the package would continue (the policy position of -1). The fifth decision, therefore, is a dichotomous, pro or con decision, for which the applicability of the present version of the exchange model is questionable.

We may expect a number of possible exchanges when not only the policy positions of the member states are different but also their saliences are differently distributed over the issues. Inspection of table 3.8 instructs us that this is partly the case, but that the opposing groups have rather high saliences on all decisions, making exchanges less profitable than would otherwise have been the case. By way of example, an exchange is possible between Greece and the United Kingdom. The saliences of the United Kingdom and Greece on the deep discount rate and the hub-regional decisions are inversely ordered. Greece, with its many airports on the Greek islands, is more interested in the hub-regional issue than in the deep discount issue, whereas the United Kingdom is more interested in the deep discount issue.

The results of the different models and the actual outcomes on the five decisions are given in table 7.7. We can hardly find any differences between the expectations from the base model and the compromise model. The one exception concerns the inclusion of hub-regional traffic in the

Table 7.7
Predicted Outcomes of Exchange Model on the Air Transport Liberalization
Decisions

	Base	Compro-mise	Base Exchange	Compromise Exchange	Actual
Deep discount fare	48.75	48.11	44.24 (.15)	47.39	45
Capacity fluctuation margin	27.5	26.51	38.22 (.05)	29.86	13.33
Duration of liberalization	0	.09	.06	.59	1 in favor
Exemption hub-regional traffic	1.92	2.1	2.74 (.03)	3.7	4
Inclusion hub-regional traffic	55.83	62.45	67.51 (.14)	59.72	80

Note: Units are percentages, except for the exemption issue. On exemptions the
scale indicates increasing support for exemptions as the values get higher.

capacity margin, where the base model does better than the compromise
model. On four of the five issues, the base exchange model gives better
predictions than the base model. The compromise exchange model also
shows an improvement on four of the five issues in comparison with its
null model, the compromise model. It is difficult, however, to evaluate
which of the two exchange models does better.

The base exchange model generates two solutions with only marginally
different outcomes, the compromise exchange model generates only one
solution. As both models do rather well, let us, by way of illustration,
concentrate on the solution of the compromise exchange model. The first
exchange is between France and the United Kingdom (this is also the first
exchange under the base model). France offers to support the liberal position on the duration of the liberalization package against a voting position
of the United Kingdom for an 11.80-percent capacity fluctuation margin
(instead of 100 percent). They both expect to gain a utility of 0.021. The
next exchange is between Italy and the United Kingdom in which the
United Kingdom supports four exemptions against Italian support for the
longer duration (.996) with an expected utility gain of 0.011. In the next
step the United Kingdom again succeeds in an effort to exchange voting
positions, this time with Greece. Greece offers to trade its voting position
on deep discount reduction against the voting position of the United Kingdom on the inclusion of hub-regional traffic. The United Kingdom is prepared to vote for a 46.64-percent inclusion of hub-regional traffic (expected
utility gain of 0.011). Next, Greece offers a voting position of 100-percent

capacity fluctuation margin to the Netherlands in exchange for a voting position by the Netherlands in favor of 3.02 exemptions (expected utility gain of 0.009). Twelve more exchanges are expected to follow, which we do not describe here.

Again, as is the case with the two radioactive contamination decisions, the exchanges sometimes result in shifts in voting positions that counterbalance shifts of other countries in the opposite direction. We can therefore expect lower realized utility gains than projected by the exchange models. When we compare the expected utility gains of all actors with those realized through the exchanges (see table 7.8), we observe that the logrolled solutions are not even Pareto optimal: the actors lose utility by exchanging voting positions. Under the base exchange model only three actors finally gain some positive utility: Greece, Italy, and Portugal. Under the compromise exchange model only one other country can be added to this list: Denmark. All other actors lose utility. Compared to the base and compromise model, the actual outcome is also a bad solution in which only Greece, Italy, Portugal, and Spain gain utility at the expense of all other member states (particularly Belgium, which held the presidency of the council at the time the final decision was taken).

If we turn to the actual decision-making process as described in chapter 3, we find that the five decisions can best be regarded as a package deal. Although some aspects of the issue were discussed extensively at an early stage, no definitive decisions were taken then. Moreover, conditions that would apply to each decision were examined at later stages and adapted repeatedly. Final decision making occurred only during the June 24–25 meeting of the Transport Council, and even then the threat that the deal would fall apart was present, as the Dutch behavior during that meeting illustrates.

The exchange model indicates that the United Kingdom was willing to trade its position on capacity fluctuation and on the hub-regional decisions in order to obtain a greater reduction in the deep discount fare and a more liberal outcome on the duration of the first phase of liberalization. This behavior corresponds to a large extent with what actually happened, as the first important steps toward a conciliation of the liberal and restrictive positions were taken under the British presidency of the council. In addition, the exchanges predicted for Greece, Spain, and Denmark on the capacity fluctuation margin and on the deep discount rate for more exemptions seem probable. It is, therefore, not surprising that a model that combines the exchange of voting positions with the weighting of final positions according to size and salience arrives at good results.

Summarizing the results of the exchange model for the air transport liberalization issues, both exchange models give good results with a very slight lead for the compromise exchange model. These results are rather close to the actual outcomes. Moreover, they form a nice example of the

Table 7.8
Expected and Realized Utility Gains: Exchanges for the Five Air Transport Liberalization Decisions

	Base Model		Compromise Model		Actual Outcome Compared to	
	Expected	Realized	Expected	Realized	Base	Compromise
Belgium	0.012	−0.339	0.005	−0.391	−0.879	−0.765
Denmark	0.022	−0.114	0.013	0.159	−0.229	−0.168
France	0.026	−0.219	0.027	−0.437	−0.326	−0.345
Germany	0.007	−0.302	0.008	−0.072	−0.126	−0.158
Greece	0.025	0.092	0.026	0.105	0.326	0.263
Ireland	0.010	−0.233	0.004	−0.058	−0.269	−0.215
Italy	0.014	0.029	0.024	0.096	0.305	0.251
Luxembourg	0.020	−0.280	0.001	−0.346	−0.703	−0.618
Netherlands	0.046	−0.050	0.018	−0.058	−0.302	−0.242
Portugal	0.008	0.076	0.003	0.157	0.328	0.209
Spain	0.008	−0.236	0.003	−0.218	0.231	0.149
United Kingdom	0.048	−0.019	0.046	−0.046	−0.179	−0.208
Utility gain	.245	−1.65 (0.04)	0.179	−1.109	−1.823	−1.776

Note: We were unable to determine the percentage gain.

Pareto problem in which utility maximizing actors arrive at a collective solution that is suboptimal. Due to the (exogenous) pressure by the commission, the European Parliament, and the Court of Justice to liberalize, the actual outcome was also suboptimal. Consequently, the exchange process arrives at rather good predictions.

Conclusion

In this chapter the results of four models have been compared on sixteen decisions. The actual outcomes are used as a yardstick, and the base model is used as a kind of null model. In the base model the actors simply vote, without taking into account differences of saliences among the actors (as the compromise model does) and without using opportunities to exchange voting positions on the basis of differentiating saliences of actors over decisions (as the exchange model does). As a consequence, we expect that the three other models should do better than the base model in predicting actual outcomes.

A first way to evaluate the three other models is, therefore, to look at how often they arrive at a better prediction of the actual outcome than the base model. If we disregard the two dichotomous decisions (all models give the same predictions), the compromise model predicts more accurately for nine of the fourteen decisions, whereas both exchange models do so for eight of the fourteen decisions. Such a comparison is very rough, however, because it does not take into account how accurate the predictions are. In order to do so, we rescaled all decisions to the interval between zero and one hundred. Moreover, for discrete issues we rounded the predicted outcomes to the closest discrete alternative. This is the case with the two yes or no votes and the number of hub-regional exemptions that can take only the alternatives of 0, 1, 2, 3, or 4. Such a normalization makes it possible to compare the deviations of the predicted outcomes over all decisions.

In table 7.9 the predicted and actual outcomes on that common scale for all sixteen decisions are given. We are now able to compute correlations between the predictions of the models and the actual outcomes in order to determine the amount of variance explained by the different models. The correlation between the predictions of the base model and the actual outcomes is a moderate .51 for an explained variance of 26 percent. It is the only model that is not significantly correlated with the actual outcomes. The next best model is the compromise model with a correlation of .65 (explained variance of 42 percent). At the same level we find the base exchange model with a correlation of .67 with the actual outcome. The compromise exchange model clearly gives the best predictions with a correlation of .73 with the actual outcomes (explained variance of 53 percent). This last model is correlated with the actual outcome at a

Table 7.9
Normalized Predictions and Actual Outcomes for Sixteen Decisions

	Base	Compro-mise	Base Exchange	Compromise Exchange	Actual
Date of Introduction					
Large	45.00	49.52	27.37	8.96	13.88
Medium	45.00	56.63	33.07	67.59	80.55
Small	45.00	70.95	73.10	82.70	80.55
Tax Incentive					
Large	50.00	49.03	77.53	88.10	73.33
Medium	50.00	32.30	30.19	13.01	73.33
Small	50.00	29.37	40.02	9.26	25.00
Emission Standards					
Large	43.00	45.36	16.05	16.14	57.00
Medium	53.80	63.22	62.18	73.10	62.32
Small	45.85	59.68	60.22	75.59	52.96
Radiation Contamination					
Level emergency	41.00	52.00	51.09	61.40	28.44
Renewal	100.00	100.00	100.00	100.00	100.00
Air Transport Liberalization					
Deep discount	62.50	60.37	47.48	57.98	50.00
Capacity fluctuation	27.50	26.51	38.22	29.86	13.33
Duration	50.00	100.00	100.00	100.00	100.00
Hub-regional exemption	50.00	50.00	75.00	100.00	100.00
Hub-regional inclusion	55.83	62.45	67.51	59.72	80.00

.001 significance level, a difficult achievement with only sixteen issues. In a multiple regression on the actual outcome, the compromise exchange model is selected as the sole predictor because of the high correlations among the predictions of the three models.

On the basis of the above results we conclude that the exchange models improve the already good predictions of the compromise model. This holds particularly for the compromise exchange model. That this model does better than the base exchange model can be explained by the fact that the compromise model gives good predictions when no exchanges are possible, but such a solution can often be improved by exchanges. It should be realized, however, that the combination of the compromise model with the exchange model often results in a suppression of the working of the saliences. In the compromise model, countries without saliences are not taken into account, which seriously limits the possibilities for exchanges over issues. We saw this happen on the first six car-emission issues where many exchange possibilities for Denmark vanished under the compromise assumption because of its zero salience on the tax incentive issues.

The small number of decisions and the high correlations among the predictions of the models make a final judgment difficult to make. Inspection of the results for the three sets of issues analyzed reveals that no model consistently predicts the outcome better. While the exchange model produced the best results in the car introduction date, tax incentive, and air transport liberalization issues, it was inferior to the compromise model in the case of the emission standards issue and in the radioactive contamination issue. This indicates that logrolling only appears to occur under certain conditions. As stated in the previous sections, there are a number of reasons why logrolling is not applicable to the emission standards and radioactive contamination issues, such as interdependency among decisions, exogenous pressure to (finally) reach a decision, the exchange rate among decisions, dichotomous decisions, and the qualified majority decision rule. This points to the need to identify a matrix of dependency relations among decisions when using the exchange model.

The high correlation between the compromise model and the two exchange models (.78 and .73 with, respectively, the base exchange model and compromise exchange model) points to another interesting aspect. The compromise model shifts the predicted outcomes of issues in the direction of countries with high saliences at the expense of countries with low saliences. If more issues are at stake on which countries have opposing saliences, the same result is obtained under the exchange models, but on the basis of another mechanism — namely, exchanges of voting positions. This latter mechanism has the advantage over the compromise model that countries can feel more satisfied because of the mutual benefits these exchanges give them. The final result is not very different, however. This makes it difficult to test which model prevails above the other.

Jacek Kugler and John H. P. Williams

8 The Politics Surrounding the Creation of the EC Bank: The Last Stumbling Block to Integration

If European unification is to progress a critical and as yet not fully resolved issue is the establishment of a banking structure that will direct monetary flows in the Community. If one believes Jean Monnet's vision of the unification process, creating a supranational bank for the European Community is the cornerstone for future integration because it reflects the willingness of countries to give up economic sovereignty to centralized institutions in exchange for the benefits of a single market. Monnet's idea parallels Mitrany's and Haas's (1964) notions that the graduated creation of institutional arrangements, of which banking is a central element, will create functional economic linkages that constrain the range of political options available to individual nations.

Many scholars, however, argue that a central bank for the Community does not represent — nor will it lead to — eventual integration. Ver Loren van Themaat (1991), among others, argues that new institutions, including banking, represent an extension of international entities started in the 1960s and do not indicate a major change in the relationship between the nation-state and the Community (Coffey 1988; Cecchini 1988; Nicholson and East 1987). However, regardless of the bank's direct impact on integration, a European Community bank would have a life of its own and will alter substantively the political and economic contours of the European Community (DeCecco and Giovanni 1989a).

The analyses discussed here examine the political process members of the European Community engaged in with respect to methods for coordinating monetary policy among the constituent nations. This investigation started prior to the

Madrid summit in June 1989 and continued through the December 1991 meeting at Maastricht. These summits provided important opportunities for Community leaders to develop joint policies on the bank's prototype.

Biannual policy discussions regarding the future of the Community evolved from a 1989 report by the Committee for the Study of Economic and Monetary Union headed by Jacques Delors. The report proposed a three-staged advance to market integration and the development of a new monetary structure for the EC. The first stage adds or refines programs to which the members have largely agreed and expands on existing plans by bringing members who have delayed compliance with the 1992 goals into line with the majority. The latter two stages, the foci of controversy and the thrust of this chapter, involve the creation of a supranational bank to govern a common monetary policy for the Community. To accomplish these goals the EC had to amend the basic Community documents to permit a supranational institution to interfere in the domestic monetary policy of individual members and to apply sanctions against individual nations for noncompliance. We shall also examine the politics of these evaluations and show that the outcomes can be predicted quite accurately by carefully appraising the political preferences of Community members. We evaluate the stability of the emerging structures with an eye to seeing how these structures are likely to evolve.

The decision-making models described in chapters 4 and 5 were used to explore the behavior of actors at the relevant summits and to evaluate alternatives available to concerned actors. Data were gathered prior to the summits at Madrid, Strasbourg, and Maastricht to evaluate the type of international banking structure that would be supported at each EC summit. Prior to Maastricht — where convergence was anticipated — data were collected on five issues that could be used by national elites to adjust the banking structure in the EC. Data were always collected before each meeting to avoid contamination of projections with the real outcome or with ex post knowledge of the negotiating process. Starting with the Madrid summit we used results from prior analyses to point the way toward the future development of a general banking policy. Our intent was not simply to forecast the outcome of each summit, but also to delineate the political dynamics that shape the eventual structure of an EC bank. Thus, beyond assessing what the winning policy would be, we explored how these decisions would be reached, evaluated how compromises achieved earlier affected future decisions, and considered the policy exchanges made to achieve the final political compromise.

First Cut: The Global Context

The structure of a supranational bank for the European Community, one that could determine monetary control and currency fluctuations in Eu-

Table 8.1
Preferred Structure of the EC Bank

---

0 = National bank in each nation. Represents the existing status quo. National banks and treasury departments in each country manage economic and monetary policy. Governments may choose to follow joint guidelines but can overrule them as needed.

20 = No Community bank but creation of cross-national linkages between the various national and private banks involved in exchanging the Community currency (ECU). Individual governments would continue interventions to protecting their economies.

50 = International bank delayed until after market-led convergence among the Community economies is achieved. National banking to promote a market-driven process of change toward the single market that eventually leads to the creation of a Community bank with loose regulatory powers.

80 = International bank during government-led convergence of the Community's economies. Creation of an international board to govern banking, the equivalent of an international reserve board. Governments remove barriers and create links between the various national and private banks. National governments can still overrule the board, but the institutionalization of inter-governmental coordinating policy would make national intervention unlikely except in extreme crises.

90 = The Community's charter is amended but the international bank created would still lack absolute authority to override governmental protests. Compromise between an international and a supranational bank.

100 = Supranational bank during government-led convergence of the Community's economies. The supranational bank is created to aid and control the evolution of the single market. Monetary policies of individual governments can be overruled by the supranational bank board despite national protests.

---

rope, is not only of concern to the member states, but also is of interest to key actors outside the Community. Before the Madrid summit there was wide disagreement within the European Community and among members of GATT, EFTA, and the collapsing COMECON about the advisability of such an institution and the responsibility that a potential supranational bank should undertake. The issue continuum displayed in table 8.1 reflects the broad spectrum of political opinions.

Several interconnected elements are represented by the scale in table 8.1. At position fifty or above on the scale, a bank for the European Community is the desired outcome, although supporters of such an institution differ widely. For example, moving from position eighty to one hundred is equivalent to increasing the level of independence allowed to the board governing the EC bank. At position ninety, an independent board would manage the banking process, but its supranational power would be limited. At position one hundred, supranational responsibilities would be extended and the implementation process would be immediate.

Table 8.2 displays the initial positions and the predicted positions of each relevant actor at the end of negotiations (i.e., the final model iteration) at the Madrid and Strasbourg summits. These predictions are based on Bueno de Mesquita's expected utility model.

We started with a broad perspective. Twenty-nine political groups were analyzed including all EC members and important foreign or domestic actors. With the exception of the United Kingdom, EC members favored the creation of a bank to coordinate monetary functions. They differed on the final structure of such a bank. External actors included nonmember nation-states and international organizations that exert some influence on the Community's banking procedures. Unlike EC members, many foreign actors reserved judgment or opposed a bank for the EC. In particular, East Germany and other Eastern European nations were concerned with the financial implications an integrated banking community would have on their own prospects for future economic development. Internationally, the GATT, COMECON, and to a lesser extent the United States and Japan were also reluctant to see the creation of a centralized banking structure for EC.

Before the Madrid summit, we posited that domestic forces would affect the negotiation ability of EC representatives at these conferences.[1] We were aware, for instance, that in the United Kingdom concerted opposition to Prime Minister Thatcher's policy led by Chancellor Lawson, and later Chancellor Major, could reflect on the United Kingdom's ability to negotiate. Likewise, in Germany, Chancellor Kohl's position was strongly affected by the independent and powerful German Central Bank (Bundesbank). Moreover, during part of this period, Germany was undergoing the process of unification and was influenced by demands from East Germany and, later, by demands from East German political groups to accelerate unification.[2] In Denmark, despite Prime Minister Poul Schlue-

1. The importance of analyzing domestic politics to understand international developments is undeniable. For example, an analysis of decisions in the Kuwait crisis shows the importance of jointly considering domestic politics in Iraq and the United States and the international community to understand the eventual outcome (Kugler 1991).
2. Recall that the Madrid summit was held June-July of 1989. Soon thereafter — on 9 November 1989 — the Berlin wall fell, starting the transition to German unification. The meeting of Security and Cooperation in Europe dealing with Eastern European nations was held in Paris, 18 and 20 November, just prior to the Strasbourg summit held 8 and 9 December 1989. An inconclusive meeting on EC unification was held in Dublin, April, June 1990. German Unification officially occurred on 2 October 1990. Important working meetings on the EC followed in Rome, October 1990; Paris, November 1990; and Rome, December 1990. These built up to the key meeting on EC integration held in Maastricht in December 1991.

Table 8.2
Positions and Forecasts on Bank Structure at Madrid and Strasbourg

	Madrid		Strasbourg	
	T_0	T_1	T_0	T_1
EC Member Countries				
France	100	85.5	100	88.6
Delors	100	89.1	100	88.9
Germany	90	93.3	80	80.0
Spain	90	85.3	100	93.8
Greece	80	82.3	80	81.2
Ireland	80	82.3	65	67.1
Belgium	80	82.3	80	81.2
Portugal	80	82.3	80	81.2
Italy	65	74.3	85	82.8
Netherlands	65	70.2	80	80.0
Denmark	65	72.4	65	67.4
Luxembourg	65	66.6	65	70.4
United Kingdom	10	10.0	10	10.0
Domestic Actors				
Bundesbank	90	82.8	80	80.0
British opposition	80	82.3	50	60.5
EEC				
External Actors				
Austria	80	82.3	80	81.2
EFTA	100	96.8	90	88.4
Sweden	80	82.3	65	72.1
Switzerland	80	82.3	80	81.2
United States	50	50.0	50	50.0
Japan	20	20.0	20	50.6
Poland	100	96.8	90	88.4
Hungary	80	82.3	80	81.2
East Germany	20	50.3	20	52.6
Czechoslovakia	10	51.8	10	53.2
Bulgaria	10	10.0	10	10.0
Romania	0	45.3	0	46.6
GATT	30	50.9	30	46.8
COMECON	30	55.0	30	52.4
Forecast	80	82.2	80	79.9

ter's support for further unification, political opinion seemed severely divided over EC developments. In the Netherlands, political consensus on the EC seemed to be conditioned by a debate on the implementation of numerous social and economic reforms. This debate was expected to spill over and weaken consensus regarding the nature of an EC bank. In France, President François Mitterrand seemingly did not face organized opposition other than on agricultural issues.

To guard against domestic distortions in our analysis, we analyzed preliminary evaluations of domestic data on a country-by-country basis. Countries considered included England, Germany, the Netherlands, France, and Italy. The results were surprising. Only in the United Kingdom and Germany did we find that domestic actors could affect the ability of elites to negotiate at the summits. Domestic divisions in other EC countries did not substantially influence the negotiation postures of their representatives at the summits. Domestic factions would, however, become important after a treaty emerged. At that juncture, of course, the proposed treaty would have to be confirmed by the domestic process appropriate to each member state.

Because of the effects we observed in our country-by-country assessments, we introduced only two domestic actors directly into the overall analysis. The British opposition that reflected Conservative challenges to Mrs. Thatcher and the German Bundesbank that could challenge the actions of the German government emerged as sufficiently important to be considered in the broader EC context. This decision resulted in a bare sketch of domestic interactions in these two countries but limited our ability to speak about powerful domestic factions within other EC member nation. Our model certainly would have permitted more detailed analyses, but we presumed that substantive consensus on negotiations would hold until a treaty was signed.

The extended forecast outlined in table 8.2 suggests that EC members were strongly in favor of an international bank and that such an entity could be formed.[3] In figure 8.1 we consider this forecast outcome from the perspective of a compromise agreement (position coincides with that of Belgium). In this figure and in all subsequent figures that reflect the political dynamics surrounding a forecast or an actor, the initial position of each actor is noted. The arrow denotes changes anticipated by the model after each iteration resulting from political adjustments in response to political pressures. An examination of the political dynamics in figure 8.1 indicates that no agreement would emerge from Madrid.

Figure 8.1 complements the results in table 8.2 but reveals a different story than one would arrive at by simply looking at the original forecast.

3.   The extended forecast arises in the expected utility model after prolonged negotiations, meaning one iteration beyond the normal stopping rule for that model.

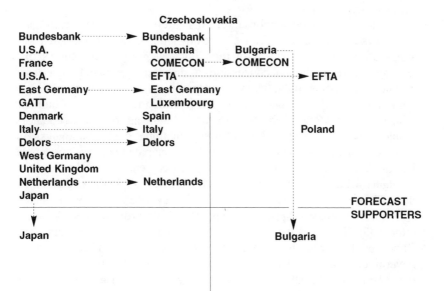

CHALLENGER

8.1: Evolution of Political Competition over Banking: Joint Perceptions at the Madrid Summit

The European Community and most non-EC actors apparently were not willing to make the concessions required to produce a treaty at Madrid. Consequently, agreement on a bank for Europe was virtually impossible. Let us move step-by-step through the logic. As noted in table 8.2 France and Delors were willing to make serious concessions and would accept a bank structure far less extreme than their initial position. Likewise, Germany would accept a stronger bank structure than originally advocated. Indeed, all EC actors but the United Kingdom were expected to make concessions during the political debate in Madrid. The United Kingdom was expected to be the one hold-out to compromise. Thus, table 8.2 shows that convergence on a solution is limited, and figure 8.1 informs us that the underlying politics were not supportive of a stable, sustainable compromise agreement.

The key actors who supported reforms differed on the specifics. Figure 8.1 shows that Delors and France were unwilling to yield further on a true supranational bank. Analysis of their political perspectives shows that they anticipated additional concessions as discussions evolved. To a lesser extent Denmark and Italy, who wanted to construct a weaker international bank, also anticipated concessions. Thus, while the estimates of political adjustments at Madrid reported in table 8.2 indicate that EC negotiators would move toward some kind of a supranational bank, the analysis of political dynamics in figure 8.1 shows that anticipated concessions would fall far short of those required for a stable agreement.

Figure 8.1 and table 8.2 disclose further particulars. In the United Kingdom, Prime Minister Thatcher opposed the compromise while many within her own party supported the proposed compromise. This discloses internal tensions that had to be resolved domestically. In Germany, the Bundesbank moved away from a supranational entity while the German government moved toward a strict bank arrangement, creating a breach between them. Moreover, East Germany, soon to enter into negotiations over unification, opposed the creation of a banking structure for Europe. Again a compromise position would have to emerge from the domestic German environment before a uniform position could be held. Finally (with the exception of Hungary and Poland), Eastern European nations and COMECON, dominated by the Soviet Union, apparently opposed further consolidation of EC rules. Their actions could lead to strained relations among EC members.

In sum, before the Madrid summit, the model accurately predicted that an agreement on an EC supranational bank would fail to materialize, recognized that EC members favored some form of international banking structure, and detected movement toward agreement. Only the United Kingdom among the EC actors continued to hold out. The remaining EC members were expected to explore the matter further. These gross expectations were fulfilled. After Madrid, the Community empowered a new group with the task of reaching a political solution acceptable to the whole community (Buchan, Stephens, and Dawson 1989). Far more important than the accurate forecast, the model provided information on the future development of the banking debate.

Table 8.2 shows that despite the defeat of banking proposals at Madrid, EC reformers in the Community had the upper hand and could converge on a reform position not far away from the compromise achieved at Madrid. The model identified several areas that required compromise prior to agreement. European Community reformers had to (1) overcome the strong opposition by the United Kingdom, (2) create a consensus in Germany for an EC banking structure, and (3) separate the EC unification process from the consequences of the breakup of the Soviet Empire.

Consider first the relations of the United Kingdom to the EC. Table 8.2 shows that the United Kingdom was the single EC member opposed to the same kind of banking structure for Europe. Figure 8.1 shows that because of this isolation, the United Kingdom was in a direct contest with other EC members. Figure 8.1 further discloses that Mrs. Thatcher was willing to risk a political confrontation with the British opposition that supported EC reform rather than seek a compromise solution. A more detailed look at this situation from the perspective of the British government, analyzed in 1990, disclosed that if Mrs. Thatcher continued to be intransigent, she would face strong domestic opposition that would threaten her government (Kugler and Williams 1990). Analysis of dynamics from the German and French perspective further show that these actors were reluctant to confront Prime Minister Thatcher (Kugler and Williams 1990).

The second issue identified was the critical role of Germany. Early analysis suggested that this country would be the key actor because it had political leverage with both the United Kingdom and France (Kugler and Williams 1990). After Madrid, Bonn moderated its position regarding an international bank. This change in position is not captured by the model. As table 8.2 indicates, Germany was expected to be accommodating toward those who favored a stronger bank structure. However, the data updated prior to Strasbourg indicate that Germany did not favor a stronger bank, but instead chose to support an international bank empowered to manage inflation but limited in other areas. This was a substantive turnaround from the previous German government position, which — along with the German Central Bank — advocated a stronger supranational institution. In our earlier effort (Kugler and Williams 1990), we speculated that Germany moved away from the expected outcome because the government was attempting to forge a coalition on this issue with the smaller EC countries and with the United Kingdom. Such a coalition could force France and Delors to comply (Kugler and Williams 1990). Reality proved to be different. France reverted to a position in support of a very strong bank. Germany moved in the other direction. On reflection, this error may be linked to the position of East Germany. When the Berlin wall fell on 9 November, a month before the Strasbourg summit, the transition toward German unification was well under way. It seems likely that the German government position was determined to a much larger degree by the domestic interaction between East Germany, West Germany, and the Bundesbank than we had anticipated. However, we did not detect this possibility, and we did not include it in our analysis, thereby failing to anticipate the German accommodation toward the EC that emerged prior to Strasbourg.

An unexpected result of figure 8.1 is that our analysis suggests that most East Europeans were prepared to challenge the policies of the major EC member states, thereby tying up discussions on EC integration. Eastern European nations could not stop the progress of the EC, but they could complicate progress toward political and economic integration. Table 8.1 shows that East Germany, COMECON — representing interests of the Soviet Union — Czechoslovakia, Bulgaria, and Romania wished to thwart advances on integration. We anticipated that these countries were concerned not with a single bank for Europe but with the consequences of an EC bank for funding their recovery programs. For this reason they wished the relationship between Eastern Europe and the EC to be clarified.

The predicted confrontation did in fact materialize. Before the Strasbourg summit, France used its role as acting president of the EC to call a special session on security and cooperation in Eastern Europe. The Paris conference formally established a European Bank for Reconstruction and Development (EBRD) and disassociated this reform from the integration of banking in the EC. Subsequently, Eastern European actors lost much of their relevance. Thus, as the model anticipated, the EC had to deal specifically with East European issues. In Paris, the Community members did, thereby removing such concerns from the Strasbourg agenda.

We continued to monitor the issues tied to banking reforms two months before the Strasbourg summit and one month before the fall of the Berlin wall. Table 8.2 shows that the political compromises worked out after the Madrid summit and before the meetings in Strasbourg had little effect on the expected utility forecast. The policy outcome forecast for the Strasbourg summit is almost identical to that derived at the Madrid summit. However, figure 8.2 shows that the political dynamics of the situation were altered dramatically between these two crucial meetings.

Analysis of the political dynamics at the Strasbourg summit shows a very different picture from that at Madrid. The forecast position now occupied by Germany emerges as the dominant outcome around which a consensus can be forged. Unlike Madrid, the EC bank structure proposed by Germany was no longer openly contested by Eastern European nations. They gave in to the demands of the EC. Only East Germany, undergoing the process of unification, was expected by the model logic to hold out for additional concessions. Other external actors like EFTA were predicted either to yield or — like GATT, the United States, and Japan — to be unwilling to oppose openly an EC bank structure.

Figure 8.2 shows fundamental progress toward the creation of an EC bank from Madrid to Strasbourg. Because of the convergence of external actors on the forecast position (see table 8.2), the model insinuates that there is no need to continue to survey the international environment in order to understand the development of a banking structure for the EC.

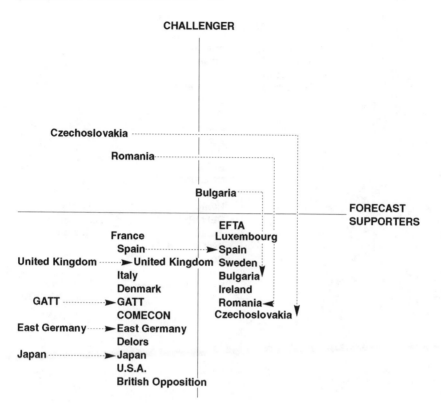

Note: See figure 8.1.

8.2: Evolution of Political Competition over Banking: Joint Perceptions at the Strasbourg Summit

While the impact of GATT, Japan, the United States, and COMECON is still felt, none of these actors are now willing to contest EC decisions openly. Moreover, the compromise outcome appears to have been gathering force within the EC.

Contrasting the results of figures 8.1 and 8.2 is quite revealing. Figure 8.1 shows that at Madrid the forecast position was fully supported by Belgium, Portugal, and Greece, while being opposed by all other EC members. At Strasbourg, as reflected in figure 8.2, the forecast, anchored by Germany, is fully supported by the Netherlands, Belgium, and Greece but — most important — was not expected to be opposed successfully by

CHALLENGERS

Germany	France	
Netherlands	Spain	
U.S.A.	Italy	
Bundesbank	Belgium	
	Luxembourg	
	Greece	
	Denmark	
	Ireland	
	GATT	
	EFTA	
	COMECON	
	Poland	
	Hungary	Portugal
	DELORS	East Germany
	Japan	Romania
	Switzerland	
	Austria	
	Sweden	
	British Opposition	

UNITED KINGDOM

COMPROMISE: Czechoslovakia, Bulgaria

8.3: British Perception of Political Competition over Banking at the Strasbourg Summit: Britain vs. Each Challenger

others. The United Kingdom perceived an opportunity for an effective challenge but was not be able to mount it successfully. For this reason, while we still did not anticipate an agreement at Strasbourg, EC actors were eventually expected to forge an agreement around the new German position that would define the form of an EC bank.

The United Kingdom entered Strasbourg embattled. As shown in figure 8.3, Prime Minister Thatcher continued to perceive the British position as both isolated and beleaguered. According to the expected utility assessment at the time, Thatcher believed that other members of the Community were vehemently opposed to her political stand and perceived that there was opposition from John Major. British isolation, however, apparently was not as profound as she believed. All EC nations that favored banking reform remained, according to our analysis, unwilling to challenge the United Kingdom's approach. Instead, the status quo with the United

Kingdom was expected to prevail as all EC actors perceived the United Kingdom to be in a position to stop them.

A break between EC members and the United Kingdom apparently was unlikely at Strasbourg. EC members preferred to negotiate further. Concurrently, the model discloses that a serious domestic conflict was erupting in the United Kingdom over the issue of banking reform. Within the logic of the expected utility model, the British opposition, unlike other EC members, seemed to believe that Mrs. Thatcher's government must be challenged (British opposition expected conflictual relations). Since both sides perceived that a political confrontation was to their advantage, the analysis strongly suggests that Mrs. Thatcher would welcome such a development. Here the model captured real dynamics quite effectively. While Prime Minister Thatcher continued her opposition to reform, the chancellor of the exchequer, Nigel Lawson resigned in October 1989 over a policy dispute centered on the EC. His replacement, John Major, adopted a compromise position that fell short of Mr. Lawson's demands but enjoyed strong and growing support within the Conservative party and the British business community. This is the position of the British opposition that challenged the prime minister's reluctance to compromise. The model indicates that the dissenting parties, summarized as British opposition, were willing to challenge Mrs. Thatcher over this key issue and suggests that Prime Minister Thatcher must give ground. Of course, ultimately she did, losing the leadership of the Conservative party and the government to John Major.

The lack of a British willingness to compromise at Strasbourg was not expected to be without consequences. As indicated in figure 8.2, Germany had staked out the pivotal position on the structure of an EC bank. Germany could compromise with either the hard stance of France that supported a more comprehensive bank, or with the position of the British opposition that wished to dilute the bank's strength. A simulation of a compromise with the United Kingdom and Germany in figure 8.4 shows that had Mrs. Thatcher adopted the position advocated by her party and her chancellor, she could have eliminated the festering domestic controversy within the United Kingdom while creating a stable but very loose banking arrangement. This outcome was more acceptable to the United Kingdom than what eventuated and would have considerably improved the United Kingdom's position relative to the rest of the Community. Developments in this direction had taken hold before Strasbourg. Pro-Europe Tories led by Chancellor Major had seemingly worked out a settlement that they hoped would provide a united front for British policy. It was reported that Mrs. Thatcher would abandon her long-held opposition to an EC bank and would adopt instead the more flexible position of Mr. Major (*Financial Times*, 5 Dec. 1989, p. 3). Figure 8.4 shows a simulation of this adjustment in the British position.

SIMULATION: Position of Germany, the Bundesbank, and the
Netherlands set at a position that weakens the
international bank, while Britain assumes the
position promoted by the chancellor of the
exchequer (Position: Germany, Bundesbank,
and the Netherlands: 75; United Kingdom: 50)

FORECAST: Position 75

CHALLENGERS

		GERMANY
United Kingdom	Belgium
France	Luxembourg
Spain	Portugal
Italy	Greece
GATT	Denmark
EFTA	Ireland
COMECON	Romania
East Germany	Czechoslovakia
U.S.A.	Hungary
Poland	Bulgaria
DELORS	Switzerland
Japan	Austria
British Opposition	Sweden

COMPROMISE: Netherlands, Bundesbank

8.4: Perception of Political Competition over Banking at the Strasbourg Summit
Assuming Britain and Germany Seek a Compromise Position

The simulation in figure 8.4, performed prior to Strasbourg, suggests a
scenario under which a stable outcome was feasible. Germany and the
United Kingdom, supported by the Netherlands, would control the outcome under this scenario, giving the British a better result than was actually realized. By adopting a hard stand, Prime Minister Thatcher's
United Kingdom bypassed the opportunity to pursue a stable compromise
with Germany that would have reduced the potential power of the international bank relative to the individual governments.

Thatcher set aside the compromise position worked out with Chancel-

Table 8.3
Contrast of Global and EC Extended Forecast during Three Summits

	Madrid	Strasbourg	Maastricht
Global forecast	82	80	85
EC forecast	86	80	79
Global minus EC forecast	−4	0	6

lor Major and argued instead in favor of her earlier position, which suggests that the compromise was a fall-back rather than an opening argument (Buchan, Mauthner, and Davidson 1989; Mauthner, Buchan, and Cassell, 1989). The result was British isolation at Strasbourg and domestic criticism at home. The long-anticipated conflict within the United Kingdom materialized and Mrs. Thatcher lost power. From the British perspective, the model indicates this was a lost opportunity. By pursuing a policy of isolation, the United Kingdom lost the chance to become an important partner in the future of Europe and instead assumed the role of a critic. Germany and France would negotiate an agreement at Maastricht that produced an outcome far less desirable for the United Kingdom, although the logic of the expected utility model led us to anticipate that the outcome would be mired in controversy.[4]

Second Cut: EC Outlook on the Summits and Banking

A more detailed look at the bargaining process among the EC nations will enable us to understand European negotiations better. In reality, the final agreement at Maastricht was affected by prospective political exchanges along five dimensions, each of which was critical to the establishment of an EC bank. A study of these aspects provides additional insights into the decision-making process.

Simplification has its costs. When the number of actors under consideration is restricted to EC members, only diplomatic interplays among EC actors are registered. Neither domestic pressures nor the effects of compromises with external actors are taken into account. Table 8.3 provides

4. A second simulation evaluating a compromise between France and Germany suggested a feasible agreement slightly beyond the preferred position of Germany (position 85). Unlike the German-British agreement, this simulated compromise between France and Germany would have been resisted by Denmark. This was the eventual outcome at Maastricht. With hindsight, one must wonder whether the defeat of the treaty by Danish voters following Maastricht could have been avoided by decisive and early British action. We cannot, however, rerun history to assess the validity of this conjecture.

Table 8.4
Estimated Positions on Bank Structure of EC Nations at
Maastricht

	T_0	T_1	T_2
Delors	100.0	100.0	100.0
France	100.0	93.6	93.6
Spain	100.0	95.1	95.1
Germany	80.0	80.0	80.0
Greece	80.0	81.3	80.0
Ireland	60.0	69.0	80.0
Belgium	80.0	81.3	80.0
Portugal	80.0	81.3	80.0
Italy	85.0	83.7	80.0
Netherlands	80.0	80.0	80.0
Luxembourg	80.0	81.3	80.0
Denmark	50.0	66.1	66.1
United Kingdom	50.0	64.9	64.9

a gross assessment of the contrasts between the global forecast obtained
using the full array of actors and the EC forecasts obtained from the more
limited sample across all three summits.

Table 8.3 shows that the differences in forecasts are not substantial,
but they are meaningful. After the Madrid summit, the result based on
interactions among only EC members suggests that a potential compromise would have favored the French and German position far more than
the British compromise. At Strasbourg, the two models (that is, with EC
actors only and with EC and external actors) coincide, indicating that the
German position would dominate. Finally, at Maastricht the global forecast suggests a compromise between France and Germany while the EC
perspective suggests a German-British compromise. We now know that
the actual outcome of Maastricht coincides with the global forecast. However, we are also aware that various compromises had to be made to
achieve the final outcome. We wish to investigate whether we can match
the final result by using the exchange models.

Table 8.4 reports the results in the post-Maastricht period. It discloses
that at Maastricht the German coalition was powerful but still had to reach
agreement with the United Kingdom and Denmark, on the one hand, and
with Delors, Spain, and France, on the other. The United Kingdom's
isolation at Madrid and Strasbourg altered its position supporting the con-

cept of an EC Bank. During the Maastricht negotiations, the United Kingdom was expected to be more conciliatory than Denmark. France and
Spain were expected to weaken demands for an independent EC bank but
would not make concessions that assured full consensus with the majority.
Thus, Germany holds the pivotal position at Maastricht. Other nations are
predicted to make more subtle adjustments that drive the political debate
from confrontation to compromise.

Post-Maastricht reports suggest that Germany reached a compromise
with France and Delors on a more highly centralized EC bank. The model
does not pick up this last move. Instead it suggests that a viable treaty
could emerge at a consensual position just six points short on our scale of
the ultimate outcome.

Exploring the political dynamics of the Maastricht summit will help us
to understand the consequences of these changes. An agreement is possible at the forecast because, with the limited convergence of Spain and
France to the German position, and the reduction of differences with the
United Kingdom and Denmark, conflict over the eventual bank structure
is reduced. This can be seen in figure 8.5.

The summary of political dynamics at Maastricht suggests that to
achieve the agreement, serious adjustments in policy were required. Denmark, the least satisfied of all nations with the treaty prospects, abandons
open opposition only during the negotiations. The United Kingdom, which
is predicted to hold out initially, eventually acquiesces to the terms of the
agreement but does not feel bound to support them. Likewise, France and
Spain are very reluctant to sign this specific agreement. However, Ireland
and Italy join other members of the EC community and fully support the
treaty according to the assessments that emerge from the model.

In retrospect we know that the EC forecast underestimated the level
of control that would be granted to the EC bank at Maastricht. To assess
more accurately the level of support or opposition to the eventual treaty,
a simulation was run where Germany adopts the actual position that
emerged from the negotiations. The forecast, as expected, follows Germany's adjustment. Figure 8.6 displays the results.

This shift in the German position produces a result less stable than that
in figure 8.5 above. Denmark remains dissatisfied by the strong bank
structure. Ireland does not join the rest of the EC in support of the new
EC bank. Italy and other smaller members of the European Community
recognize their inability to affect the outcome, but they do not join the
new agreement voluntarily, as they would have done had the bank been
less rigid in structure. Finally, Delors seems to prefers prolonging the
negotiations rather than acquiescing at Maastricht.

At Maastricht, Germany made extensive concessions to France. In the
long run, the resulting agreement was far more vulnerable and less sustainable politically than a slightly weaker arrangement would have been.

FORECAST: Position 80

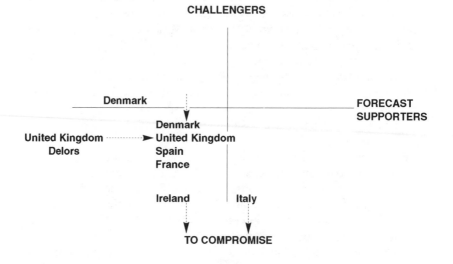

Note: See figure 8.1.

8.5: Political Competition over Banking at the Maastricht Summit: Movement from Base to Extended Forecast

Whatever the economic merits or limitations of the proposed relatively independent EC bank, our political analysis suggests that a weaker banking structure would have been far more agreeable to all EC parties and would have generated far less political opposition. If these evaluations are correct, the marginal economic gains suggested by the EC bank's independence fostered the political acrimony that followed the signing of the Maastricht treaty.

Using the EC perspective alone, we underestimated the ultimate outcome at Maastricht. In the following section we shall model the prospective concessions among EC members across issues using the exchange models. We are interested in determining whether logrolling across issues might have produced shifts in the positions of dissatisfied parties that would lead to the policy positions embedded in the treaty.

Effects of Political Exchanges on the EC Bank Structure

The treaty signed at Maastricht represents a position six percentage points removed from the position forecast by the expected utility approach. Why

SIMULATION: **Germany adopts position 85 at the Maastricht Summit**

FORECAST: **Position 85 to 84 concurrent with ultimate outcome**

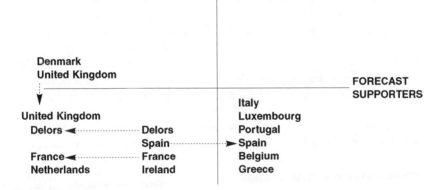

COMPROMISE: None

Note: See figure 8.1.

8.6: Simulated Political Competition over Banking at the Maastricht Summit If Germany Adopts the Ultimate Outcome: Movement from Base to Extended Forecast

the disparity? Prior analysis suggests that several factors may have caused this small amount of error.

One reason could be oversimplification. By including only EC members, we may have underestimated the residual impact of foreign actors. The global forecast outlined in figure 8.3 correctly anticipated the position reached at Maastricht (position 85). This argument is implausible, however, because we also show in the analysis of the political dynamics that concerns with Eastern European nations were removed from the integration debate at the Paris meeting prior to the Strasbourg summit. Moreover, other foreign actors alone do not affect the results materially. Thus, despite the accurate forecast from the global model, this outcome is not consistent with the political realities our model describes for Europe and — although accurate — may simply be coincidental.

Second, internal explanations may account for this discrepancy. We can show that Germany anticipated little opposition from other EC actors whether the Germans compromised with the United Kingdom or France (adopt 75, 80, or 85) to gain the final decision. Perhaps this German misperception led to too many concessions to the French–Delors position, inadvertently generating far more dissension within the EC than was necessary. This explanation is plausible, but it is driven by hindsight rather than by foresight. The persuasive alternative explanation we decided to explore before Maastricht was whether some nations made side deals to arrive at the Maastricht treaty. Such tradeoffs would have been missed in our previous analysis based on a single dimension across time.

Before the Maastricht summit, data were collected on five banking issues that potentiality could be used to make substantive policy exchanges among EC nations, altering the eventual outcome. All are in the same domain of banking but allow individual nations to gain particular concessions from other EC members on specific components of banking policy.

We anticipated that compromises along five issues could alter the overall agreement. The *time* dimension considers how long each member country wants to delay before allowing the EC central bank to control monetary matters. At one extreme, full institutionalization by 1992 was demanded, and at the other extreme an undefined future date was proposed. The second dimension — *control* — assessed who would be responsible for the EC bank's policy. Options ranged from a board of finance ministers responsible to individual governments, to an independent Euro-bank board that would set and execute policy with little or no governmental interference. The issue of *scope* addressed the spectrum of proposed responsibilities assigned to the EC bank. At one extreme the EC bank would have no capacity to intervene directly to control inflation, while at the opposite extreme the EC bank would have wide latitude to interfere in domestic economies to control inflation. The fourth is *harmony* and concerns the coordination of economic tasks. Alternatives range from allowing the market place to determine the major conditions, to managing the EC merger through existing institutions. Finally, the *ECU* dimension assesses the levels of fluctuations that would be allowed for this currency. Alternatives ranged from managing fluctuations through the European Monetary System or fixing exchange rates against all currencies. (See the appendix for further details on the scales.)

The hypothesis we explore is whether the exchange models improve the accuracy of the EC forecast. If the analyses indicate that the forecast shifts from 80 to 85 by employing an exchange strategy, then we could argue that the real negotiations at Maastricht involved complex bargaining among the member states of the sort that would have been missed by the single-dimensional analysis conducted thus far. Consider the results in table 8.5

Table 8.5 displays the expected utility outcomes and the forecasts from the exchange and compromise models. The individual dimension section shows the forecasts and estimates the accuracy of the expected utility assessment for each dimension related to the EC bank structure. The EC bank structure refers directly to the institutional developments we have followed throughout this chapter.

Consider first the individual dimensions. Our conjecture was that the exchange and compromise models would bring forecasts for each dimension closer to the actual outcome than did the expected utility model. This hypothesis was not supported. Across individual dimensions, the expected utility model is off the mark by 6.4 percent, but the compromise and exchange models do not improve on this overall performance. Moreover, the exchange models fail to improve the forecasts on the individual dimensions. In actuality, the expected utility forecasts are somewhat superior on the average to those from the exchange and compromise models. Thus, we surmise that exchanges and compromises do not improve the expected utility prediction. When compromises occur, they tend to shift outcomes slightly in the wrong direction. These are disappointing results since we hoped to use these dimensions to increase the accuracy of forecasts obtained for the overall EC bank structure.

The results of the banking dimensions are also inconsistent with our expectations. The expected utility forecast misses the actual outcome by six points, while the compromise forecast deviates by ten, and the exchange forecast errs by 9 percent. At first glance it seems that compromises along any of these dimensions had a minimal effect on the Maastricht negotiations.   There is, however, room for a more positive interpretation. These results imply that a compromise between Germany and the United Kingdom, rather than between Germany and France, should have evolved. Such results differ from reality at Maastricht but are not inconsistent with forecasts that we have shown starting with the Madrid summit. Germany's compromise with France (figure 8.6) is politically less stable than a simulated compromise that Germany and the United Kingdom could reach (figure 8.4). The results of the compromise and exchange model suggest exactly the same pattern — increased stability could be attained by a compromise between the United Kingdom and Germany. Given these cumulative results, we strongly suspect that all forecasts may be missing the actual outcomes because the terms and conditions settled on were not optimal. If this is the case, had Germany adopted the stable outcome that we forecasted, the political dissension that followed the implementation of the Maastricht treaty would have been reduced. Of course, treaties are not simply a search for equilibrium. Other, far more pertinent reasons may have prevailed during the negotiations that

Table 8.5
Impact of Exchanges among EC Countries on the EC Bank Structure at Maastricht

	Expected Utility		Exchange Model		Compromise Model		Actual Outcome
	Forecast	Accuracy[a]	Forecast	Accuracy	Forecast	Accuracy	
Individual Dimensions							
Time	61	(11)	67	(17)	67	(17)	50
Control	70	(0)	70	(0)	71	(1)	70
Scope	66	(−4)	66	(−4)	65	(−5)	70
Harmony	55	(−5)	42	(−18)	42	(−18)	60
ECU	63	(−12)	62	(−13)	61	(−14)	75
Mean of absolute value for accuracy (in percent)		6.4		10.4		11	
EC Bank Structure	79	(−6)	75	(−10)	76	(−9)	85

[a] Accuracy is calculated as the difference between each forecast and the actual outcome.

dictated the actual outcome. However, perhaps this type of intelligence could help anticipate the degree of political bickering that will take place after an agreement, and adjustments could be made to minimize such dissension.

In sum, the disparities between the forecasts and reality were not reduced through logrolling. The available compromises did not take place. Rather, the Community agreement on the structure of the EC bank is seemingly unrelated to other important issues raised about monetary functions at these negotiations. Finally, expected utility simulations and the exchange and compromise models strongly suggest that the German-French compromise was too drastic, and that the British-German option that was overlooked or abandoned after Strasbourg may have produced a less controversial Maastricht treaty. This assessment is supported by the post-Maastricht dissent by Denmark and the bare approval Maastricht obtained in the French referendum.

Our attempt to anticipate and specify the bank structure was fairly successful. Our analyses anticipated the collapse of the Madrid summit, indicated the progress at Strasbourg, and anticipated — within 5 percent — the eventual outcome at Maastricht. The expected utility model consistently suggested that a stable outcome would result if the EC bank structures reflected a compromise between the German and British proposals. A more complex study using the compromise and exchange models did likewise. However, neither of these models improved on the precision of the expected utility forecasts. Both shared with the expected utility assessment the feature that they isolated the German-British compromise as the most stable solution. The actual outcome differed from these forecasts, reflecting a German-French compromise.

On side issues, the study of political dynamics after the Madrid summit isolated the need to separate the push toward integration from pressing issues created by Eastern Europe's detachment from the Soviet bloc. The model anticipated the separation accomplished at the Paris conference. The analysis also accurately anticipated the serious domestic dissent created by British policies. This dissent resulted in a challenge to Mrs. Thatcher's authority and led to the emergence of Mr. Major as the United Kingdom's prime minister. Once the United Kingdom moderated its position, the analysis revealed an opportunity for British-German compromise at Maastricht. This compromise did not materialize. Finally, the analysis shows that dissension was not minimized by the Maastricht German-French compromise, and indicated that Denmark would be likely to challenge the treaty. Our analysis anticipated less resistance elsewhere. For this reason we expect that after the positive vote in France, the Community will approve the Maastricht treaty. Recently progress has been made in this direction.

Let us detail a major failure. The study failed to identify the German–French compromise either through the expected utility process or with the aid of the compromise and exchange models. We consistently identified two salient possible compromises: the German–French compromise which lead to a relatively strong but contested bank structure (the Maastricht outcome); and the German–British compromise that could lead to a unanimous, largely uncontested solution. All models suggested that the more stable German–British compromise would emerge. However, in reality the less stable German–French compromise materialized. One is tempted to conclude that an opportunity to minimize political dissent was missed by the Maastricht negotiators. This research allows us to conclude that the integration process has been advanced, but the implementation process — now just beginning — will be contentious.

Given the Maastricht treaty and the advances forecasted, the impact on European integration should resemble the "spillover" concept originally advocated by Monnet. The last major stumbling block to European integration has been tackled, but it is too early to tell if opposition to further integration has disappeared.

APPENDIX: SUPPLEMENTARY DATA ON EXCHANGE DIMENSIONS

Issue 1. Time

Time required for the institutionalization of an EC bank.

Nation	Capabilities	Position	Salience
United Kingdom	85	30	60
France	85	100	90
Germany	90	30	100
Spain	40	80	60
Italy	60	80	70
Netherlands	75	50	50
Belgium	55	50	50
Luxembourg	20	50	70
Greece	30	50	30
Portugal	15	30	30
Denmark	50	30	70
Ireland	20	30	25
Delors	60	100	100

Note: 1 = Never — maintain status quo indefinitely
   30 = Delay — Post-convergence institutionalization of bank
   50 = Luxembourg compromise
   80 = Shift when some market activities in place
   100 = 1992 — earliest possible

Issue 2. Control
Who will direct bank policy and execution.

Nation	Capabilities	Position	Salience
United Kingdom	85	60	90
France	85	70	90
Germany	90	100	100
Spain	40	60	70
Italy	60	60	50
Netherlands	75	70	60
Belgium	55	70	90
Luxembourg	20	70	40
Greece	30	60	40
Portugal	15	60	50
Denmark	50	60	75
Ireland	20	60	40
Delors	60	70	100

Note: 1 = Finance ministers
40 = Council of National Bank Governor's (CNB) alone
60 = CNB directs policy; Euro-based bank board (EBB) only
         executes policy
70 = CNB and EBB share policy powers
100 = Independent EBB sets and executes policy

Issue 3. Scope
Scope of bank responsibilities: inflation control vs. intervention in domestic economics.

Nation	Capabilities	Position	Salience
United Kingdom	85	40	90
France	85	90	80
Germany	90	65	100
Spain	40	80	50
Italy	60	75	60
Netherlands	75	65	60
Belgium	55	65	50
Luxembourg	20	75	50
Greece	30	100	60
Portugal	15	30	70
Denmark	50	30	80
Ireland	20	80	50
Delors	60	100	95

Note: 1 = No intervention account management
        65 = Advise on inflation
        85 = Control inflation in ECU rates
       100 = Intervene in domestic economies to control inflation

Issue 4. Harmony
Harmonization of economic talks within market.

Nation	Capabilities	Position	Salience
United Kingdom	85	30	90
France	85	100	70
Germany	90	50	70
Spain	40	30	50
Italy	60	30	30
Netherlands	75	60	50
Belgium	55	60	50
Luxembourg	20	60	40
Greece	30	30	50
Portugal	15	30	40
Denmark	50	25	50
Ireland	20	30	20
Delors	60	100	60

Note: 1 = Market directed
         30 = Government-directed harmonization of all economies
         60 = Link major economies letting others catch up as they can
        100 = Tracks managed — immediate link of major economies and
              managed merger of minor economies

Issue 5. ECU
Variability to be allowed for currency fluctuations

Nation	Capabilities	Position	Salience
United Kingdom	85	100	50
France	85	40	80
Germany	90	40	90
Spain	40	70	60
Italy	60	70	60
Netherlands	75	60	50
Belgium	55	70	50
Luxembourg	20	60	40
Greece	30	70	40
Portugal	15	70	30
Denmark	50	40	50
Ireland	20	70	40
Delors	60	100	60

Note: 1 = United basket — European Monetary System (EMS)
        40 = Full EMS with basket of currency
        70 = German mark for full EMS
       100 = Hard ECU — fixed exchange with other currencies

IV Comparison and Evaluation of the Models

In the next chapter the predictions of the two classes of models confront each other and reality. To our knowledge, this is the first time that two classes of models with opposing views of the political process are placed side by side by their developers and compared so directly to the evidence. Such a direct confrontation and demanding test is facilitated by the fact that both models are based on the same fundamental variables and are built on similar basic assumptions. Consequently, the two models differ solely and fundamentally in terms of the assumed underlying process: conflict versus exchange.

To our surprise, both sets of models do well, although meaningful differences can be discerned between them. The high predictive capacity of both types of models implies that actual outcomes of EC decision making can be predicted from completely opposing underlying processes. This might well be a main reason why scholars of the opposing schools have been able to persist in their respective views.

On the basis of these findings, we may wonder whether this controversy between conflict or exchange as the fundamental mechanism for political decision making will ever be solved. Chapter 9 provides one clue for hope, namely, that the errors of the predictions of the models are not so highly correlated with each other. This indicates that under certain, not yet known, conditions the conflict model gives better predictions and that under other conditions the exchange model does. This implies that an investigation of these conditions might be a fruitful path for future investigations.

The final chapter gives a summary of the main conclusions and implications to be drawn from this book. It does so in nontechnical terms and explains the importance of the chosen approach for the different audiences of the book.

Bruce Bueno de Mesquita and Frans N. Stokman

9 Models of Exchange and of Expected Utility Maximization: A Comparison of Accuracy

Several methods for predicting policy decisions have been delineated and applied to policy choices in the European Community. Each model relies on information about policy issues that is available to decision makers and to analysts before a decision is actually made. Consequently, each method holds out the prospect of being a tool for political analysis that can be done before the fact. Such a tool could be a valuable instrument for policymakers as well as policy analysts by helping to avoid or minimize highly conflictual or politically unpalatable decisions. Although each method makes use of the same data, the base, compromise, expected utility, and exchange models are quite different in terms of the assumptions they make about the specific process of decision making. This provides an opportunity to make a direct comparison between the two core methodologies tested here: maximization of welfare through logrolling or through bargaining on one issue at a time.

Four questions lie at the heart of this evaluation. They are:

1. Do the network and exchange (or logrolling) models or does the expected utility model predict accurately?
2. Do the models make different predictions?
3. Is either approach more accurate than the other?
4. Are there advantages to pursuing either or both types of models in combination in the future or are these methods inadequate as prospective tools for predicting political behavior?

Sixteen issues have been investigated in common using the network and exchange models and the expected utility model. An additional six banking issues were examined using the expected utility model, the compromise model, and the exchange model, but not including the base or combined models. The network and exchange models provide four different predictions: the base prediction, the compromise prediction (sometimes referred to as comp.), the base exchange prediction and the compromise exchange prediction. In addition, we have constructed tests linking the expected utility model to the base and compromise models. One such linked model is referred to as EU-B (or EU-base) because it ties the base model to predicted positions from the expected utility model. The other, which joins predicted positions from the expected utility model to the logic of the compromise model is denoted as EU-C (or EU-compromise).

The expected utility model is combined with the base and the compromise model by assuming that decision makers first try to reconcile their differences on an issue by issue basis and then look for opportunities to logroll across issues if they remain dissatisfied. The linkage is achieved by treating the predicted position of each decision maker at the end of the expected utility model's bargaining rounds as the input policy position of the decision maker for the compromise or the base exchange model. The notion is that it is easier to reach agreement and build coalitions on one issue at a time than it is across issues. Consequently, we surmise that logrolling efforts are reserved for a later stage when decision makers have exhausted the avenues available to them to resolve their dissatisfaction on particular issues.

Table 9.1 summarizes the results for each of the sixteen core issues using the four network or exchange models, the two linked models, and the expected utility model. The table also identifies the actual outcome for each issue. The predicted and actual outcomes on six EC banking issues have also been calculated. Because these issues have not been solved using all of our models, they are not included in most of our summary statistics. In any event, they do not fundamentally alter any of our answers to the four evaluative questions that motivate this chapter. Occasionally we will also provide summary statistics that include the banking issues when it seems especially helpful or informative.

In order to answer our four motivating questions it is necessary to normalize each of the values in table 9.1 so that cross-issue comparisons can be made. For instance, we want to know whether a prediction of 4.67 years relative to an actual outcome of 4.83 years is closer or farther from reality than a prediction of 1,500 deutsche marks compared to an actuality of 2,200 deutsche marks. To normalize each issue, we first calculate the range of possible outcomes as the difference between the maximum and minimum preferred outcome. For dichotomous, yes-no issues, yes is coded as 1, no as 0, and indifference or neutrality as .5. The normalized prediction equals the value of the difference between the predicted out-

Table 9.1
Predicted and Actual Results

	Actual	Expected Utility	Base	Compromise	Base Exchange	Compromise Exchange	Linked	
							EU-Base	EU-Compromise
Introduction Date								
Large autos	4.8	4.7	6.7	7.0	5.6	4.5	6.2	5.8
Mid-sized autos	8.8	8.4	6.7	7.4	6.0	8.1	7.9	8.8
Small autos	8.8	9.0	6.7	8.3	8.4	9.0	7.4	7.9
Tax Incentives								
Large autos	2,200	2,372	1,500	1,471	2,326	2,643	2,874	2,970
Mid-sized autos	2,200	1,459	1,500	969	906	390	1,834	1,931
Small autos	750	1,271	1,500	881	1,201	278	1,633	1,343
Emission Standards								
Large autos	.78	.58	.71	.72	.57	.57	.53	.55
Mid-sized autos	.79	.72	.75	.80	.79	.85	.61	.60
Small autos	.76	.87	.73	.80	.80	.88	.77	.77
Radiation[a]								
Maximum level	.36	.81	.47	.57	.56	.65	.56	.65
Extension	yes	yes	yes	yes	yes	yes	yes	yes
Air Transport Liberalization								
Deep discount	45.0	50.0	48.8	48.1	44.2	47.4	40.8	41.1
Capacity margin	13.3	19.9	27.5	26.5	38.2	29.9	34.7	24.7
Duration	yes	yes	neutral	yes	yes	yes	no	yes
Hub-regional exemption	4	3	2	2	3	4	2	2
Hub-regional traffic capacity	80.0	70.0	55.8	62.5	67.5	59.7	61.6	69.3

a Qualified majority rule.

come and the minimum policy preference divided by the range, as denoted in the following equation:

normalized prediction =

$$\frac{|\text{predicted outcome} - \text{minimum preference}|}{\text{maximum preference} - \text{minimum preference}} \times 100$$

The normalized prediction places all values on a scale from zero to 100. Thus, the issues denoted in chapter 3 are all recast in normalized form. For instance, the maximum possible value on each of the tax incentive issues listed in table 3.3 is 3,000 deutsche marks and the minimum value is 0 so that the range of preferences encompasses everything from 0 to DM 3,000. Therefore, each tax incentive value (predicted outcome or actual outcome) is divided by 3,000 so that a predicted value of DM 1,500 is equivalent to a normalized prediction of 50. Likewise, the issues concerned with the date for introducing emission standards fell on a continuum that ranged from four years up to a ten-year delay. Consequently, an actual outcome of 8.83 years is equivalent, in normalized form, to $[(8.83 - 4)/(10 - 4) \times 100] = 80.5$. Thus, the normalization process converts each value into a percentage of the maximum value that was predicted or adopted. Of course, we can compare percentages to each other much more straightforwardly than we can compare values in years to values measured in DM for tax incentives. Table 9.2 displays the normalized predictions.[1]

Do the Models Predict Accurately?

Several methods are employed to evaluate the accuracy of the predictions of the contending models. In the first test, the normalized actual outcomes and the normalized predicted outcomes are compared to one another. The statistical procedure used addresses the question: "How likely is it that the predicted outcome and the actual outcome are the same?" The test is a comparison of predicted means and observed means, with the probability evaluated using a t-test for differences in means assuming equal variances and paired observations. By pairing observations, the test asks not only if the means of the two series are alike, but also whether the specific distribution of observations is also alike. The answer to these question is

---

1. It should be noted that we have rounded predicted values to the nearest whole number for one issue, denoted hub-regional exemption, among the air transport liberalization issues. The reason is that the dependent variable is coded as a four-point ordinal scale with no meaning attached to values between the possible outcomes of 1, 2, 3, and 4. The actual predictions of the models were 2.7 for expected utility, 2.1 for the base model, 2.0 for the compromise model, 1.9 for the base-exchange, 2.7 for the compromise-exchange, and 3.7 and 4.0, respectively, for the expected utility-base and expected utility-compromise linked models.

Table 9.2
Normalized Predictions and Actuality (percent)

	Actual	Expected Utility	Base	Compromise	Base Exchange	Compromise Exchange	EU-Base	EU-Compromise
Introduction Date								
Large autos	13.9	11.1	45.0	49.5	27.3	9.0	36.2	29.3
Mid-sized autos	80.6	72.5	45.0	56.6	33.0	67.7	65.2	79.5
Small autos	80.6	82.7	45.0	71.0	73.2	82.7	56.5	65.3
Tax Incentives								
Large autos	73.3	79.1	50.0	49.0	77.5	88.1	95.8	99.0
Mid-sized autos	73.3	48.6	50.0	32.3	30.2	13.0	61.1	64.4
Small autos	25.0	42.4	50.0	29.4	40.0	9.3	54.4	44.8
Emission Standards								
Large autos	57.0	16.6	43.0	45.4	15.2	15.2	7.3	11.2
Mid-sized autos	62.3	48.7	53.8	63.2	62.0	72.8	29.3	27.5
Small autos	53.0	74.5	45.8	59.7	60.5	76.3	54.5	54.5
Radiation								
Maximum level	28.4	79.2	41.0	52.0	51.1	61.4	51.1	61.4
Extension	100.0	100.0	100.0	100.0	100.0	100.0	100.0	100.0
Air Transport Liberalization								
Deep discount	50.0	66.7	62.5	60.4	47.5	58.0	36.1	37.1
Capacity margin	13.3	19.9	27.5	26.5	38.2	30.0	34.7	24.7
Duration	100.0	100.0	50.0	100.0	100.0	100.0	0	100.0
Hub-regional exemption	100.0	75.0	50.0	50.0	75.0	100.0	50.0	50.0
Hub-regional traffic capacity	80.0	70.0	55.8	62.5	67.5	59.7	61.6	69.3

Table 9.3
Probability That the Predicted Outcome Equals the Actual Outcome

	Probability	Mean	Standard Deviation
Actual		61.9	29.5
Expected utility	0.97	61.7	27.8
Base	0.10	50.9	15.1
Compromise	0.37	56.7	21.0
Base exchange	0.33	56.1	25.2
Compromise exchange	0.62	58.9	33.5
EU-base	0.18	49.6	26.5
EU-compromise	0.46	57.4	27.8

summarized in table 9.3, along with the mean and standard deviation for the predicted values and the actual values.

Table 9.3 suggests several interpretations. The likelihood that the expected utility predictions (EU) are within statistical error of the true values is very high. There is a 97-percent chance that the predicted outcome and the true outcome value are statistically the same and only a 3-percent chance that they are sufficiently different to reject the hypothesis that they are equal.[2] This is a very strong finding. The two compromise models fair better than the two base models, although by this particular test none do nearly as well as the expected utility model.

We cannot express much confidence that the compromise predictions

2. The accuracy rate of the expected utility model may be understated. The model proved to be egregiously inaccurate on one issue — the first radiation issue analyzed. In that one case the model predicted an outcome equal to .813 while the actual outcome on the issue of tolerable radiation contamination in food was .356. However, the model's prediction is equal to the recommendation made by the European Commission in the first stage of the decision process. The issue — one of only two in the data set decided under the qualified majority rule — then was subjected to protracted negotiations among the members of the Community. In the end, after about five rounds of bargaining, the commission's recommendation was replaced by an agreement to set the acceptable level of radioactive contaminants in foodstuffs at .356. If the expected utility model is permitted to iterate through an extra five rounds of bargaining we find that the model's logic no longer supports the initial prediction of .813. Instead, our prediction derived from the expected utility model becomes .475, a value rather close to the true outcome. Had we utilized this extended prediction, the expected utility model's error rate would drop significantly.

Having said that, we do not use the extended prediction because we cannot be certain that the decision makers knew, ex ante, how long discussions would last on this issue.

Table 9.4
Errors of Prediction

	Mean Error Percentage	Standard Deviation
Expected utility	15.3	14.5
Base	22.9	14.6
Compromise	17.0	15.1
Base exchange	16.8	16.0
Compromise exchange	16.5	16.7
EU-base	27.3	23.8
EU-compromise	17.9	15.9

and the actual outcome values are the same. We find for the compromise and compromise exchange models that there is a 37-percent and 62-percent chance, respectively, that the differences between the observed, true values and the predicted values are due to chance. On average, then, the compromise models produce a fifty-fifty chance of being equal to the true values by the test of differences in paired values. For the base exchange model, the equivalent chance is 33 percent, while for the base model the chance that the actual outcomes and the predicted outcomes are the same is only 10 percent. Clearly the null, base model fits reality quite poorly, with all of the other models being a clear improvement over the null hypothesis and with the expected utility model proving dominant by this test. Second place goes to the compromise exchange model.

The two linked models are somewhat disappointing in that they do not improve on the initial expected utility results (EU). Still, we are examining only a small sample of issues and the linked predictions using the compromise model are rather good. We reserve judgment on whether the EU-compromise linkage represents an improvement or an unnecessary sacrifice of parsimony pending further investigations.

A second test evaluates the percentage error associated with the predictions from each model to see how much larger they are than zero. Table 9.4 summarizes tests of the magnitude of the errors for the sixteen European Community issues studied here. Errors for the six banking issues are summarized below.

Table 9.4 provides an alternative angle of vision from that given in table 9.3. The lowest average error of prediction across the sixteen issues (or the twenty-two issues that include the six banking decisions) is associated with the expected utility model. For the expected utility model, the average error is 15.3 percent, reduced to 14.3 percent when the banking issues are included in the assessment. This is substantially better than the average error rate for the base or the linked expected utility-base model, but it is only slightly better than the error rate produced by the exchange models and the compromise model. The probability that the predictive errors for those models are as small as the predictive error for the expected utility model varies between 70 percent and 73 percent. That is, there is only a 25- to 30-percent chance that the expected utility errors are really smaller than the errors from the exchange or compromise models. This probability rises to between 55 and 65 percent if we include the assessments of the six banking issues from chapter 8 in our overall evaluation.

We should be concerned about the distribution of predictive errors as well as their magnitude. The smaller the magnitude, the more accurate the predictions, of course. The fewer the extremely inaccurate predictions, the more confident that we can be that future errors will be close to the mean. Figure 9.1 displays the distribution of predictive errors for each model. Figure 9.2 replicates figure 9.1, but just for the three models for which we have assessments on the expanded data set that includes the banking issues from chapter 8. Each figure divides the predictive errors into five groups. The groups are divided into intervals of 12 percent each. No model produced predictive errors in excess of 60 percent. On several issues one or more models had predictive errors of 0 percent.

These figures tell an important story. Only the expected utility model and the compromise model can boast that as many as half of their predictions in our sample of issues deviated from the true outcome by less than 12 percent. With the banking issues included, the compromise model maintains this record of performance, while the expected utility model improves on it somewhat, with about 55 percent of all errors falling at or below a 12-percent deviation from the true outcome. For these models, errors also drop off quickly as we move above a 12-percent deviation from the true value. The other models do not do as well. And, as we have come to expect, the base model (our null model) performs quite poorly by comparison with any of the other methods we have investigated. Finally, we note that about 80 percent of the errors of prediction from the expected utility, compromise, and compromise exchange models fall within 24 percent of the true value. These seem like rather strong performances, encouraging us to conclude that at least these three models provide strong evidence that politics can be predicted and that these are models that have considerable potential value for analysts and decision makers.

Table 9.5 provides further evidence of the predictive capacity of these models. In the table we present the bivariate correlations among the various models we have evaluated, as well as their correlation with the actual outcomes on the issues. The table also summarizes the correlations among the predictive errors of the various models.

We note that there is a substantial correlation between the expected utility results and the various compromise and base models. The highest

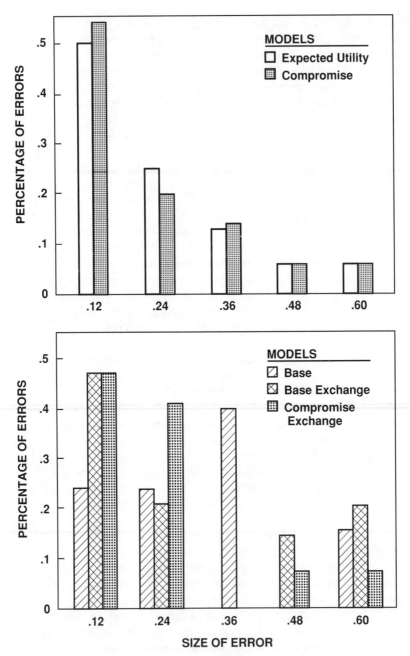

9.1: Error Rates in Predictions, Not Including Banking Issues

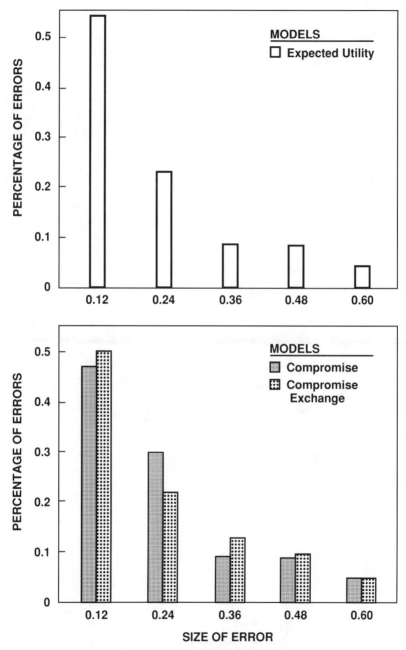

9.2: Error Rates in Predictions, Including Banking Issues

Table 9.5
Predictive Capacity of the Models

	Actual	Expected Utility	Base	Compromise	Base Exchange	Compromise Exchange	EU-B	EU-C
Correlations among contending models and reality								
Actual	1.00							
Expected utility	0.72	1.00						
Base	0.51	0.49	1.00					
Compromise	0.65	0.72	0.64	1.00				
Base exchange	0.66	0.83	0.54	0.77	1.00			
Compromise exchange	0.73	0.87	0.40	0.73	0.88	1.00		
EU-base	0.24	0.41	0.48	0.03	0.29	0.28	1.00	
EU-compromise	0.65	0.84	0.45	0.59	0.71	0.65	0.56	1.00
Correlations among prediction errors								
Expected utility		1.00						
Base		-0.24	1.00					
Compromise		0.26	0.43	1.00				
Base exchange		0.47	0.16	0.54	1.00			
Compromise exchange		0.65	-0.31	0.26	0.63	1.00		
EU-base		-0.01	0.64	-0.09	-0.07	-0.21	1.00	
EU-compromise		0.60	0.07	0.35	0.20	0.14	0.26	1.00

$N = 16$

of these correlations — that between the predictions for the EU and the compromise exchange model, for instance — is .87, suggesting that about 25 percent of the variance in each is unrelated to the other. While the two exchange models are highly correlated with the EU model, the nonexchange models share less than half their variance in common with the EU predictions. Perhaps the differences are due to the possibility that both kinds of deal making — issue by issue and logrolling across issues — take place. When one or the other is most likely remains an unanswered question.

The correlation between the respective errors of prediction between the expected utility model and the other models ranges between a high of .65 and a low of −.01, indicating that the models do not generally make the same mistakes in their predictions. Of course, this can be seen in greater detail by inspecting table 9.2 or figures 9.1 and 9.2.

It seems evident from the various tests we have performed that, overall, the two best models are the expected utility model and the compromise exchange model. Other models perform well on one or another test, but these two consistently do well, with some advantage seeming to favor the expected utility model. The latter seems favored because it has the smallest average error of prediction and the lowest variance in its predictive errors, and because of the extraordinarily high probability that the predicted value and the true outcome are the same. Still, the compromise exchange model seems like a powerful tool for capturing likely outcomes when logrolling or issue-position exchanges are expected to play a prominent part in the resolution of issues. It remains for future research to better specify when expected utility type agreements are reached and when exchange agreements are reached.

While the models tested here have performed very well, we should not lose sight of their limitations. Each model depends upon expert inputs. This is both a virtue and a limitation. It is a virtue in that expert knowledge is readily available on many important questions, but it is a limitation in that it means that considerable skill has to be developed in turning expertise into the numerical inputs required by each of the models we have investigated. Beyond data issues, the models differ in their approach to politics and in the assumptions they make about decision making. Each assumption (of these, or of any other approach, of course) represent prospective limitations.

The expected utility model, on the one hand, treats issues as separate areas for negotiations, bargaining, conflict, and agreement. It assumes that issues are resolved one at a time without an opportunity for decision makers to trade benefits on one issue for concessions on another. The exchange models, on the other hand, link issues to each other and search for best trades across issues while ignoring possible bargains between decision makers within the context of a single issue. Thus, the expected utility model sacrifices the reasonable notion that decision makers engage in logrolling, whereas the exchange models sacrifice the equally reasonable notion that decision makers negotiate compromises within the context of a single issue.

The expected utility model assumes that decision makers are sophisticated and strategic. The decision makers in this model are engaged in a complicated game of strategic maneuvering aimed at improving their individual welfare. Indeed, it is their strategic sophistication that contributes the dynamic component to the model and that distinguishes it from simply predicting the initial position of the median voter as the outcome of the game. Instead, the expected utility model allows for the possibility that strategic maneuvers will alter the location of the median voter by the time an issue is finally resolved. But by treating issues as unidimensional and preferences as single-peaked, the expected utility model precludes the possibility that cyclical preferences will emerge, thereby forcing deterministic outcomes in some circumstances when such outcomes are improbable in reality. Such circumstances probably account for some of the predictive error reported in our assessments.

The exchange models assume that players are sincere and are risk neutral. These are strong assumptions that facilitate the development of cooperative agreements among players across issues. Without these restrictions, the exchange models would presumably reveal that for sophisticated "voters" there is a possible trade that can defeat any proposed exchange and that can, in turn, be defeated by still another trade. By assuming away this possibility of trading cycles, the model becomes a practical tool of real use to policy analysts and decision makers. But, of course, it is likely here, as in the expected utility model, that these assumptions are violated in reality from time to time and that such violations are a source of some of the predictive errors. That the predictive errors in both sets of models are small is testimony to the fact that the restrictive conditions of the models do not violate reality so much as to render the models incapable of addressing important aspects of politics.

The success of the expected utility model and the failure of the linked models to improve upon its predictions suggests that a wide array of issues are settled without critical dependence on logrolling or position trading among decision makers across issues. However, the successful performance of the exchange models indicates that it would be premature to dismiss issue trading as a central feature of policy formation. There is some parsimony advantage to focusing on issues one at a time, but experienced observers of politics recognize that even single-issue decisions are often influenced by the tacit possibility that if there is no agreement, then trades may take place across issues. Such threats of issue linkage were, for instance, a common feature of U.S.–Soviet maneuvering during the cold war.

In political science in general and among EC researchers in particular, we find a longstanding discussion among two contending groups of scholars. The first group maintains that the nature of politics is primarily conflictual and that social outcomes are obtained primarily by conflicts among individuals and groups over the social use of material things or values. The second group emphasizes the cooperative nature of many political processes and their similarity with exchange processes in economics where social outcomes are determined by cooperation among buyers and sellers. One reason for the insolubility of this dispute is that results of noncooperative and cooperative models have been difficult to compare. In this book, however, directly comparable cooperative and noncooperative models have been developed and applied. The comparability of the models is insured by the fact that they are based on exactly the same three variables — namely, power, salience, and policy position.

The expected utility model and the compromise model can be classified as noncooperative models, whereas the three exchange models are cooperative in structure. We expected therefore to be able to contribute to the solution of the conflict between the cooperative and noncooperative approaches, at least within the context of the EC. To our surprise, however, we are not, as the predictions of both types of models are very close to the actual outcomes.

We believe that decision makers engage in some bargaining within the confines of an issue and some bargaining across issues in an effort to maximize their welfare. Exactly when and how such bargaining takes place remains unresolved by our research. A theory of when each type of bargaining takes place remains as a question for future study. It requires the elaboration of conditions under which both cooperative and noncooperative processes are feasible, but with different predicted outcomes of the political processes. The conditions under which cooperative processes are feasible were given in chapter 5; formulation of the conditions (if any) under which the two processes subsequently result in different outcomes is the main element still to be elaborated.

Six distinct models for predicting policy choices have been delineated. Several have been found to make rather accurate predictions on their own. Some advantage goes to the expected utility model because of its overall slightly better performance. Still, the average accuracy of prediction of the compromise exchange model is not significantly different from the expected utility model's accuracy. Of course, the individual predictions on an issue-by-issue basis are certainly different. The average percentage error and the correlations between the actual outcomes and the predicted outcomes probably are the best indicators of just how similar is the effectiveness of each model.

The models evaluated here provide a firm basis in replicable methodologies for believing that important features of politics are predictable. What is more, these methodologies imply that accurate predictions can be extracted from readily available information well in advance of the taking of actual decisions. Reliable prediction about fundamental policy questions need not be viewed as a distant hope, but rather as a firm reality.

A. F. K. Organski and Samuel Eldersveld

10 Modeling the EC

For the third time in the modern era, Western Europeans are presenting the world with social inventions that promise to reshape their future and that of the industrial world. Europeans have been responsible for such inventions before. They "invented" the nation-state; they "invented" the industrial revolution; and they are currently "inventing" the instruments and changes to bring about the unification of Western Europe. If unification succeeds — and the process to bring it about is likely to be longer, more tortuous, and far more scabrous an experience than its proponents ever imagined — there can be little question that Europeans will again have a decisive voice in fundamental world decisions. In Europe and elsewhere, the European Community's unification is the event to watch.

The trajectory of Europe's unification clearly presents a major laboratory for scholars in the social sciences, and particularly for students of politics interested in the stream of negotiations along the road toward economic, political, social, and military unification of the twelve nations of the European Community. The political and economic elites guiding unification not only seek to undo the obstacles blocking interaction, but also to create new linkages among twelve previously unconnected national societies. The success of European unification depends on decisions by political and economic leaders in Brussels and the governments of its member nations and the private sector. The ability of the leaders to execute their decisions is critical. Consensual international unification of fully developed countries is a unique and enormously complex phenomenon. Studying European unification requires new instruments and procedures to understand fully the dynamics of the decision-making process.

The explanations described in this book are through the

lenses of game theoretic models. This report on research efforts by European and American scholars represents a major step toward our understanding of current European decision making.

Looking Back: The Essentials of This Book

There is no need to go into great detail here about what has been reported in this volume. Some points, however, should be noted. The presentation illumines the kind of things that must be known to understand the process of Western European unification. Knowledge of the European Community's governmental institutions and their powers, along with the formal treatment by governmental organs of the issues being analyzed, is insufficient to provide an understanding of the dynamics that propelled participants in their dealings with issues of nuclear contamination, gas emissions, air traffic, and the institutionalization of the Community's banking system. The discussion of the development of the institutions and the policy issues is an essential first step to any analysis, yet much more is required to understand the entire decision-making process.

This volume provides a mapping of the huge space stretching between the knowledge of the governmental institutions and their powers, on the one hand, and the results represented by the decisions that governments make, on the other. The dynamic that is critical to capture occurs outside the formal structures, although these structures are an important element in giving shape to decisions and setting limits. The calculations and behavior of all players — which generate the pressures to move the institutions to act as they do — remain largely invisible without the rigorous logical structures that permit the simulation of the data. Without these tools the researcher is left to guess what has been going on, why precisely the actions and decisions in question have been taken. The chapters making up this book have presented these instruments and the results of their use when they are applied to the analyses of critical decisions of the European Community.

Unification of the European Community is clearly dependent on success in building central political and economic institutions that will further bind together the members states. It also depends on the Community's success in removing obstacles to cross-national interaction and cooperation. Both sets of issues are illustrated by the cases analyzed in this book. The push and pull of institution-building is explored by a review of the major decisions that eventuated in the creation of the central banking system for the Community. The choices were at the very heart of the struggle over unification. They were stretched over three meetings (Strasbourg, Madrid, and Maastricht) of the heads of the governments of the members and were bitterly contested. The analysis revealed the dynamics of the tug-of-war over the decision and forecast inter alia that the strongest opponent to the compromise that was eventually reached would lose its position. The victors, we now know, would also pay a heavy price for their choices of compromises over the creation of the central bank. The very process of unification was put to its most severe test.

The issues chosen to illustrate the operation of the Council of Ministers in the negotiations were equally revealing of the core process that has been pushing unification of the European Community forward. The issues concerned three critical areas of governmental responsibility: (1) the question of the maximum permissible levels of radioactive contamination in food stuffs; (2) the setting of emission levels for the exhaust gases of motor vehicles; and (3) the liberalization of intra-EC air traffic during an experimental three-year period.

The substantive issues explored were not chosen solely to provide tests of the models. In selecting these issues the authors also sought to show how decisions could be made on questions involving a wide range of policy fields. The issues reflect controversial and critical national interests that engaged different configurations of the Council of Ministers. Therefore, the resolution of these issues provides an important insight as to how the twelve nations of Europe resolve their differences.

It is clear that the major contribution of this book is the manner in which decision making is analyzed by the models. Their performance in analyzing the issues and forecasting the outcomes make this book unique. There is no other work in the literature that presents the deployment and comparison of applied formal models in this way.

No governmental decision can ever be satisfactorily explained or predicted solely from the contextual setting in which the decision is made. This rule certainly applies to the central organs of the European Community. The structure of the decision-making institutions and the rules by which they operate serve as constraints within which decisions will be made, yet the range of choices is still very large. Structural analysis can never really tell why decisions were made the way they were. Most decisions are fueled by activities carried on outside the decision-making structures. These activities include the proposals and counterproposals that the actors make to one another, searching for common ground and advantage; the alliances they forge to strengthen their own positions; and the defections from agreements or coalitions that arise in the course of finally resolving an issue. The environment of negotiations is ever changing. Consequently, information on how actors perceive their environment, what demands they can make, what the traffic will bear, and what is advantageous for them is most important. Even the best and most sophisticated analysts can only grasp at most a tiny fraction of the comprehensive picture. The bargaining and cajoling that is at the heart of decision making remains largely invisible to the analyst, but at least the existence of rigorous, logical structures that permit the simulation of the data makes it possible to formulate convincing hypotheses about what may have gone on.

All such information is precisely what the expected utility models provide for the analyst. The logrolling models developed by Frans Stokman, though they lack the strategic component of the expected utility models, capture the cases where the actors make trades across issues. The tug-of-war process through which collectivities make choices had not been seen before. By exploring decisions with these models, analysts have the sensation Galileo Galilei probably had when he looked at the night sky with his naked eye and then put his eye to the telescope. The models represent a sea change in the study of decisions.

There is no need here to go over how the models work. The description of their construction and operation was done very well in chapters 4 and 5. One or two points will suffice. As Roy Pierce indicated in the introductory chapter, modelers put a lot of stock in the performance and the predictive power of the models they develop.The issue of prediction is critical to the scientific process. The attempt to put researchers preoccupied with the predictive capacity of their models on the defensive with the argument that they should be more concerned with explanation displays an embarrassing confusion about the relation between the two.

The expected utility and logrolling models share a good deal in common. They are built on the same assumptions of single-peakedness and unidimensionality, and they use the same data and method of collection. They are complementary in some respects but also differ in important ways. The two sets of models do not measure the same things, and they differ in their performance in different issue areas. Most important, they differ in their angle of vision on the decision-making process.

The difference between the angles of vision of the expected utility and logrolling models on the process of decision making is fundamental. The expected utility models take the position that decision makers solve issues one at the time. The logrolling models, as their name implies, view decision making as a process where those involved resolve differences by trading compromises on one issue in one decision process with a compromise on another decision. This latter view of what negotiators do is the more general and accepted view. The findings of this volume, however, suggest that this is not the case; conventional wisdom on this point is incorrect. Trading across issues does occur, but is a less common event than usually assumed. This should not be surprising. It is reasonable to think that decision makers exhaust all options within the confines of one issue before relying on bargaining across issues.

The most important and relevant aspect of the models deployed in these analyses is their performance and, specifically, their predictive power. The performance of the models has been described in detail in chapters 6, 7, and 8. In this regard, the models presented in this volume are clearly remarkable. In the case of the expected utility models, the probability that the predicted outcome was what indeed occurred was an astounding 97 percent. The probability of correct predictions with the logrolling models, though quite high by conventional political science standards, is substantially lower. There is clearly a solid basis in the analyses conducted here for the claim that reliable predictions about fundamental policy questions need not be viewed as a distant hope, but rather as a firm reality. The statement is a clear signal about a new revolutionary condition in the study of decision making.

The Readers of This Book

The materials in this book are directed to a wider audience than was presumed when the work first began. The materials are addressed particularly to two sets of potential readers: scholars and policymakers. Social scientists are clearly a very important audience. Scholars in most branches of the social sciences deal at least indirectly with decision making and its consequences, and this is doubly true of students of politics and policy. A partial list of the scholars among political scientists would include Europeanists, comparativists, students of foreign policy, elite behavior, institutions, and political development, and, of course, modelers. Modelers do not usually have expertise in the substance of the myriad of problems that are part and parcel of the unification of Europe. This condition holds the other way around: students with great substantive knowledge of European unification generally have little, if any, domesticity with game theoretic approaches and techniques. There is general agreement that communication between the two sets of researchers is difficult. Yet, as this work demonstrates, what each set knows is essential to the other.

This book represents a strong signal of what modeling — and specifically the models presented here — can contribute to the work of scholars interested in political decisions related to European unification and to students of decision making in general. The models also indicate the power of the logical structures applied to the issues treated here. Clearly, the two sets of readers may regard differently what has been accomplished in this research effort. The scholars interested in European politics may be entirely taken with what can be learned through the use of these models in understanding the decision making shaping European unification. The scholars interested in modeling may regard the phenomenon of European unification as no more than the setting for testing of their models and may view the performance of the models as the main event. Most important, however, this book is an illustration of what can be achieved in both modeling and comparative politics if modelers and substantive scholars cooperate. The book sets down clearly the rules of engagement between the two sets of scholars for maximum results.

The other set of readers to whom this book is addressed is the very large community of policymakers. Their interest in how decisions are made and how outcomes are determined requires no lengthy explanation. Making decisions, implementing them, and dealing with their consequences is what policymakers do. The studies here offer a penetrating view of how policymakers in the public and private sectors make decisions affecting the European unification process. But clearly the analyses and findings should be of equal interest to policymakers operating in other political environments.

It is often argued that the interests of these audiences are not the same; that policymakers, interested — as they are — in constructs with immediate application to practical problems, and scholars, interested for the most part in basic research, want fundamentally different things. We would argue the opposite, that the interests of these sets of readers are not too dissimilar. Where they differ is the way they would use the procedures and the product presented here.

Explanations and Predictions

The logrolling and expected utility models presented in this book should be helpful to scholars in two ways. They enable analysts to capture the dynamics involved in the negotiation process underpinning all collective decisions. They permit a very rapid, elegant, and highly rigorous logical procedure to simulate the dynamics of decision making to represent the explanation of what happened, why all the participants acted as they did and produced the result they did. In some sense, therefore, the models produce an explanation of the behavior and the results of that behavior. What other meaning does "an explanation of the way a decision was taken" have? The core of any explanation, of any decision, by any collectivity is the pinpointing of the expectations and perceptions of the actors and the resulting actions taken by these actors. This allows a complete presentation of the push and pull and bargaining dynamics leading to the final decision. The systematic and rigorous tracing of all steps that players take on the basis of their perceptions and expectations constitutes a comprehensive explanation of the decision-making process. How can scholars in the social sciences provide any more explanation than this in any analysis of decisions of collectivities?

Far more important, the models really do explain, because the dynamic they portray eventuates in a forecast of the outcomes of the decision-making process. Such forecasts have been found accurate nine out of ten times. This ability is new in the study of political decisions, and it is of major importance. Until a very few years ago, forecasting in the social sciences could be done mainly in two ways. One could ask an expert, that is, someone who spent his or her professional life absorbing and evaluating all information available on an issue, and the expert would render his or her best judgment of what would be reasonable to expect as an outcome when the issue is finally joined. Such forecasts tend to be "on the one hand this and on the other that" variety or provide so wide a range of possible outcomes as to be of reduced value. Forecasts based largely on intuition render it difficult for their authors to retrace the analytic process followed in reaching such conclusions. Dean Acheson was known to have complained that George Kennan's forecasts of, and judgments on, the budding rivalry between the United States and the Soviet Union at the beginning of the cold war were often quite arresting, but he could not get Kennan to explain (to Acheson's satisfaction) why he had come to the conclusions he did and why alternative explanations should be rejected. We know Kennan's estimates and policy recommendations were not followed. Events, of course, proved Kennan to have been prophetic. An advantage of the models presented here is that they meet the problem head-on. They specify each component of the process by which a decision has been made and permit a logical explanation of why things happened the way they did.

The other major approach to forecasting is rooted in the use of econometric techniques. At its core it involves fitting a line through data summarizing past and present behavior and extrapolating the central trend into the future. This fitting and extrapolation process does not establish how the data points, representing what has already occurred, are related to one another. There is no theory. The method works best, obviously, when past trends continue into the future and does badly when they do not. The models presented in this book differ in that they are based on solid theory rooted in the assumption that individuals and collectivities of individuals act in what they believe are their own interests. Their preferences may appear — and may be — unreasonable, or they may misperceive realities, yet individuals and groups act in accordance with the belief that what they choose to do will bring them what they want.

In the social sciences one has heard very frequently two discordant voices. One hears opined that the claim of this new ability to forecast is unrealistic so far as human behavior is concerned. The obstacles to surmount are just too large. This is particularly true in the field of decision making. But this extraordinary view is contradicted by what has already been achieved in the field of politics, at a time when forecasts of elections — clearly collective decisions — have over and again proven accurate within sampling error.

A second and even more troubling view is that this capacity to forecast decisions is of little consequence because it is mere prediction, at most irrelevant to the real commitment of the social sciences, which is to explain social phenomena. The argument strikes us as absurd, displaying an embarrassing ignorance about science and scientific research. We confronted the issue of the models' explanation above and argued that the models do explain; indeed, they provide the undergirding of any explanation of what actually happened. It would be hard to imagine any way of presenting the dynamics of negotiation or of trade-offs more efficiently and more powerfully than done in the models presented here. So the view that the forecasting the models produce is mere prediction has no merit. Anyone who attempts to elevate "explanation" and denigrate "prediction" misunderstands the critical link between prediction and explanation. The two are not separate. They are inextricably linked, and each leads to the other.

Prediction holds the answer to the question, "how is one to know whether an explanation is not correct" in scientific research. It is the highest standard test for any undertaking aiming to discard the incorrect explanation among competing hypotheses. In the sciences, accurate, replicable prediction is the most powerful validation procedure of the explanation one gives for events that have occurred or are yet to occur. Indeed, it is the best validation procedure available.

This is obviously true not only for pre-diction but also for post-diction. There is no difference in principle between the two. Once an outcome has been achieved, a number of explanations — sometimes very different ones — will probably fit the outcome. Indeed, this is precisely what most of the discussions and disagreements in the social sciences are really about: which of the competing explanations that fit the outcome is really the correct one? When one engages in seeking to explain phenomena where outcomes are known, it is a cardinal rule that the data on which the hypothesis is based should be totally separate and different from the data on which the hypothesis is tested. The simulation of prediction is the key to the whole procedure, and if violated, it disqualifies the test. For unless the post-diction has taken place according to these rules, the hypothesis purporting to explain the phenomenon cannot be said to have been validated. All this is clearly elementary but should be repeated because now, at long last, in the field of decision making the possibility to make predictions is finally here. The importance of what has been done cannot be overestimated. Those who refer to it as mere predictions know not what they say.

The Models and the Study of Elites

Students of elite behavior should prove special beneficiaries of the models presented here. Much of the decision making that is studied in the political arena is made by elites alone or in conjunction with the mass public. Elites, by definition, are the decision makers. They define foreign policy, economic policy, social policy, defense policy, and municipal policy, among other things. Elites are the ones who direct the execution of these policies and regulate the changes they want to put in place. In the issues analyzed in this research, it was clearly elites who determined rules regarding emissions, air traffic, banking regulations, and nuclear standards. The public becomes important when intra-elite disagreements cannot be resolved at the elite level, and the disputants turn to broader constituencies to help them defeat their rivals.

One has the impression that elite studies, no matter how approached and executed, do not get at what scholars really want to know. They present social, psychological, or economic explanations of why elites appear to decide as they do. They suggest that upbringing or class or income are factors in decisions by cohorts of specific leaders. But such explanations seldom are of much use when one seeks to explain specific decisions or to forecast how elites will behave on other issues — which allies they will select and which players they will try to defeat. One could go on and on. The behavior of elites and the decisions they make is accounted for in the most vague and general terms. Much of what falls under the rubric of elite studies remind one of music appreciation courses, where students talk of music but do not write or play music.

These deficits cannot be made up unless somehow it is made possible for the scholar to observe the elites as they make decisions. Because such direct observation is highly unlikely, researchers are left to guess what happened — or will happen — and why. The models presented here enable the researcher to simulate the dynamic that led to the outcome and to monitor with system and rigor, decision by decision, the behavior of elites in their most important work.

Two Cultures in the Social Sciences

An unintended consequence of using the models presented here is that they present the hoped-for and often-discussed possibility of collaboration between two cultures in the social sciences that, despite all protestations to the contrary, have kept one another at arm's length since the beginning of the behavioral revolution. One culture is that of scholars deeply involved in sifting through and evaluating the substance of the problems under review, and the other is a culture committed to the study of social phenomena through quantitative, inductive and deductive approaches. The gap between the two cultures has been widening. Rarely do members of one culture acquire competence in the domain of the other, in large part because of the high costs in time and effort required.

A second, more important reason has been the lack of a mechanism through which one set of scholars could make immediate use of the knowledge of the other. The models presented in this book have changed this condition for mathematical modelers and area and issue experts concerned with the general process of decision making. The models require data that represent the distillation of an incredible amount of information on the part of scholars. Scholars with expertise in the issues being analyzed are asked to evaluate four critical pieces of information to any question involving decisions: (1) the identity of the actors with influence over the process of decision making in that specific issue; (2) the specific preference of each actor on that specific issue; (3) the importance of the issue to each actor; and (4) the potential power that each actor has on that specific issue. The evaluations are rendered readily usable by the two sets of mathematical models by transforming the qualitative and substantive information in the expert's possession into numerical estimates on scales from 0 to 100. It is important to emphasize that it requires tremendous substantive knowledge to be able to make the judgments required to provide the models with the necessary information. A good standard for the claim of expertise in a substantive issue is precisely the ability of a scholar to be able to estimate accurately the values the models require. Whether or not the standard has been met is empirically testable in that if the inputs are within acceptable levels of accuracy, they permit the models to forecast the outcome.

Few will disagree with the notion that the identity of the actors, their preferences, the importance they assign to the issue, and their power are the keys to understanding what makes for decisions and that knowing these inputs makes the researcher an expert. It is important to point out that experience indicates that most people who are considered experts can provide the needed information. Once the inputs are known, the calculations required to reach the outcome escalate rapidly in such large numbers that it is impossible to retain all of the components of the process without the help of computers. It is also clear,however, that the logical structures embodied in the models cannot make up for errors in the data. The old rule inevitably applies here as well: garbage in, garbage out.

The actual bringing together of these two cultures mobilizes an incredible research potential. It makes it possible for each group of scholars to use the materials of the other. The modelers are empowered in testing substantive propositions because the data required to feed the models are distilled for them in such a fashion that they need not invest their professional life to learn what substantive experts already know. The same thing is true the other way around. The models make it possible for substantive scholars to become users of powerful analytic procedures beyond their reach in the past. The scholar who is deeply involved in the substance of the problems under review will be the one able to use the new instruments to maximum advantage. This same scholar, with an interest in using the most powerful instruments available to explore substantive problems but disinterested in contributing to the development of such instruments, is the greatest beneficiary of the work reported here. The modeling effort presented here points to the possibility of a collaboration between the two cultures that would enhance immensely the scholarly productivity of the two communities.

Models and the Policymakers

The materials of this book are also addressed to a second set of readers. This community of potential users is as large, or larger, than the community of scholars. Policymakers involved at all levels of the process of European unification — and policymakers in general — should be clearly interested in the models and their applications.

Policymakers are not involved in the peripheral preoccupations of scholars who have vested interests in their disciplines' particular descriptions and explanations of the decision-making process. The policymaker, by virtue of his or her responsibilities, is interested in the essentials of the process: what are the views of all other participants to the game, who can be convinced to make compromises, what each side will have to give to make a deal a reality. The product of the models assists the policymaker directly in solving the problem of how best to navigate through the often turbulent currents that move the decision process to an outcome. Critical to the decision maker is a precise knowledge of the results of negotiations before the decisions have been made.

In addition, policymakers have a special interest in one other aspect of the expected utility models' output. This is what Bueno de Mesquita called the intervention model. Perhaps more than the scholar, the policymaker is interested in the questions: "Can the outcome be changed? What can one do to bring that change about?" Can results that are inimical to the interests represented by the policymaker — or are only minimally acceptable — be improved upon? It may be that what the policymaker would wish cannot be achieved, but the results could be made more acceptable. It is the policymakers' responsibility to manage things so as to minimize their losses and maximize gains.

In short, the policymaker wants to know precise answers to two sets of questions. First, if things are left to run their course, what is to happen on the issue under consideration and why? The models presented above provide accurate answers to that question. But knowing the outcome and even the dynamics that brought about the results are half of the answers the policymaker wishes to know. Equally important is the answer to the question of whether the outcome can be improved. Can he or she take action to obtain a better solution than would result if things were left to unfold without any intervention?

Critical, then, is how policymakers change outcomes to coincide with their preferences, or if that is not possible, how they improve outcomes at least part of the way from what would have otherwise resulted. The answers to these questions are essential for all who make policy. A policymaker works with very imperfect information. Very few things are known; inevitably much is left to educated guess work. For policymakers, negotiations often resemble groping in the dark.

The intervention model illumines this part of the decision-making process. It takes advantage of its ability to simulate the changing expectations and calculations of the players over the entire process of negotiation, which may include several rounds of discussions, moves, and countermoves. The model identifies the relevant players, as well as the actors whose views of the situation might be conducive to a strategic compromise. This information permits the development of a meaningful strategy as to what to do to improve the outcome. This strategy is based on the simulation by the model of expectations, perceptions, and moves that the actors can take. The model delineates strategies that map in detail who the policymaker should contact and in what sequence, what deals to propose, and which players to avoid.

The intervention model takes as given that actors prefer gains to losses. From this simple premise it identifies who believes that what is being asked of them is less than they would lose if it came to a confrontation. Given such expectations, they prefer giving in to a confrontation. These are clearly the players who can be most fruitfully approached. It is easiest to convince someone who already believes that it is in his or her interest to accept the deal that is being proposed. The model also identifies a set of players who expect to lose less in a confrontation than they would by giving in. Under such conditions a compromise is still possible. It may make sense for the policymaker to invest the time and resources necessary to bring a deal about. These examples do not exhaust the opportunities that the policymaker can seize from the negotiating dynamics. But to seize the opportunities, the policymaker must be aware of them. Missed opportunities are losses. This is precisely the information that policymakers would wish to know.

Two additional points should be made. Intervention in the decision process may require that strategy and operational plans be worked out quickly. Knowing what to do is of little value to the policymaker after the opportunity has passed. The intervention model provides answers in a very short time (if an expert with the required expertise is available) and imposes very low costs on its users when compared with other approaches. The major costs have already been absorbed by the expert who spent a lifetime sifting and evaluating the information on the issue.

Laying out a strategy and executing it are two different things. Even after one knows who to approach and who to avoid, what compromises to offer or reject, the execution of the plan may be a lengthy and uncertain task. It would be terribly wrong to believe that having developed the correct strategy and tactics, the implementation of the strategy is easy or even trivial. Implementation is often an onerous business requiring both resources and skill. For example, a strategy requiring a policymaker to raise the importance of an issue may be opposed by members of the policymaker's own organization with interests in other issues now threatened with being downgraded in the organization's plans.

In a nutshell, then, the models tell in advance what the outcome will be if things are left to run their course, and what, if anything, can be done to change it. One is reminded of the serenity prayer: "God grant me the serenity to accept the things I cannot change, the courage to change the things I can, and the wisdom to know the difference." The intervention models appear to make it possible for the policymaker to do just that.

A unified European Community will alter significantly the distribution of wealth and power in the world. That is probably reason enough to monitor the phenomenon with great care. But scholars have an additional reason to be concerned with the process of European unification. The process of integration offers a unique opportunity to explore directly the way twelve different developed societies grope toward becoming one. One set of data essential if one wishes to monitor and understand the phenomenon of European unification is the stream of decisions by the European Community and member governments (and elites in the private sectors) creating central institutions, coordinating national policies, and removing obstacles in the way of greater interaction among Europe's people. These decisions are the critical component of the politics of European unification. However, much of such decision making is hidden from view, rendering attempts to explain why and how decisions were made very much of a guessing game.

Much of the material in this volume is directed to solving this problem. Models that have been deployed and proven successful in other arenas are presented and shown to illuminate the decision-making process. The authors provide a direct comparison of the performance of two contending sets of models. The critical standard applied here is performance in predicting outcomes. This alone represents a major contribution. Also, the view of the decision-making process in the European Community that the models provide should prove arresting to the reader. The models made possible the presentation of detailed and comprehensive views of the dynamics that bring about Community outcomes. Without these tools this dynamic remains almost completely invisible to the observer. Finally, but very important, the expected utility models are a useful aid to decision makers in their policy formulation and execution. The ability of the models to pinpoint in advance opportunities that may be missed or gains not originally considered represent major assistance for policymakers.

The work presented here reaffirms that the key to future success in the study of political decision making in Europe and elsewhere is in the collaboration of two separate, and often antagonistic, scholarly cultures: the culture of modelers and that of the area or functional expert. Their collaboration is essential for a deeper understanding of the processes governing the decisions of the European community and collectivities everywhere.

References

Agence Europe. 1985–89. *Bulletin Quotidien Europe.* Luxembourg: Agence Internationale d'Information pour la Presse.

Axline, W. A. 1968. *European Community Law and Organizational Developement.* New York: Oceana Publications.

Banks, J. 1990. "Equilibrium Behavior in Crisis Bargaining Games." *American Journal of Political Science* 34:599–614.

Beck, D., and B. Bueno de Mesquita. 1985. "Forecasting Policy Decisions: An Expected Utility Approach." In S. Andriole, ed., *Corporate Crisis Management.* Princeton: Petrocelli Books.

Black, D. 1958. *Theory of Committees and Elections.* Cambridge: Cambridge University Press.

Boudon, R., and F. Bourricaud. 1982. *Dictionnaire critique de la sociologie.* Paris: Presses Universitaires de France.

Buchan, D., R. Mauthner, and I. Davidson. 1989. "EC Heads Isolate Thatcher." *Financial Times,* December 9–10:1.

Buchan, D., P. Stephens, and W. Dawkins. 1989. "EC Compromise Sets Stage for Economic Union in Early 1990s." *Financial Times,* June 28:1.

Bueno de Mesquita, B. 1975. *Strategy, Risk, and Personality in Coalition Politics: The Case of India.* Cambridge: Cambridge University Press.

———. 1981. *The War Trap.* New Haven: Yale University Press.

———. 1984. "Forecasting Policy Decisions: An Expected Utility Approach to Post-Khomeini Iran." *PS* 17:226–36.

———. 1985. "The War Trap Revisited." *American Political Science Review* 79:157(ENDASH)76.

———. 1990. "Multilateral Negotiations: A Spatial Analysis of the Arab-Israeli Dispute," *International Organization* 44:317–40.

Bueno de Mesquita, B., and D. Lalman. 1986. "Reason and War." *American Political Science Review* 80:1113–31.

———. 1992. *War and Reason. Domestic and International Imperatives.* New Haven: Yale University Press.

Bueno de Mesquita, B., D. Newman, and A. Rabushka. 1985. *Forecasting Political Events. The Future of Hong Kong.* New Haven: Yale University Press.

Camus, A. 1956. *The Rebel.* New York: Vintage Books.

Cecchini, P. 1988. *The European Challenge, 1992: The Benefits of a Single Market.* Aldershot: Wildwood House/Gower Pub.

Coffey, P., ed. 1988. *Main Economic Policy Areas of the EEC, Towards 1992: The Challenge of the Community's Economic Policies When the "Real" Common Market Is Created by the End of 1992.* 2d ed. Boston: Kluwer Academic Publishers.

Coleman, J. S. 1970. "Political Money." *American Political Science Review* 64:1074–87.

——. 1972. "Systems of Social Exchange." *Journal of Mathematical Sociology* 2:145–63.

——. 1973. *The Mathematics of Collective Action*. London: Heinemann Educational Books.

——. 1986. "Micro Foundations and Macrosocial Theory." In S. Lindenberg, J. S. Coleman, and S. Nowak, eds., *Approaches to Social Theory*. New York: Russell Sage Foundation.

——. 1990. *Foundations of Social Theory*. Cambridge: Belknap Press of the Harvard University Press.

Conybeare, J. 1992. "A Portfolio Diversification Model of Alliances." *Journal of Conflict Resolution*. 36:53–85.

Davis, O., M. DeGroot, and M. Hinich. 1974. "Social Preference Orderings and Majority Rule." *Econometrica* 40:147–57.

DeCecco, M., and A. Giovanni, eds. 1989. *A European Central Bank? Perspectives on Monetary Unification after Ten Years of the EMS*. New York: Cambridge University Press.

DeCecco, M., and A. Giovanni. 1989a. "Supporters Rush to Claim Historic Success." *Financial Times,* June 28:1.

——. 1989b. "Compromise in Madrid." *Financial Times,* June 28:14.

——. 1989c. "Bruges Group Warns against Early Entry to EMS." *Financial Times,* December 5:3.

Downs, A. 1957. *An Economic Theory of Democracy*. New York: Harper and Brothers.

Fiorina, M. P. 1975. "Formal Models in Political Science." *American Journal of Political Science* 19:133–59.

Friedman, J. W. 1990. *Game Theory: With Applications to Economics*. 2d ed. New York: Oxford University Press.

Friedman, M. 1953. "The Methodology of Positive Economics." In M. Friedman, ed., *Essays in Positive Economics*. Chicago: University of Chicago Press.

Goldberg, A., and D. Robson. 1983. *Smalltalk-80. The Language and its Implementation*. Reading, Mass.: Addison-Wesley.

Haas, E. B. 1964. *Beyond the Nation State: Functionalism and International Organization*. Stanford: Stanford University Press.

——. 1968. *The Uniting of Europe: Political, Social, and Economic Forces, 1950–1957*. 2d ed. London: Stevens.

Hoede, C., and R. R. Bakker. 1982. "A Theory of Decisional Power." *Journal of Mathematical Sociology* 8:309–22.

Hoede, C., and A. Meek. 1983. "Structural Aspects of Decisional Power." *Journal of Mathematical Sociology* 9:242–52.

Hoede, C., and J. S. Redfern. 1985. "Optimization of Decisional Power in Representational Systems with Voting Power." *Journal of Mathematical Sociology* 11:331–40.

Hoffmann, S. 1966. "Obstinate or Obsolete: The Fate of the Nation State and the Case of Western Europe." *Daedalus* 95:862–915.

——. 1982. "Reflections on the Nation-State in Western Europe Today." *Journal of Common Market Studies* 21:21–37.

Jansen, M., and J. K. De Vree. 1988. *The Ordeal of Unity: The Politics of European Integration*. 2d ed. Bilthoven, Neth.: Prime Press.

Kapteyn, P. J. G., and P. VerLoren van Themaat. 1989. In L. W. Gormley, ed., *Introduction to the Law of the European Communities: After the Coming into Force of the Single European Act*. 2d ed. Deventer, Neth.: Kluwer.

Kenis, P., and V. Schneider. 1989. "Policy Networks as an Analytic Tool for Policy Analysis: A Review of Some Applications." Unpublished paper.

Kramer, G. 1972. "Sophisticated Voting over Multidimensional Choice Spaces." *Journal of Mathematical Sociology* 2:165–80.

Krislov, S., C. D. Ehlermann, and J. Weiler. 1986. "The Political Organs and the Decision-Making Process in the United States and the European Community." In M. Cappelletti, M. Seccombe, and J. Weiler, eds., *Integration through Law: Europe and the American Federal Experience*. Vol. 1: *Tools and Institutions*. Bk. 2: *Political Organs, Integration Techniques and Judicial Process*. Berlin: De Gruyter.

Kugler, J., and J. H. P. Williams. 1990. "The Last Stumbling Block to Integration: Exploring the Politics of Banking Reform in Europe." Paper presented at the Conference on European Integration, Groningen, Netherlands.

Lalman, D. 1988. "Conflict Resolution and Peace." *American Journal of Political Science* 32:590–615.

Lalman, D., and D. Newman. 1991. "Alliance Formation and National Security." *International Interactions*. 16:239–55.

Laumann, E. O., and D. Knoke. 1987. *The Organizational State: Social Change in National Policy Domains*. Madison: University of Wisconsin Press.

Laver, M., and K. A. Shepsle. 1990. "Coalitions and Cabinet Government." *American Political Science Review* 84:873–90.

Laver, M., and N. Schofield. 1990. *The Politics of Coalition in Western Europe*. Oxford: Oxford University Press.

Lehermann Madsen, O., and B. Moller-Pedersen. 1988. "What Object- Oriented Programming May Be — and What It Does Not Have to Be." In S. Gjessing and K. Nygaard, eds., *ECOOP 88. European Conference on Object-Oriented Programming*. Berlin: Springer Verlag.

Lindberg, L. N. 1963. *The Political Dynamics of European Economic Integration*. Stanford: Stanford University Press.

Lindenberg, S. 1985. "An Assessment of the New Political Economy: Its Potential for the Social Sciences and for Sociology in Particular." *Sociological Theory* 3:99–114.

———. 1990. "Homo Socio-oeconomicus: The Emergence of a General Model of Man in the Social Sciences." *Journal of Institutional and Theoretical Economics (JITE)* 146:727–48.

———. 1992. "The Method of Decreasing Abstraction." In J. S. Coleman and T. J. Fararo, eds., *Rational Choice Theory: Advocacy and Critique*. Newbury Park: Sage.

Lodge, J. 1989. "EC Policymaking: Institutional Considerations." In J. Lodge, ed., *The European Community and the Challenge of the Future*. London: Pinter.

Marsden, P. V. 1983. "Restricted Access in Networks and Models of Power." *American Journal of Sociology* 88:686–717.

Mauthner, R., D. Buchan, and M. Cassell. 1989. "Wrangle on German Unity Formula." *Financial Times,* December 9–10:3.

McKelvey, R. 1976. "Intransitivities in Multidimensional Voting Models and Some Implications for Agenda Control." *Journal of Economic Theory* 16:472–82.

McPhee, W. N. 1963. *Formal Theories of Mass Behavior*. New York: Free Press.

Mitrany, D. 1933. *The Progress of International Government*. New Haven: Yale University Press.

Morgan, T. C. 1984. "A Spatial Model of Crisis Bargaining." *International Studies Quarterly* 28:407–26.

———. 1989. "Power, Resolve, and Bargaining in International Crises: A Spatial Theory." *International Interactions* 15:289–312.

———. 1990. "Issue Linkages in International Crisis Bargaining." *American Journal of Political Science* 34:311–33.

Morrow, J. D. 1986. "A Spatial Model of International Conflict." *American Political Science Review* 80:1131–50.

———. 1987. "On the Theoretical Basis of a Measure of National Risk Attitudes." *International Studies Quarterly* 31:423–38.

Nicholson, F., and R. East. 1987. *From the Six to the Twelve: The Enlargement of the European Communities*. London: Longman.

Parsons, T., and N. J. Smelser. 1956. *Economy and Society*. New York: Free Press.

Podolny, J. 1990. "On the Formation of Exchange Relations in Political Systems." *Rationality and Society* 2:359–78.

Ray, J. 1992. *Global Politics*. 5th ed. Boston: Houghton Mifflin.

Riker, W. H. 1986. *The Art of Political Manipulation*. New Haven: Yale University Press.

Ruigrok, W. 1990. "De Beperkte Mondialisering van de Europese Industrie: Handelspolitieke Consequenties" (The Limited Mondialisation of the European Industry: Trade Political Consequences). *Internationale Spectator* 44:306–11.

Rumelhart, D. E., and J. L. McClelland, eds. 1987. *Parallel Distributed Processing. Explorations in the Microstructure of Cognition*. Vol. 1: *Foundations*. Cambridge: MIT Press.

Scheingold. S. 1965. *The Rule of Law in European Integration: The Path of the Schuman Plan*. New Haven: Yale University Press.

Schofield, N. 1976. "Instability of Simple Dynamic Games." *Review of Economic Studies* 45:575–94.

Shapley, L. S., and M. Shubik. 1954. "A Method for Evaluating the Distribution of Power in a Committee System." *American Political Science Review* 48:787–92.

Stokman, F. N., and R. Van Oosten. 1990. "A Dynamic Model of Policy Networks." Unpublished paper, ICS.

Stokman, F. N., and J. M. M. Van den Bos. 1992. "A Two-Stage Model of Policy Making with an Empirical Test in the U.S. Energy Policy Domain." In G. Moore and J. A. Whitt, eds., *The Political Consequences of Social Networks. Research in Politics and Society,* vol. 4. Greenwich, Conn.: JAI Press.

Stokman, F. N., and J. V. Stokman. 1992. "Strategic Control and Interests: Its Effects on Decision Outcomes." Paper presented at the 87th annual meeting of the American Sociological Association, Pittsburg, Penn., 20–24 August.

Van den Bos, J. M. M. 1991. *Dutch EC Policy Making: A Model Guided Approach to Coordination and Negotiation*. Amsterdam: Thesis Publishers.

VerLoren van Themaat, P. 1991. "Some Preliminary Observations on IGCs: Relationships between the Concepts of a Common Market, a Monetary Union, an Economic Union, a Political Union, and Sovereignty." *Common Market Law Review* 28:275–89.

Wallace, H. 1973. *National Governments and the European Communities*. London: Chatham House.

Wallace, W. 1983. "Less Than a Federation, More Than a Regime: The Community as a Political System." In H. Wallace, W. Wallace, and C. Webb, eds., *Policy-Making in the European Community*. 2d ed. Chichester, Eng.: Wiley.

Weesie, J. 1987. "On Coleman's Theory of Collective Action." University of Utrecht, Netherlands. Mimeographed.

Williams, J. H. P. 1991. "The Major Difference? Negotiating a European Central Bank." Unpublished paper.

Williamson, O. E. 1991. "Comparative Economic Organization: The Analysis of Discrete Structural Alternatives." *Administrative Science Quarterly* 36:269–96.

Wippler, R. 1978. "The Structural-Individualistic Approach in Dutch Sociology: Toward an Explanatory Social Science." *The Netherlands Journal of Sociology* 14:135–55.

Zeggelink, E. P. H. 1993. *Strangers into Friends: The Evolution of Friendship Networks Using an Individual Oriented Modeling Approach*. Amsterdam: Thesis Publishers.

Contributors

Bruce Bueno de Mesquita is a senior fellow at the Hoover Institution on War, Revolution and Peace, Stanford University, and professor of political science at the University of Rochester.

Samuel Eldersveld is professor emeritus in the Department of Political Science at the University of Michigan.

Jacek Kugler is the Elisabeth Helm Rosecrans Professor of International Relations at the Center for Politics and Economics of the Claremont Graduate School.

A. F. K. Organski is a program director at the Center for Political Studies, Institute for Social Research, and professor of political science at the University of Michigan.

Roy Pierce is professor emeritus in the Department of Political Science and associate research scientist emeritus at the Center for Political Studies, Institute for Social Research, at the University of Michigan.

Frans N. Stokman is scientific director of the Interuniversity Center for Social Science Theory and Methodology and professor of social science research methodology at the University of Groningen.

Jan M. M. Van den Bos is a senior researcher at the Netherlands Court of Audit.

Reinier Van Oosten is a researcher at the Interuniversity Center for Social Science Theory and Methodology at the University of Groningen.

John H. P. Williams is an associate of Decision Insights Incorporated specializing in Western Europe.

Index

Abstraction, method of decreasing: 111, 122
Accountability: 13, 14
Acheson, D.: 235
Acquiescence. *See* Capitulation
Agence Europe: 35–45, 47, 56
Agenda: 3, 12, 14, 26, 77, 194
Agriculture Council: 23
Airfares, deep discount: 45–47, 59, 60, 148, 178–80
Air pollution. *See* Environment
Air transport: 10, 33, 72, 131, 184; background, 43–46, 48; development of data, 56, 59–62; expected utility assessment of, 148–50, 217; exchange assessment of, 176–80, 217. *See also* Seating capacity
A-item: 26
Applied modeling: 15, 67, 72, 79, 86, 103, 111, 122, 123, 231. *See also* Object-oriented modeling; Simulation
Articles of EEC. *See* European Economic Community
Assumptions: role of, in models, 3–7, 32, 122, 130; comparison of expected utility and exchange models, 67–69, 105, 213, 214, 225, 226, 232; in expected utility model, 73–79, 83–85, 87, 89, 95, 96, 103, 143; in example, 81, 96, 113, 120; in bargaining over issue positions, 95–97, 100; in controlling strategy, 101, 153; in exchange models, 105, 108–12, 119, 121, 124, 163, 167, 168; of linked models, 215
Austria: 19
Automobile industry: national characteristics of, 34–37, 115, 116, 145, 154, 156–58; catalytic converters, 35, 37, 38; large cars, 36, 116, 134, 140, 165, 167–71; small cars, 37, 38, 133, 134, 138, 141, 145, 164, 165, 167–71; emissions, 56, 57, 95, 132–36, 138, 143, 145, 154, 163–65; data on, 58, 132, 183; analysis of, 77, 78, 118, 120, 139, 145, 164–71, 183; tax incentives, 139–41, 164, 167, 173; performance of models on, 36, 116, 134, 140, 165, 167–71, 184
Aviation, civil: 33, 34, 43, 45, 46, 59, 176

Bakker, R. R.: 112
Banking system: background on, 9–10, 49–54, 185–88, 237; data on, 33, 56, 62–65, 187, 188, 204, 215; creation of a supranational, 50–52, 54, 62, 63, 71, 130, 186, 192; discussed at Strasbourg, 52, 53–54, 193, 194; discussed at Maastricht, 130, 201, 202, 204, 208; discussed at Madrid, 190, 191, 193, 194, 207; political attitudes toward, 190–99, 201–8; model differences, 202, 205, 215, 220, 221
Banks, J.: 74, 75, 87, 88
Bargaining: characteristics of agents, 6, 7, 13, 77; models for assessing, 12; hypothesized process in EC, 71–75, 79, 88–89, 94, 136–38, 145; beliefs and, 87, 99; Nash solution, 97; computational intuition in expected utility model, 97–100, 136–38; Raiffa–Kalai–Smorodinsky solution, 111, 124; computational intuition in exchange models, 126, 127; costs of, 138; and comparative statics, 150–53; accuracy of predictions about, 159, 232; over banking policy, 199, 204, 214, 215; comparison of models, 214, 215, 225